# On Hunger

# On Hunger

*Violence and Craving in America,
from Starvation to Ozempic*

Dana Simmons

UNIVERSITY OF CALIFORNIA PRESS

University of California Press
Oakland, California



Suggested citation: Simmons, D. *On Hunger: Violence and Craving in America, from Starvation to Ozempic*. Oakland: University of California Press, 2025.
DOI: https://doi.org/10.1525/luminos.232

Library of Congress Cataloging-in-Publication Data

Names: Simmons, Dana (Dana Jean), author.
Title: On hunger : violence and craving in America, from starvation
    to Ozempic / Dana Simmons.
Other titles: California studies in food and culture ; 85.
Description: Oakland, California : University of California Press, [2025] |
    Series: California studies in food and culture ; 85 | Includes bibliographical
    references and index.
Identifiers: LCCN 2025001873 (print) | LCCN 2025001874 (ebook) |
    ISBN 9780520412989 (paperback) | ISBN 9780520412996 (ebook)
Subjects: LCSH: Hunger—United States—History. | Food industry
    and trade—Social aspects—United States. | Hunger—Political aspects—
    United States.
Classification: LCC HD9005 .S555 2025 (print) | LCC HD9005 (ebook) |
    DDC 363.8/5610973—dc23/eng/20250208

LC record available at https://lccn.loc.gov/2025001873
LC ebook record available at https://lccn.loc.gov/2025001874

GPSR Authorized Representative: Easy Access System Europe,
Mustamäe tee 50, 10621 Tallinn, Estonia, gpsr.requests@easproject.com

publication supported by a grant from

**The Community Foundation for Greater New Haven**

as part of the *Urban Haven Project*

*To UCR students*

*Why should you take by force that from us which you can have by love? Why should you destroy us, who have provided you with food?*

—WAHUNSENACAWH (POWHATAN), CA. 1609

*Down in Mississippi they are killing Negroes of all ages, on the installment plan, through starvation. If you are a Negro and vote, if you persist in dreams of black power to win some measure of freedom in white-controlled communities, you go hungry.*

—FANNIE LOU HAMER, "GOING HUNGRY FOR FREEDOM," 1968

*Here we describe three racial projects significant for the production of hunger in today's Karuk community. These projects are outright genocide, lack of recognition of land occupancy and title, and forced assimilation. . . . Lest readers fall into the myth that the production of hunger took place in the past, we emphasize that lack of recognition of land title and forced assimilation are very much ongoing today.*

—KARI NORGAARD, RON REID, AND CAROLINA VAN HORNE, "A CONTINUING LEGACY: INSTITUTIONAL RACISM, HUNGER, AND NUTRITIONAL JUSTICE ON THE KLAMATH," 2011

*He who can say to his fellow-man, "You shall serve me or starve," is a master and his subject is a slave.*

—FREDERICK DOUGLASS, "SPEECH AT ELMIRA. WEST INDIA EMANCIPATION," 1882

*There are differences between the bareness of subsistence poverty, particularly in poor nations, and the poverty of the poor in wealthy consumerist nations that is produced by industries of deprivation, where the detritus of commodity artifacts and the cheaply produced and polluted accumulate around the "least of these" who are both defined and constrained by deprived productions.*

—IMANI PERRY, "STICKS BROKEN AT THE RIVER: THE SECURITY STATE AND THE VIOLENCE OF MANHOOD," 2018

*You're not you when you're hungry.*™

—MARS INC. ADVERTISEMENT FOR SNICKERS BAR

CONTENTS

# Introduction

There is a valley in Tennessee named after my ancestor. Samuel Wear (1753–1817) is buried by Wears Valley, in the Fort Wear cemetery. A monument "erected by his descendents [*sic*]" honors him as a "Pioneer, Soldier of four Wars; Colonial, Revolution, Indian, 1812; One of the Heroes of Kings Mountain, and a Founder of the State of Franklin." When the War of American Independence broke out, Wear moved his family from Virginia to occupy land beyond the borders of the British colonies. He took advantage of a weakened colonial state authority to grab territory within Cherokee treaty lands. He built a stockade, Wears Fort, right in the middle of a Cherokee pedestrian highway that traveled from Virginia through the Great Smoky mountains to the Overhill Cherokee towns along the Little Tennessee River.[1]

Wear was responsible for the starvation and destruction of many Cherokee people. Alongside other "Overmountain Men," many of them Scots-Irish like himself, he engaged in a campaign of uncontrolled and illegal dispossession and ethnic cleansing. The newly formed US government prohibited settlements and violent excursions into Cherokee territory, but Wear and his neighbors refused to recognize state authority over their right to seize land. In 1785 he helped to lead the first secession from the United States, the self-proclaimed State of Franklin. The following year, Wear was one of the pseudo-state's "commissioners" who held Cherokee leaders Kaiyah-tahee (Old Tassel) and Uskwa'li-gu'ta (Hanging Maw) at gunpoint and forced them to sign the so-called Treaty of Coyatee, which repudiated US guarantees of Cherokee land sovereignty and ceded enormous swathes of territory to the settlers. As historian Kevin Barksdale (2009, 107) put it: "Perhaps in the entire history of Euroamerican Indian diplomacy, no single treaty contained the level of intimidation as that [Treaty of Coyatee]."

Within a year the State of Franklin opened a land office and began to sell off the forcibly ceded lands to settlers in exchange for cash or animal pelts (Barksdale 2009, 108). The Franklin settlers even tried to make a secret deal with the King of Spain, to guarantee their ownership over that land. "It is well known that you have taken almost all our country from us without our consent," Kaiyah-tahee charged. "They [the settlers] may take what little land we have left, which is very little, not sufficient to keep us much longer from perishing" (Palmer 1884, 306). Kaiyah-tahee's accusation that settlers were starving his people went unheeded. When some Overhill Cherokee resisted the occupation of their land, Wear was probably among the leaders of a Franklin militia invasion that burned down several Cherokee towns and killed their inhabitants. The invaders took an ax and murdered Kaiyah-tahee, Uskwa'li-gu'ta, and Coskuah (Old Abram), who had gathered for peace talks with US representatives (Barksdale 2009, 111). By 1795 the United States legitimated this violent and illegal seizure of land and power. Samuel Wear served as a delegate to the constitutional convention that year establishing a new state. "Right of Occupancy" grants turned squatted land into private property. Wear received a grant for five hundred acres of flat and fertile land, from the mouth of Walden's Creek to Pigeon Forge (Sharp 2014b). His violence was subsumed under the pioneer mythology, and his property rights vested in the legal authority of the State of Tennessee.

Technically I am a descendant of Samuel's brother John. John seems to have followed his brother around, so Samuel's story can stand in for his, perhaps with the exception of the landed wealth. I know that at least one of John's children owned chattel property, including an enslaved woman named Mima. John's lineage down to my mother's father left a record of a hardscrabble settler family, moving with each generation (or sooner) to claim new lands and livelihoods. My great-grandmother Daisy, who married a Wear and lived for over a century, told me childhood stories of horse-drawn covered wagons and one-room schoolhouses on the prairie. Wears traveled to Oklahoma, Kentucky, Texas, Nebraska, Kansas City, and Palo Alto. Sod huts to executive offices.[2]

For as long as I can remember, I held this history distant from my own sense of self. I imagined myself in another world. I remember as a child holding tight the conviction that I was a visitor to Earth from another planet, whose days were equivalent to Earth years. I sought every opportunity to live and study abroad, seeking identity in rootlessness. I studied French history, delving into questions that I carefully kept distant from my own experience. I imagined myself a cosmopolitan. A reader might see a reenactment of the settler-colonial imagination, projecting itself onto maps of territories yet to be seen and occupied (Veracini 2021). It has taken me some time to enter into the questions that animate this book, which call up my own implication in time and place. Today I live and work on the ancestral lands of the Gabrieleño Tongva, Cahuilla, Luiseño, and Serrano peoples.

The University of California, where I teach, was founded with proceeds from the sale of expropriated Indigenous land (Joseph A. Meyers Center 2021, 23). I exist in the form I have taken because of this inheritance of violence and dispossession. I am an "accessory after the fact" (Morris-Suzuki 2005, 26). Kaiyah-tahee's people suffered, directly and indirectly, by my ancestors' hands. The lands they lost ceased to provide sustenance, and many must have died of hunger. Thousands more perished of starvation during the Cherokee peoples' forced removal to Indian territory in the 1830s. Colonizers failed to eliminate Cherokee lands, people, and culture, though many paid a heavy price for their collective survival into the present. As Tessa Morris-Suzuki (2005, 27) has written, "though we may not be responsible for such acts of aggression in the sense of having caused them, we are 'implicated' in them, in the sense that they cause us" (also see Rothberg 2019, 79). I am an inheritor and a beneficiary of a history of hunger and starvation.

This book is about an enduring pattern in US history: *the production of hunger*. On multiple occasions, from the eighteenth through the twentieth century, state agents, and private (settler-) citizens colluded in large-scale campaigns of ethnic cleansing and political control by starvation. Food sources were destroyed, blocked, denied, altered, or substituted to force people to obey, move, clear lands, accede to white power, and make way for new regimes of land and labor. Hunger served as an instrument to consolidate the modern United States. At certain moments this dynamic became so severe and visible that it entered into historical consciousness. History records the programmatic starvation of Indigenous peoples on the Plains in the late nineteenth century, when US authorities and their civilian allies carried out a genocidal slaughter of bison and withheld government rations on Indian reservations. A century later, plantation owners and White Citizens Councils withheld wages and food welfare (commodities) to starve Black residents, especially those involved in civil rights, out of the South. Historians and journalists often refer to the latter moment as the "discovery of hunger in the United States." But hunger had not disappeared in those intervening decades.

What does it mean to say that hunger is produced? Across the twentieth century, food and nourishment were withheld to get people and animals to do things. Sometimes this was explicit, as when people in power said, "Do this or you will starve." (It happened, and happens, more often than you might think.) Other times hunger was produced in more subtle ways, as when food processors designed cheese puffs to melt so fast that your body doesn't have time to register that you ate something. Or when welfare officers made it harder for people to get benefits. Workfare requirements are a way to produce hunger, to get people to do work. Hunger is still systematically produced for political and economic ends. Just look at the way some politicians condemn food-based welfare benefits like SNAP (food stamps) and you'll see that people in power are actively producing hunger today. Few of them would say out loud that some folks must be kept hungry so that they will go to work. But that subtext is really not hard to detect. Another example: the rise of "cheap food" suggests that hunger is intensifying by design. Processed goods, with intense flavors and low nutritive value, are formulated to provoke craving for more. In the late twentieth and twenty-first centuries, food itself produces hunger.

Hunger is produced by depriving people of access to food. Hunger is also produced by food, by commodities designed to stimulate cravings. The power to control hunger carries huge economic, political, and medical consequences. This is an era defined by an obsession with thinness and metabolic diseases such as obesity and diabetes. Vast profits are to be reaped by the inventor of a safe and effective hunger-suppressant drug. The ability to produce, to suppress, or to control hunger is a continuing struggle. Hunger is an ongoing form of racial, economic, and environmental violence over regimes of land and labor (Goldstein 2018, 83). Hunger in the Americas is produced through the continuing negation of Indigenous land occupancy, forced assimilation, welfare policy, low wages, long hours, debts, deceptive packaging, agricultural subsidies, unlivable geographies, and contaminated soils and waters. These are structural relations, and it is necessary to trace their continuities and shifts. The past intrudes on the present.

These topics—starvation and resistance on the Plains, the struggle for Black liberation, welfare politics, and processed food—appear discrete and independent. To find the continuities and parallels between them, I look to the scientific record. I first began to wonder about the role of hunger in US history when I noticed it appear over and over in scientific experiments. Hunger has inspired thousands of scientific publications, surveys, case reports, theories, and conference presentations since the late nineteenth century. The entire field of experimental psychology was built on studies of hunger. Early work in the field of neuroscience focused on identifying brain centers for hunger and thirst. Medical researchers continue to search for a pharmaceutical holy grail, a drug that suppresses hunger (Ozempic and Wegovy are just the latest in a long line of pharmaceutical appetite suppressants). If you study the history of science, you find evidence that hunger has remained a systemic and continuous presence in American society, politics, and economy.

When I began this project, I searched for historical context to understand why hunger held such a salient position in twentieth-century human science. Quickly I found that object and context, figure and ground, background and foreground, collapsed. I found that US Indian Agents employed a "starving process," making Native people hungry to get them to do work. Plantation owners kept Black sharecroppers hungry, in debt, and dependent on food advances. Welfare agencies made food support contingent on relief work and moral standards of behavior. Food processors designed products that maximize consumers' cravings. American prisons used (and use) food and hunger to enforce compliance. Science and politics, welfare and knowledge, acted recursively one upon the other and in tandem. Political ideologies, utilitarianism, and colonial racial hierarchies informed scientific assumptions and experiments. Scientists made hunger and scarcity into natural objects, fit for political regulation. There is a direct connection between the production of scientific knowledge about hunger and the production and weaponization of hunger itself.

Relative to other more mechanized forms of violence, hunger appears as a footnote in most accounts of modern history.[3] Why? Perhaps because hunger seems to belong to a time outside of modernity. Unlike mechanical mass death, hunger appears neither modern nor spectacular. Contemporary images of hungry children copy visual conventions established already in the nineteenth century (Vernon 2007, 81). Every decade or two, international leaders pledge to end hunger and/or poverty by a plausibly distant target date. (The most recent pledge, to reach Zero Hunger by 2030, is certain to fail like its predecessors.) It is as if hunger were an old mess to be mopped up. But hunger is no anachronism. Hunger does not disappear with modernity; hunger is integral to it. The history of hunger and starvation in the twentieth century complicates any account, which views hunger as an early stage in the foundation of the modern world. We often speak about hunger as an "age-old" problem. I argue that hunger has never been more modern. Hunger is a systemic product of capitalist, settler-colonial society.

. . .

Hunger takes various forms at different times and places. Sometimes deprivation is visibly violent; in other cases, hunger appears an unfortunate by-product of consensual market mechanisms. Hunger is produced by neurochemical signals, emotional and physical sensations, agro-industrial infrastructures, scientific experiments, violence, and inequity. The range of words that describe hunger suggest the multiplicity of forms and scales (from individuals to households to nations and continents) that hunger has taken historically.[4] A history of hunger must account for complexity, continuity, and change at specific historical moments. How do these historical processes themselves produce particular kinds of historical subjects? Who becomes hungry, and why?

Hunger is biosocial and as such is bound to natural histories and social histories. Archives of science let us see how the natural and the social were cleaved in specific ways at particular points in history. To borrow Scott Vrecko's (2010a, 37) observation about addiction, "What is most interesting is not that [hunger] is an admixture of biology and politics, but how that particular mix changes over time and how such changes relate to important social, personal and political issues." This book follows hunger as it appears in different forms and contexts: a sensation, an emotion, a genetic function, a bodily regulator, an economic status, a social norm, a nutritional insufficiency, a psychological effect, or a cultural expression. The paragraphs below outline some of the terms and concepts that define hunger.

Starvation, in the modern era, is an act of violence. From the mid-nineteenth century on, starvation has followed the colonial commodity frontier. Britain and its former colonies turned much of the world into plantations, mobilizing massive amounts of plants and animals. Food was a tool of colonial power, and colonized peoples in Ireland, India, and the Americas starved by dispossession and by force (Otter 2020, 15). In the twentieth century, mass starvation became a standard weapon of war. Postcolonial authoritarian rulers used famine events to leverage international aid. As Alex de Waal (2005, xii) has argued, speaking of Sudan: "'to starve' is transitive: it is something people do to each other." Starvation is a form of elimination.

Dietary deficiencies represent a quantitative, biomedical form of hunger (Yates-Doerr 2015a, 232; Mudry 2009). Deficiency diseases and malnutrition are medical conditions diagnosed and treated by doctors; a person could be deficient and not know it, or claim to be hungry and be diagnosed without any deficiencies (Carolan 2013, 4). Deficiency appears as an abnormality to be treated and reformed, with nutrition education or supplements like "Plumpy'Nut" formula and vitamin tablets (Escobar 2011, 72; Tappan 2017; Scott-Smith 2017). For example, doctors in the 1920s and 1930s feared that masses of American children, even the well-off, lacked key nutrients for high-level functioning, and prescribed vitamin fortification for the general populace (Biltekoff 2013, 46–76; Apple 1996; LeBlanc 2019, 18). Deficiency diseases call for technical measures, like the small plastic arm bracelets that Doctors Without Borders carry to diagnose malnutrition in children (Redfield 2013, 16). This kind of operation lends to thinking about hungry people as a population rather than as specific individuals and communities. "World hunger" counts up all those people in one global sum of malnourishment, 850 million worldwide (Philipps and Ilcan 2003, 135). In these ways "deficiency" can operate like an "anti-politics machine," reducing complex social, economic, cultural, and political dynamics to a single quantifiable disease (Ferguson 1994; Biltekoff 2024, 14).

By the mid-twentieth century, the terms "deficiency" and "deprivation" expanded far beyond nutrition to mark a whole category of people as inadequate, incapable, inferior (Moran 2018, 133; Williams-Forson 2022, 14). Entire countries and regions (especially in Africa) are labelled as deficient, whether in food supplies, knowledge, or governance (Tappan 2017, 47). In the United States, experts and politicians accuse poor, Black, and immigrant mothers of failing to properly nourish and educate their children (Gálvez 2019; Valdez 2021). Nonwhite food cultures are denigrated as unhealthy, and neighborhoods described as "food deserts," neglecting their complexity, vibrancy, and resourcefulness (Reese and Garth 2020; Yates-Doer 2024).

In a very different mode, "hunger" can stand in for a politics of the poor, a public claim on the collective commons. Hunger elicits outrage and justifies demands for economic justice. In this way hunger is a "rhetorical weapon of the weak" (Allen 2007, 24). Hunger, especially among children, is an indictment of a system that condemns people to suffer. Colonial famines, hunger strikes for political rights, and hunger marches during the Great Depression politicized hunger in the early twentieth century (Vernon 2007, 44). In the late twentieth century, movements for social and economic justice resonated with the rallying cry "We Are Hungry" (Potorti 2017). The human right to be free of hunger was enshrined in the United Nations Covenant on Economic, Social, and Cultural Rights (Office of the United Nations and FAO 2010). By contrast with medical definitions, "political hunger" is grounded in emotion (anger, pity), economic rights, and claims to social justice (Alkon and Agyeman 2014).

Partly in response to the politicization of hunger, "food insecurity" has come to substitute for hunger in official and expert discourse over the past forty years. Starting in the 1980s, the United Nations laid out a plan to guarantee world food security, defined as a household's ability to access healthy and culturally appropriate foods at all times.[5] Instead of political rights, "food security" focuses attention on individual purchasing power and consumers' access to local and global food markets (Jarosz 2011, 124; Jarosz 2014). The solution to food insecurity appears to be to grow more food, more quickly (Philips and Ilcan 2003). With its focus on household units and personal consumption, food insecurity policy can make it easy to blame individuals for their own poverty, instead of addressing structural change (Carney 2015; Vaughn 2017).

"Food insecurity" also refers to fear, anxiety, and stress about having enough food. Researchers in the 1990s developed a household survey instrument that marked people as food insecure if they worried that they would run out of money to buy food, or skipped meals to make their household food supply last longer (Radimer 2002; Olson 2010). The survey was grounded in poor women's descriptions of their lived experiences (Radimer 1990). The US Department of Agriculture (USDA) quickly picked up this instrument and bureaucratized it; now the USDA runs an annual national food insecurity survey. By contrast, food justice activists politicized food insecurity. Community food security, for activists, meant collective self-determination and autonomy over food (Ashman et al. 1993).

By the turn of the twenty-first century, hunger came to represent a complex of danger, anxiety, deficiency, and individual responsibility. Public fears around weight, fatness, and the so-called obesity epidemic turned uncontrolled hunger into a threat that needed to be neutralized (Biltekoff 2013, 114). Increasingly health experts and neuroscientists came to describe hunger and food craving as a form of addiction. Sugar, carbohydrates, chocolates, and other palatable foods seem to hold some people in "the thrall of external forces" that characterizes addiction (Campbell 2007, 20). Sweet and fatty foods stimulate cannabinoids and opioids within the body, provoking reactions that medical researchers analogize to drug responses (Pelchat 2002). Some people appear more vulnerable than others to such diseases of the will; this is the underlying assumption for most obesity research today, which seeks to identify an obesogenic typology, genetic profile, character, or environment. This typology is frequently associated with Black and Indigenous people, often women (Moran 2018, 137; Strings 2019). Some people's hungers, cravings, and desires appear uniquely dangerous, unhealthy, maladapted to the modern consumer market.

Although these versions of hunger have dissimilar political, psychological, and physiological effects, they share a common logic of negation. Hunger corresponds to a negation of the desires, relations, and material substances that nourish and sustain life. Hunger characterizes what Sylvia Wynter (2003, 321) has called the "archipelago of Human Otherness," an archipelago of the unlivable. Hunger appears natural because this mode of understanding has dominated in the West since the dawn of the age of empire. Eugenics and free-market ideologies require that some people—marked by class, color, and indigeneity—be sacrificed (Wynter 2003, 329). This pattern of negation and sacrifice often seems like just how things work in "normal life." "This normal way of life is rooted in racial condemnation," writes Katherine McKittrick (2013, 7), "it is spatially evident in . . . geographies described as battlegrounds or as burned, horrific, occupied, sieged, unhealthy, incarcerated, extinct, starved." Hunger describes an existence recognized only in its negation, that which "must be sacrificed" to the free market and natural selection.

. . .

I wrote much of this book during the Coronavirus outbreak. Donald Trump, Mitch McConnell, and the House Freedom Caucus did all they could to punish and purge recipients of SNAP benefits, even as a global pandemic wreaked havoc on employment and wages. In cities across the United States cars lined up for miles for drive-through food bank distributions. Almost 30 percent of US households with children were food insecure as of June 2020; one in eight children was not getting enough to eat because their families couldn't afford to feed them. These numbers were unprecedented in the contemporary era, many times higher than during the worst of the 2008 Great Recession. Racist disparities in food insecurity widened; insecurity early in the pandemic increased moderately for white families and catastrophically for Black and Latinx families (Bauer 2020). Meanwhile, Republicans resisted expanding food benefits out of fear they will "create a moral hazard for people to be on welfare," a thinly veiled racial condemnation (DeParle 2020). If someone is hungry, antiwelfare politicians suggest, then they must be lazy, fraudulent, or biologically unfit.

Hunger in the United States is often described as a paradox: want in the midst of plenty, scarcity in the midst of abundance. There is, in fact, no paradox. Janet Poppendieck, in her study of food assistance during the Great Depression, has pointedly rejected this framing. This apparent paradox described "the normal, predictable working of the economy rendered extreme by the Depression" (Poppendieck 2014, xvii). Hunger does not appear only by accident or hard luck and is not simply an effect of inequitable purchasing power. As Ashanté Reese and Hanna Garth (2020, 4) put it, the food system is not "broken"; it is working exactly as it was intended to. In a state of hunger, it is unclear where compulsion and desire end and begin. Hunger mixes desire and addiction, coercion and control, in what Patricia Williams (1988) has called "antiwill." What does it mean to stop by a fast food joint or skip a meal because you're in a hurry? To eat food that tastes or feels good instead of food that is labelled "good for you"? What does it mean to choose to purchase health insurance, a car repair, textbooks, or nice shoes instead of eating? Or to refuse poor working conditions and choose to survive on welfare or food bank donations?

This ambiguity, this mixture of compulsion and desire, is advantageous for those who would blame individual choices for hunger and metabolic disease. In these situations violence is masked as an individual's inability to adapt to market conditions or to modern life. Coercion is masked as autonomy. Extermination is masked as poverty. A different kind of antiwill gets produced by the economy of processed foods. People, when hungry, may want to eat what is fast, nearby, cheap, easy, sweet, fatty, salty, filling, satisfying. Liquid energy drinks, extruded corn-based cheese puffs, and potato-flour chips are designed to escape detection by the mouth so that eaters don't stop eating. What does it even mean to be hungry in that context? As Mars Inc. says in its ads for Snickers chocolate candy bars, "You're not you when you're hungry."

Hunger is violence. "It is unacceptable," states the United Nations, "that in a world that produces enough food to feed its entire population, more than 1.5 billion people cannot afford a diet that meets the required levels of essential nutrients and over 3 billion people cannot even afford the cheapest healthy diet" (FAO et al. 2020, ix). There is nothing natural or inevitable in those numbers. To cite Liz Theoharis (2020), leader of the Poor People's Campaign, the universal potential for abundance is a "well-kept secret," obscured by free-market ideologies. "Scarcity is a myth." Even in an era when overconsumption churns through unprecedented quantities of fuel and matter, scarcity and hunger seem ever-present. Everywhere there is fear and anxiety about running out, spending too much, losing out, not having enough. How is this? What happens when we stop thinking about scarcity as a natural fact of life, a given? What if we asked how and why hunger, scarcity, deprivation, desire, and need are produced? An inventory of the past is necessary for imagining otherwise.

• • •

This research emerged through many encounters. The first class I ever taught was on hunger and famine in modern history. I've since taught many versions of that class at the University of California–Riverside (UCR); over time our discussions have shifted from a focus on historical famines to very personal conversations about the hunger that UCR students are experiencing every day in their classrooms. My first book, *Vital Minimum*, looked at the science and politics behind how to define the "life" in a "living wage" (Simmons 2015; Simmons 2017). That book focused on France, although I always had an eye on parallel debates and experiments in the United States.

I wrote a history of Impostor Syndrome (Simmons 2016) and was astounded to find in my research that mid-twentieth-century psychologists constantly were talking about hunger. Psychologists used hunger as a tool to model other, more abstract drives and motivations, such as the motivation to solve a puzzle, to score an A on a test, or to succeed in life. One particularly oddball yet very influential psychologist, Donald McClelland, came up with a numerical scale of the "Need to Achieve" that he initially tested using a scale of hunger and food deprivation (McClelland and Atkinson 1948; see Luissier 2017). *Where on earth did that come from*, I wondered. I discovered, as I write in chapter 1, that hunger figured at the very beginning of experimental psychology. Hunger became a tool for testing the effects of rewards and punishments on animals' and people's ability to learn.

I knew from my UCR colleague Cliff Trafzer that hunger has been used historically to force people to learn: the US Bureau of Indian Affairs withheld rations to get Native families to send their children to Indian schools (Trafzer, Keller, and Sisquoc 2006). This connection pointed me toward a field of research in Native history, from James Daschuk's (2014) powerful story of hunger and genocide in *Clearing the Plains* to contemporary work on Native food sovereignty. More than anything, this research was impelled by UCR students' advocacy for recognition and repair of food insecurity on campus. Even before the pandemic, half of UCR undergraduates were food insecure. Half again of those met the US Department of Agriculture criteria for "very food insecure," meaning that they regularly skipped meals for financial reasons (University of California 2024). UCR student activists politicized hunger and demanded solutions. (For more on this topic, see the conclusion.)

My research is responsible to these students and others who may feel shame or alienation due to hunger and food insecurity. For them, I want to get this story right. By which methods could I weave together these multiple and intersecting threads? I began with a history of science. But "background" histories intruded and demanded to be treated with great care. Readers of my early drafts also wanted more. What exactly did cats, dogs, and rats in puzzle cages have to do with Indian schools? What did white supremacist violence in the American South have to do with medical definitions of starvation and malnutrition? These are not distinct, parallel, or analogous histories. There is a direct connection between the production of scientific knowledge about hunger and the production and weaponization of hunger itself.

This book explores the intersection of racial capitalism and human biology. As Matthew Wolf-Meyer (2011, 878) has written, "American [racial] capitalism produces human biologies that accord with its claims and ends." This dynamic has two parts: one is the experience of living in specific bodies in space and time. The other part is the way that lived experience and bodies are understood, explained, and pathologized in terms that line up with specific political and economic ends. This work requires a materialist method, which treats hormones, neurons, microbiomes, bones, and brains as historical entities. Bodies shape and are shaped by historical developments, alongside economies, political power, labor relations, commodity flows, spatial infrastructures, and so on. There is no determinism here, neither biological nor cultural. This history operates on uneven time scales, incorporating scars and traces of deep generational pasts and the flows of everyday. This is a history of life chances and antichances, choices and antichoices, possibilities for health and liveliness.

Michel Foucault (2009) coined the term "biopolitics" to describe a specific phase in the government of life, which was concerned with the health, quality, and discipline of people as populations. This project needs something else, more like a socio-econ-psycho-bio-political history. A "material-semiotic-affective-infrastructural" history (Murphy 2017, 7). We could call it biohistory, but that word is already used to describe the findings of physical archaeology; anyway, perhaps the bio- prefix has been used enough already and we don't need any new words to do this. As Nancy Krieger (2011) has explained, there is a long history of critical sociopolitical epidemiology going back to Rudolf Virchow (2006 [1848]). This kind of method is evident in Rupa Marya and Raj Patel's (2021) biopolitical history of colonialism and inflammation, Lundy Braun's (2014) history of medical race correction, Wolf-Meyer's (2012) ethnography of sleep, Elizabeth Wilson's (2015) *Gut Feminism*, M. Murphy's (2011; 2017) work on distributed reproduction and populationism, and Anne Fausto-Sterling's (2008) work on bone density, race, and gender.

This book strengthens connections between histories of welfare, histories of science, and food studies. I am inspired by many scholars of food justice and welfare. Ashanté Reese (2021; 2022), Hanna Garth (Reese and Garth 2020), Monica M. White (2018), Bobby Smith II (2023), Julie Guthman (2011), Emily Yates-Doerr (2024), and Greta de Jong (2016) are models for engaged scholarship that links contemporary forms of neoliberal work and consumption to ongoing plantation histories. Annelise Orleck (2011), Felicia Kornbluh (2015), Premilla Nadasen (2004), Alyosha Goldstein (2018), and Alondra Nelson (2011) show how to work as scholar-activists with and for the long struggle for welfare and health, rights and survival. Nancy Fraser and Linda Gordon (1994), Jill Quadagno (1990), Gwendolyn Mink (1996), Janet Poppendieck (1999), Marion Nestle and Sally Guttmacher (1992), Dána-Ain Davis (2007), Elizabeth Hinton (2016), Julilly Kohler-Hausmann

(2017), and Maggie Dickinson (2019) have fought scholarly battles against the violently reductionist ideologies behind late-twentieth-century welfare reform. Unfortunately that work is never done.

. . .

Hunger is a technology. By that I mean that hunger is not a natural event but a product of human agency.[6] Hunger is a "lever," in the words of a presidential staffer in the Johnson administration, to "get something done" (Riley 2017, 262). Technologies align material realities with specific ideas about how the world should be (Wise 1993, 207; Hecht 2011; Clarke and Fujimura 1992, 6). In that sense, technologies only really become apparent through their use, when they are put into repeat operation (Morrison and Morgan 1992, 6). Technologies are also designed to be reproduced (Coleman 2009, 178). I call hunger a technology because I see a pattern repeating across different times and places in twentieth-century America: hunger is produced, on purpose, to get people (or animals) to do something. In many areas of American life, hunger has become a "default setting" that quietly and powerfully reinforces existing social hierarchies (Benjamin 2019, 2).

What kind of technology is hunger? In this book I describe three uses of hunger: as method, as weapon, and as policy. Any psychologist will recognize food deprivation (hunger) as a standard method. Open any number of psychology reports, and you will find experimental subjects deprived of food for twelve to forty-eight hours before taking a taste test, running a maze, or some such. Hunger is a method for motivating and modifying specific behaviors. Hunger is also, relatedly, a weapon. In carceral spaces (Indian agencies, plantations, prisons) hunger is deployed to control and to punish. Extreme hunger (starvation) can be used to eliminate whole groups or peoples and erase them from the land. Finally, hunger is a policy. Federal law, government agency rules, and executive policies, across the twentieth century, created and fostered hunger by design. Policies, laws, and rules were enacted to make people hungry—incarcerated people, Black Hills Sioux, welfare recipients, beneficiaries of foreign food aid—to comply with specific demands (moving off the land, getting a job, following a directive).

Hunger is often presented as natural, inevitable, or the result of bad choices. Because of this, many people with hunger have come to see themselves as maladapted, as lacking in self-control, or as predestined to suffer because of an unfortunate genetic or economic heritage. Hunger appears as an individual psychological or physiological affliction. We know that there are strong correlations between hunger and social conditions such as stress, but the neuroscience of hormonal flows and neural pathways captures only a limited view of this dynamic. This book offers a historical counterpoint to ahistorical, internalizing, and moralizing tendencies.

Each chapter describes a particular form of hunger, one way in which hunger was produced and deployed. People in power used hunger to suppress dissent and difference as well as to impose control and compliance. But they never fully succeeded. Hunger misfired. Experiments failed. Hungry people and animals found ways to resist and subsist. The chapters track two interwoven threads: politics and science. Chapters 1, 3, 6, and 7 describe political struggles over hunger, and how hunger has been deployed to control land, labor, and freedom. Chapters 2, 4, 5, and 8 focus on the history of science, and what that history tells us about the biopolitics of hunger. Each chapter unpacks a concept or framework for understanding hunger and follows how it was used in the world, its effects, and how it was resisted. Sometimes the connections between ideas, experiments, practices, and politics were direct, as in the way that deficiency theories shaped midcentury welfare policy. Or the way that eugenic commitments informed how scientists and politicians dealt with hunger. Other times they were indirect, like the connection between early twentieth-century Indian schools and animal intelligence experiments. Each chapter is about a different material-epistemic technology. Chronologically, the chapters focus on one theme at a moment in time.

Scientists were often much more explicit about what they were doing than were food companies, employers, or politicians. Hunger experiments were almost always designed to model something happening outside of the lab, in human society: elementary education, motivation to work, behavior modification. Scientists had no compunction about appearing cruel or stingy. They said it straight-up: they deprived their subjects of food so that they would do things, change their habits, solve a puzzle, press a lever, run to a target, or respond to a psychological test. Scientists manipulated their subjects' ability to control their own eating, to see what happened. As a result, scientists left some of the clearest descriptions of what hunger meant and how it worked at particular moments in time.

Scientists also made hunger into something natural, seemingly without a history. Even as scientists drew upon surrounding ideologies about hunger, learning, desire, and control, they smoothed out the particularities and turned these ideologies into universal statements about how nature functioned (Williams 2020). Not all scientists reinforced the status quo so smoothly. Some researchers followed the political traditions of scientific materialism and social medicine. Physiologists called out food companies for manipulating consumers' taste and hormonal signaling and causing addictions to sugar or carbs. Doctors diagnosed malnutrition and demanded free food for their patients. Neuroscientists named stress, racism, and exploitation as social determinants of health. Still, scientists created an epistemic infrastructure for what Katherine McKittrick (2013, 7) has called "the normal way of life," where exploitation is every day. Scientists' naturalizing work allowed certain kinds of relationships to seem normal and acceptable.

Chapter 1 defines what one nineteenth-century Indian agent called "the starving process": coercion by starvation. Nineteenth-century US agents programmatically and explicitly produced hunger to force Native people to sell territory, to move from their ancestral lands, and to accommodate settler-colonial regimes of labor and land use. Starvation was also mobilized against Black economic and political enfranchisement during Reconstruction. The starving process was designed to create a state of antiwill, in which people had to "agree" to accommodate white settler demands in order to survive. Chapter 2 shows how scientists at the turn of the twentieth century replicated the "starving process" in their animal experiments. Hunger was at the origin of the field of experimental psychology, in studies of animal learning. Countless experiments tested the effects of "punishment" (electric shocks) versus "reward" (the relief of hunger) on the speed of learning. By the mid-twentieth century, producing hunger was understood as a standard, normative method, associated especially with educational and behaviorist psychology.

Chapter 3 tells the story of the Hunger Marchers, a mass movement of hunger activism that spread across the United States during the Great Depression. Employers and welfare agents withheld food to enforce particular forms of labor, displacement, and political action. Poor people mobilized to oppose these practices of power. In the early years of the Great Depression, a coalition led by sharecroppers, miners, unemployed people, women, and Black activists and Communist Party members organized Hunger Marches under the banner "Fight—Don't Starve." Chapter 4 describes how the United States mobilized and controlled hunger at the close of the Second World War. American officials and experts viewed food as a vehicle to reconstruct war-damaged cultures and societies. Scientists at the University of Minnesota put volunteer subjects on a semistarvation diet and observed its effects on their physical and mental health as well as their social and political capacities. The Minnesota researchers, alongside social scientists in Europe and Asia after the war, defined "the hungry" as a political subject. Hunger appeared as a threat to political stability and a stimulus to violence and revolution.

Chapter 5 is about how food itself can provoke or suppress hunger. Sugar advertisements sold the public on the idea that sugar could help them curb their own hunger. At the same time, physiologists began to suspect that homeostasis, the body's ability to self-regulate, was a myth. Food commodities could themselves produce hunger in the form of uncontrollable cravings. Midcentury sugar cravings created the conditions for new forms of addiction research and food marketing. This was a different instance of antiwill: hunger as addiction. Chapter 6 is about starvation as a weapon of white supremacy. The chapter studies survival experiments undertaken by poor Black residents of the South, in response to their systematic starvation by plantation owners and the white power structure. Medical experts, mobilized in parallel to the Civil Rights movement, documented malnutrition and starvation not just in the South but across the whole United States. Scientific debates over how to define and explain malnutrition revealed ideological differences over the nature of poverty. Activists proclaimed that "hunger is *real*" and directly connected poor people's hunger to histories of racism, labor exploitation, and dispossession.

Chapter 7 examines carceral hunger. Hunger is produced every day in American prisons and jails. In the 1970s, prisons across the country shifted to from regimes of starvation to regimes of hunger based on cheap food and behavior control. From this perspective, carceral hunger offers insight on broader regimes of food insecurity that emerged in the 1980s, in the context of punitive welfare reform. Although raw starvation is widely condemned today as a form of torture, feeding people impoverished foods, under conditions of violence and unpredictability, has become normal and normative. Chapter 8 offers a history of the science of hunger suppression, desire, longing, and capitalism. I trace a scientific history of Ozempic (semaglutide), in which I consider what semaglutide reveals about hunger. In an extractive, violent, and stochastically changing world, hunger expresses a gut feeling that things are not right. This kind of hunger is a combination of wanting and longing, a constant, fixed, involuntary attention. I show how Ozempic could be understood by one of Novo Nordisk's own research affiliates as a project of Marxist pharmacology.

I close the book with a reflection on hunger and learning at UC Riverside, where I work and teach. Student activists at the university and elsewhere are pointing a way forward, toward collective care and a nourishing university.

. . .

Hunger, in American foundation stories, ended at the first Thanksgiving. The American dream is all about security and plenty. I remember one Thanksgiving, a day of collective food abundance that also marks the history of Native people's dispossession. I was a small and very skinny child. My aunts would declare loudly, more to each other rather than to me, "You can take another piece of pie, Dana, you don't have anything to worry about. You can eat as much as you want!" Which of course was their way of declaring their own desire and its willful thwarting. I remember the shame of being in a position to eat all I wanted, in contrast to the self-control and abnegation of those I loved. Needless to say, I did not take a second piece of pie, and I still do not to this day.

My research for this book has led me to interrogate the racialized history of that interaction. (The gender dynamic was already obvious to me at age twelve.) Suppressing hunger was clearly marked as white and middle class, an identity some members of my family (not the Wear side) clung to tenuously as descendants of poor Jewish Eastern European immigrants (Roediger 2006). My great-grandmother's handwritten memoir of her childhood in a Chicago tenement, run by a Bolshevik landlord, is an unceasing account of her desire for a dollar and some nice food. There is shame in hunger, and there is shame in failing to enact self-control in the face of desire and abundance.

With this project I try to reckon with how hunger gets embedded in everyday relations, and violence becomes a norm by its very repetition. Hunger is telegraphed at supermarket checkouts, in school cafeterias, and in charity campaigns for local food pantries. Major industrial food processors publicize national and international hunger in "public service" announcements. In 2000 advertising strategists at Philip Morris, which owned Kraft General Foods at the time, recommended to "use PM's [Philip Morris's] involvement in hunger as a recurring theme in ongoing mix of ads" and to "heavy up use of hunger ads against ethnic opinion leaders, women opinion leaders and active moms" (Philip Morris 2000, 15). Food vendors have long seen hunger as a growth opportunity (Guthman 2011, 163). The everyday violence of hunger is not a relic of history or an effect of underdevelopment. It is not a side effect of progress, history, or the expansion of capital. It is integral to those very processes. Because this violence is visible every day, one must conclude that hunger has become normal. I hope to disrupt that normalcy.

1

# The Starving Process

Mrs. Mattie Grinnell traveled from the Fort Berthold Reservation in North Dakota to Washington, DC, with the 1968 Poor People's March. "Gentlemen," she told the Senate Subcommittee on Employment, Manpower, and Poverty, "I came over here to Washington, DC. I am old enough to stay home and rest. But the councilmen over there at home don't try to do anything for us." She testified:

> In my young days, we had a good time. We got lots of game going on, buffaloes and deer and antelopes and prairie chicken and fish and everything else which comes handy. So, we never starved or anything. . . . Now the white people came on our reservation and killed off all our buffalo and all these game here so we have nothing to eat and we are starving half the time. The white people killed all our buffaloes out and they gave us commodities, which was just cornmeal, oats, and rice and all that; that is not really our food. But we have to eat that. Most of it is all wormy. . . . That is what I was trying to explain to President Johnson, and I came. (*Hunger and Malnutrition in US* 1968, 113–114)

She was 101 years old at the time. "I am the only full Mandan left," said Mrs. Grinnell.

Mattie Grinnell's story of hunger and dispossession bridges the nineteenth century and the late twentieth-century Poor People's campaign for economic and political rights. Hunger, in her account, was a tool of white power. Grinnell chose a transitive verb—to starve—to emphasize that her hunger was made, produced, by white settlers and their political and military administration. She connected the history of slaughtered bison to poor government commodity rations and punitive local administrators. Starvation came from the mass slaughter of traditional game; starvation also came from the impoverished commodities on which

17

the government forced her to live. Once her food relations "came handy"; later, food was "given" by the US government, sparingly and neglectfully. Cornmeal, oats, and rice themselves caused hunger. They were "not really our food," rather spoiled and wormy substitutes for varied, local, seasonal food sources. Grinnell experienced government provisioning as an act of violence, making her eat what she defined as nonfood. Mrs. Lucille Knight, also from Fort Berthold, accused the US government of killing her with commodities: "They are slowly driving me to my grave, pushing me along with that starchy food" (*Hunger and Malnutrition in US* 116).

In 1968, Grinnell and her community at the Fort Berthold Reservation were still struggling for control over their own subsistence. This outcome was neither accidental nor unintended. US agents produced hunger on purpose. Indian agent P. B. Hunt called it "the starving process": "It is necessary you should keep the Indian hungry if you wish him to do anything" (Hunt 1881, 80).[1] Hunger was a technology used to coerce social, political, economic, and cultural changes in the direction of private property, wage work, as well as land and capital accumulation. The starving process was designed to make its targets "do" things, change their behavior, their labor and subsistence strategies, and give up their land and political autonomy. Almost always this meant moving off their ancestral lands, making way for privatization and white ownership, and working for wages on farms and rural industries.

The starving process involved several strategies. Indian agents and military operatives tried to force Native people to give up hunting and gathering for European-style agriculture, even on lands not appropriate for farming. Hunting grounds were enclosed, lands privatized, plowed and fenced, and wild game killed off. The US Army cut off access to hunting supplies, horses, guns, and ammunition. The army facilitated a genocidal slaughter of bison on the Plains in the 1870s through the 1890s. Once sources of autonomous subsistence grew short, Indian agents used commodity rations to force other changes in foodways, labor, and culture. Rations were withheld or made conditional on agreeing to cede territories, move, plow up horse pastures for planting, or work on agency initiatives. US forces programmatically sought to destroy autonomous Native people and lifeways. They used commodity rations as instruments of political violence.

Even as US agents methodically employed hunger as a tool of coercion, they obfuscated their violence in a language of nature and history. Recursively hunger was made to appear natural and inevitable. It appeared as a side effect of the flow of history toward "progress and civilization," privatized land and agrarian cultivation. Hunger was explained by poverty rather than violent dispossession. By the twentieth century, anthropologists and scientists portrayed Native hunger as ahistorical. Some explained hunger as a character defect, the consequence of an indolent culture and an inability to work hard. Others posited that periodic starvation was an evolutionary inheritance, part of the hunting-and-gathering lifestyle. Hunger appeared as a natural consequence and a maladaptation to modernity.

But that hunger was made. American authorities imposed hunger as a cost or punishment to Native people who refused to concede power and land, as a tool of elimination. As the *Santa Cruz Sentinel* opined in 1889, "if the individual Indian cannot hold his farm and make a living . . . he can not by virtue of 'nationalization' of his land bar out someone who will make good use of it. He must work, sell or starve."

. . .

In 1872, Oglala Sioux chief Maȟpíya Lúta (Red Cloud) came to a council with military officers, commissioners, and agents who insisted that the Sioux give up their sovereign land in the Black Hills and move to a new agency in Indian Territory. A clerk recorded their conversation:

> *General Smith:*  I want all to know that I expect, before next moon, to have orders to give no more rations here, and but little time is left in which to put up your buildings [on a new Indian agency site]. . . .
>
> *Red Cloud:*  If you are going to stop the rations say so, and tell the truth.
>
> *General Smith:*  I do tell the truth. I expect the order. There is plenty on the way to go to the place you select, but the Great Father will not send it here.
>
> *Red Cloud:*  Before the houses are built the provisions will be spoiled.
>
> *General Smith:*  We want you to decide now, and the houses will be built at once. . . .
>
> *Red Cloud:*  This is the last time I will come here. I am going to leave now. . . .
>
> *General Smith:*  Very well. I want you to remember that what I say is the truth, and after next moon no more rations will be given here to anybody; and for this reason we want you to decide now where you will have your agency. If you don't and your women and children are hungry, it is your own fault. (*Report of the Commissioner* 1872, 25)

Just four years earlier, the 1868 Fort Laramie Treaty had established the boundaries of sovereign Sioux territory. Gold was discovered in the Black Hills soon after, however, and prospectors illegally poured in. The United States set out to extract the Black Hills from the Sioux for white exploitation and settlement, by convincing the Sioux to sell their sacred treaty land and to move to Indian Territory. These proposals met with a wall of refusal. Commissioners finagled agreement from only 10 percent of tribal men, far fewer than the three-quarters vote required by treaty to pass a deal (Cook-Lynn and Gonzales 1999, 240). In response the US government chose a strategy of starvation.

US agents wielded hunger as a technology of antiwill, to take up Patricia Williams's term (Williams 1988; Nichols 2020, 131). General John Smith demanded that Maȟpíya Lúta and the Sioux give legal consent to alienate their sacred land. Consent had to be willful, in the form of a "decision" to sell and move elsewhere, to fulfill the formal requirements of treaty and contract. When Maȟpíya Lúta exercised his will and refused, Smith blamed this antidecision for the resulting violence ("if . . . your women and children are hungry, it is your own fault"). US agents used hunger to turn will into antiwill, refusal into violence, destruction into self-destruction. And yet, Maȟpíya Lúta and his people refused. Sioux people continue to refuse to this day (Estes 2019; Robertson 2022).[2]

Because of commissioners' failure to produce concession, and the strength of Sioux refusal, the Black Hills case left a clear archival record of the starving process. Commissioners did not manage to bring back to Washington, DC, a valid agreement to cede the land. In response, and in the wake of the US defeat at the Battle of Little Big Horn, Congress contravened the 1868 treaty and enacted a patently unconstitutional law seizing the Black Hills. The act of August 15, 1876, became known as the "Sell or Starve Act." The 1876 act explicitly made survival conditional on acquiescence and set starvation as the price of refusal: "hereafter there shall be no appropriation made for the subsistence of the Sioux, unless they first relinquished their rights to the hunting grounds outside the [1868 treaty] reservation, ceded the Black Hills to the United States, and reached some accommodation with the Government that would be calculated to enable them to become self-supporting" (Cook-Lynn and Gonzales 1999, 239). A follow-up act in February 1877, when the government still could not prevail, stipulated the rations that Sioux would receive if they did concede: beef or bacon, flour, corn, and a little coffee, sugar, and beans. "Such rations, or so much thereof as may be necessary, shall be continued until the Indians are able to support themselves" (Cook-Lynn and Gonzales 1999, 240). "Self-supporting" in this context referred to permanent settlement, agricultural cultivation, and integration into markets for goods and labor.

Three further conditions in the act reflected standard policies on many Indian agencies: First, rations would be issued to the "head of each separate family," thus reinforcing individualism and patriarchy at the expense of tribal identity. Second, no rations would be issued for children between the ages of six and fourteen, unless they enrolled in Indian schools designed to assimilate children to Euro-American culture and wage work. Third, "whenever the said Indians shall be located upon lands which are suitable for cultivation, rations shall be issued only to the persons and families of those persons who labor" (Cook-Lynn and Gonzales 1999, 240). "Patriarchy or starve," "assimilate or starve," and "work or starve" were logical extensions of "sell or starve." Each proposed a nonchoice between self-negation and extinction.

Government rations themselves were designed to force assimilation at the cost of hunger. As Mattie Grinnell testified, wheat flour, sugar, and coffee did not constitute nourishing food for her. Rations on Indian agencies were often spoiled, insufficient, or entirely lacking (Ostler 2001, 118). At first, Indian agents distributed beef rations to the Sioux "on the hoof"; herds of cattle were released every two weeks at different locations on the reservation, and men were able to hunt cattle in a way similar to how they once hunted bison. Some Indian Bureau officials objected to this arrangement as "barbaric" and sought to replace it with pre-slaughtered cuts of meat (Ostler 2001, 118). Thus commodity rations were designed intentionally to negate long-standing relations with specific seeds, plants, and animals (Hubbard 2014, 301).

Archival traces suggest that this pattern, the starving process, repeated across the nineteenth century and beyond. In 1866, General William Tecumseh Sherman tried to convince Ute leaders to move onto a reservation. Utes refused to give up their seasonal subsistence rounds of hunting-and-gathering; they argued that immobility represented death (Lewis 1994, 40). Sherman "tried to explain and reason with them in various ways, but at last broke up the council in disgust, and blurted out in his peculiar way, as he strode back to his quarters, 'They will have to freeze and starve a little more, I reckon, before they will listen to common sense!'" (Lewis 1994, 42). Similarly, Canadian authorities withheld rations in 1882 to force Cree dissident Big Bear and his band to surrender, making way for railroad construction and white settlement. As James Daschuk (2014, 123) has written, "once the Indians were settled on reserves (and dependent on rations), the government could counter protests by withholding food."

In 1887 the US Congress mandated the enclosure of unincorporated Native American territories into private allotments, annexed to the United States. With the Dawes Act, Congress sought to complete the task of assimilating Native people into an individualist, agrarian mode of existence, while appropriating "extra" lands for white settler occupation (Adams 1988, 5). Four years later, in 1891, Congress mandated schoolhouse education of Native American children. If a family refused to send children to Indian schools, often boarding schools miles from home, Congress authorized the Indian Bureau to withhold that family's rations (Adams 1988, 3). An Indian agent at the New Mexico reservation of the Mescalero Apaches wrote in 1897 that "the deprivation of supplies . . . worked a change" in families unwilling to let their children go. "Willing or unwilling every child five years of age was forced into school" (Jacob 2006, 215). The Dawes Act required the president to certify that a tribe was ready to adopt a sedentary agrarian life, before the Indian Bureau could convert their territory to allotments and sell the remaining land to white settlers. Hunger was a tool to open those lands quickly to dispossession (Adams 1988, 19).

The "starving process" led to mass extermination of Native people's nonhuman relations. On the West Coast, dams and industrial fisheries eliminated Chinook salmon (Norgaard 2019, 150). On the Plains, US government agents and private citizens empowered (and often supplied) by the military carried out extermination at an unprecedented scale. Tasha Hubbard (2014) has argued convincingly that the slaughter of millions of bison should be characterized as a genocide of the Plains "first people." The *United States Army and Navy Journal* reported in 1868 on a remark by Sherman "that the quickest way to compel the Indians to settle down to civilized life was to send ten regiments of soldiers to the Plains, with orders to shoot buffaloes until they became too scarce to support the r******s" ("Buffalo Campaign" 1869, cited in Smits 1994, 317). Although Sherman did not call up these regiments, he and other army officials facilitated and encouraged bison slaughter across the Plains. General Philip Sheridan called for "destroying the Indians' commissary" (Smits 1994, 330) and advised Sherman to "make [Indians] poor by the destruction of their stock, and then settle them on the lands allotted to them" (Smits 1994, 323).

. . .

The presence of Generals Sherman and Sheridan, architects of scorched-earth tactics during the Civil War, alerts us to connections between the American South and West. During the Civil War, Southerners called the Union blockade of their ports "the starvation policy" (Smith 2011, 13). Sherman (1875, 211) demanded that Confederates at Savannah surrender or suffer starvation. Sheridan destroyed the fields and railroads that provided subsistence to residents and enemy troops in the Shenandoah Valley (Sherman 1875, 210–211). Union policies toward formerly enslaved refugees, housing them in "contraband camps" and requiring labor in exchange for food, echoed and prefigured later Indian policy; like Sherman and Sheridan, many officers served consecutively in the South and West (Downs 2012, 171). Officials in the Freedmen's Bureau and Indian agents were excessively concerned about their charges' indolence and their dependency on government rations and believed that hunger was a stimulus to work (Downs 2012, 55).

Following Emancipation, formerly enslaved people entered the "free labor" force in a context of hunger, failed harvests, policing, and vigilante violence. In the chaotic years after the end of the Civil War, Southern plantation owners and formerly enslaved workers engaged in asymmetrical struggles over the meaning and value of labor. The bondage of chattel slavery gave way to "free" contracts, sanctioned by federal authorities, and debt peonage. As a Union army commander put it, "the liberty given [freedpeople] simply means liberty to work, work or starve" (cited in Saville 1994, 3). Plantation landowners restricted freedpeople's access to food as a means of labor discipline. Formerly enslaved people planted corn, beans, potatoes, and other food crops where they could, and some acquired land for themselves (Wallach 2019, 65; Green, Green, and Kleiner 2014, 52). But plantation landowners leveraged their property rights to block such attempts at independence. Owners locked up harvested seed cotton, including the workers' shares, and distributed the proceeds only at the end of the harvesting season. Planters who paid cash wages similarly delayed payments until the end of the year. Some planters refused to allow workers to grow their own food at all; many prohibited workers from seeking extra work elsewhere or from selling their share of the cash crop directly on the market. Emancipation overturned customary rights that had allowed enslaved people to grow and manage some of their own food supplies (Saville 1994, 112–136).

Landowners were backed by federal authorities, many of whom believed in the "instructive" power of hunger to get people to work (Emberton 2013, 72).[3] The

Freedmen's Bureau, established by Congress to manage the transition from slavery to free labor, provided food rations for many formerly enslaved people in the immediate aftermath of war but refused aid for able-bodied adults; within a year the Bureau cut off almost all rations (Emberton 2013, 58–59; Farmer-Kaiser 2010, 39). A Bureau agent in South Carolina wrote that "only actual suffering, starvation and punishment will drive many [formerly enslaved people] to work" (cited in Emberton 2013, 57). Another Bureau official reported that starving freedpeople in his district were reduced to eating green corn, pond lilies, and alligators (Emberton 2013, 57). In some areas federal officers actively encouraged landowners to lock up the means of subsistence to "keep the freedman true to his [labor contract] agreement" (Saville 1994, 116). Landowners or federal agents stored food supplies in a centralized warehouse and rationed them to workers. As chapters 3 and 6 recount, food advances and debt obligations severely limited plantation workers' autonomy well into the twentieth century.

Political coercion took place through direct violence (lynching) and threats of starvation. In the same year as the passage of the "Sell or Starve" act (1876), newspapers reported that Southern plantation owners were threatening freedmen's voting rights. The *Chicago Daily Tribune* quoted a speech by Colonel Edwards of South Carolina on the eve of the 1876 elections: "We have taken and subscribed to a solemn oath before God . . . to make no advances of food or permit any one to occupy our houses or premises who votes the Radical ticket again. We know what we are talking about. The colored people will starve, but we will not. Now is your last time. Become Democrats or you are ruined" ("Starvation and Death" 1876). Republicans accused Southern politicians of "presenting to the colored man the alternative of starvation or support of the Democratic party" (XLIV Congress 1876). These tactics echo threats against Black voter registration issued by plantation owners and White Citizens' Councils in the twentieth century at the time of the Poor People's March.

By debt and hunger, Emancipation spawned a state of "indebted servitude," "an anomalous condition betwixt and between freedom and servitude" (Hartman 1997, 126–131).[4] Frederick Douglass accused the Southern states of reinstituting slavery, in the form of the "power to starve." Douglass argued that control over the means of subsistence gave former slaveholders "power over life and death, which was the soul of the relation between master and slave." Plantation owners "could not, of course, sell [freedpeople], but they retained the power to starve them to death, and wherever this power is held there is the power of slavery" (Douglass 1882, 611–612).

. . .

By the late nineteenth century, the use of hunger as technology was widely practiced and publicly known.[5] Hunger was produced for economic and political ends. Indian agents and the press recast elimination by hunger as poverty. One could reproduce a litany of sources describing Native people as "a lot of paupers" dependent on public handouts, for whom "only the pinchings of hunger will drive them to work" ("Black Hills" 1875; Forney 1858, 211). But that serves no purpose other than to rehearse the insult. The ideology of pauperism, imported from English political economy, led Indian agents across North America to make rations conditional on farm work or wage labor. Indian agents styled themselves as directors of almshouses, where hunger figured as an "incentive to industry" (*Report of the Commissioner of Indian Affairs* 1878, 31, 140; Winslow 1882, 10; Daschuk 2014, 116). Hunger and poverty then served to justify the taking of lands that were not cultivated "industriously."

Through the twentieth century, ideologies of pauperism covered over material theft. Some imagined that both Native Americans and Black Americans would perish "naturally" as a result of underdevelopment (Emberton 2013, 71). Cultural ecologists associated a "bare subsistence" diet with a "meager" culture. As Ned Blackhawk has shown, anthropologist Julian Steward claimed in the 1940s that food scarcity had prevented Nevada Shoshone from developing a coherent tribal identity or culture. As a consequence, Steward argued, Nevada Shoshone should not be recognized as a sovereign tribe (Blackhawk 1997, 62–69). This is just one example of how hunger and starvation were offered as evidence of Indians' "natural" and inevitable dissipation. Recursively hunger appeared simultaneously a cause, an effect, and a reason for dispossession. But Native people resisted and did not succumb to assimilation, starvation, and destruction. In some cases, tribes turned US strategies to their own advantage, "alternately trading, raiding, accommodating and vanishing" (Heaton 2005, 37). Even after confinement to reservations, some recycled government annuity items into goods for prestige and sale. Sioux people used hides from government-issued cattle to make moccasins for sale to traders (Ostler 2001, 119). Shoshone Bannocks cut agency flannel into trim for horses and fashioned agency blankets into leggings for sale (Heaton 2005, 49). Utah and Colorado Utes collected government rations as part of their subsistence rounds, "incorporating traditional resources with crops and rations." Uintahs traveling through Colorado passed as White River Utes to receive rations there; in turn, Colorado Utes collected rations as Uintahs while visiting the Utah agency (Lewis 1994, 40). These peoples used rations as a form of resistance.

Native leaders across the nineteenth century named and contested the use of hunger as a tool of white power. To Maȟpíya Lúta, to leave hunger unfed was the greatest breach of his people's social bond. He warned that white men had deceived the Sioux with "shining things that pleased our eyes." Possessiveness, he warned, overturned "the wisdom of your fathers." He sarcastically described how to assimilate to possessive white culture: "you must lay up food, and forget the hungry. . . . Look around for a neighbor whom you can take at a disadvantage, and seize all that he has! Give away only what you do not want; or rather, do not part with any of your possessions unless in exchange for another's" (Red Cloud 2000 [1866], 130). Rejecting an ethos of dispossession, Maȟpíya Lúta articulated an ideal of mutual aid. In this, he echoed the words of other Indigenous leaders who associated food giving with solidarity and equated hunger with willful destruction.[6]

This history of the production of hunger, of the starving process, was largely ignored by mainstream culture during most of the twentieth century. Hunger seemed to burst upon the public scene in the late 1960s like a bad surprise. At the 1968 Senate Subcommittee hearing where Mattie Grinnell testified, officials expressed shock at discovering widespread hunger in prosperous postwar America. Senator Joseph Clark lamented: "For far too long, we have buried our heads in the sand like an ostrich, unwilling and, indeed, unprepared to face the truth" (*Hunger and Malnutrition in US* 1968, 1). But for many of the poor people in attendance, such as Grinnell, long histories of hunger as violence remained very much alive and present. The Reverend Ralph Abernathy, president of the Southern Christian Leadership Council and leader of the Poor People's Campaign, told the Senators that the US government had "let our people starve" (*Hunger and Malnutrition in US* 1968, 68). Andrés de Pineda, of Denver, Colorado, testified: "We speak for the oppressed, for the hungry thousands that exist in this country, to the tortures of many kinds that have been applied to us. . . . We are the ghosts, the sons of chiefs, gods, kings, and revolutionists, here to haunt you for what is rightfully ours, the human right to exist" (*Hunger and Malnutrition in US* 1968, 105).

These stories are well known to Native people and Native scholars alike. They are not mine. These stories belong to James Daschuk (2014), Hiʻilei Julia Hobart (2019), Kyle Powys Whyte (2016), Leanne Betasamosake Simpson (2017), Nick Estes (2019), Audra Simpson (2014), Ron Reid, Leaf Hillard (Norgaard, Reid, and Van Horn 2011), the Native American Food Sovereignty Alliance (NAFSA 2020), and many others active in the movement for Indigenous food sovereignty as well as to Reconstruction scholars such as Julie Saville (1994) and Saidiya Hartman (1997). I share these stories here because land dispossession, assimilation, and hunger were and are still reproduced in North America every day. Because right now I live and work on stolen land. Because these stories were just the beginning.

2

---

# Punishment and Reward

The first one to be hungry, on purpose and experimentally, was the cat. The cat was in a wooden box, and around her hung strings and wooden buttons and levers. She could smell fish outside. She hadn't eaten since the previous daylight. Edward Thorndike, who made the box and who held the fish, called the cat's state "utter hunger." Driven by hunger and the smell of fish, the cat swiped and clawed and pushed against the box and all the things around her. She moved impulsively, randomly, reaching at whatever she could grasp. All at once, the box opened and the cat leaped out toward the fish smell. The man offered her a tiny morsel; this was her "reward." The man picked the cat up and returned her to the box. Still driven by utter hunger, the cat began again to move about until the box door gave way, again and again, gaining very small pieces of fish, until the time when she no longer returned to the box. At the end of the day, at last, she and the other cats could eat "abundant food to maintain health, growth and spirits, but commonly some what [*sic*] less than they would of their own accord have taken" (Thorndike 1911, 27).

Dogs came after the cats, but the dogs howled loudly at night when Thorndike left them hungry and their cries awoke William James and his family sleeping upstairs. The dogs, like the cats, lived experimentally in James's basement, which James had lent to his postgraduate student as no suitable space could be found at Harvard University. Because of their howls, the dogs could not live in "utter hunger." They exercised in the wooden boxes at morning-time, when they had not yet eaten, and they "made great effort for a bit of meat," if somewhat irregularly (Thorndike 1911, 59).

I begin this chapter with a piece of what Steven Shaviro has called "speculative extrapolation." Shaviro (2016, 11) suggests that scientists and humanists both

26

practice a form of controlled free imagination, constructing hypothesis and testing them to see whether they work. I do not know whether Thorndike's cat was female. I do not know if she would recognize him as a "man," or if her experience matched his description of it. The anecdote is an attempt to extrapolate the hungry animal's subject position and to test this extrapolation against the known evidence. It matters to me to begin this narrative with a cat and her situation. I prefer to risk an imperfect speculation rather than to reproduce only the voice of a scientist-narrator (whose account of the same events appears below). I seek to pay attention to those who were hungry.

Edward Thorndike made starvation into a tool for the new field of experimental psychology. Within a decade after publication of his thesis, hunger became a standard instrument. Animal behavior labs spread to Harvard, Clark University, Cornell, Johns Hopkins, and the University of Texas, and psychologists in all of these labs adopted hunger as an epistemic tool. Hunger became a standard psychological apparatus, alongside new introductions such as Willard Small's (1900) animal maze and Robert Yerkes's (1907) electric shock apparatus. Psychologists tested hungry turtles, mice, rats, rhesus monkeys, and crows. This setup became standard to the extent that a young psychologist in 1911 could state his method simply and without elaboration, "hunger was used as a motive" (Hicks 1911, 142). Throughout the twentieth century, hunger remained an essential tool for comparative psychology. Hunger (mostly mouse hunger) remains an important model system today, in the fields of behavioral genetics and neurochemistry.

Hunger became a technology to produce behaviors and emotions. Scientists deprived kittens, monkeys, chicks, turtles, children, and soldiers of food for four, eight, twenty-four, or forty-eight hours and observed the effects. Hunger became a standard tool in part because its intensity could be controlled on an objectively measured scale, hours of deprivation. I want to think through the meaning and context of this choice. Why did producing hunger appear to Thorndike and his colleagues at the turn of the twentieth century as a reasonable and generative relation with their animal subjects? What led Thorndike to introduce hunger to these formative experiments in comparative psychology, and why does hunger remain so central to this field? What preexisting relations made hunger an obvious choice? What relations, in the end, did hunger experiments produce?

. . .

Edward Thorndike began his work on animal psychology at the same time that the US government implemented a program of Native American containment and reeducation through hunger (see chapter 1). I suggest that Thorndike's experiments, at the turn of the twentieth century, replicated this same relation in the animal laboratory.

FIGURE 1. Edward L. Thorndike's puzzle-box B1. *Source*: Robert Mearns Yerkes Papers, 1822–1985 (inclusive), Manuscripts & Archives, Yale University Library.

In 1897, Thorndike put a young cat in an uncomfortable situation:

> If we take a box twenty by fifteen by twelve inches, replace its cover and the front side by bars an inch apart . . . we shall have means to observe [a] *simple case of learning*. A kitten, three to six months old, if put in this box when hungry, a bit of fish being left outside, reacts as follows: it tries to squeeze through the bars, and bites at its confining walls. Some one of all these promiscuous clawings, squeezings, and bitings turns round the wooden button, and the kitten gains freedom and food. By repeating the experience again and again, the animal gradually comes to omit all the useless clawing, etc. . . . It has formed an association between the situation, "confinement in a box of a certain appearance," and the impulse to the act of clawing at a certain point of that box in a certain definite way. (Thorndike 1907, 22)

Many questions arise from this experimental description. What elements define this setup as a model of learning? How is it a "simple case"? Why kittens, and why were they hungry? What does it mean to think of this setup, described as "confinement in a box of a certain appearance," as a "situation"? One set of clues can be found in the history of Thorndike's menagerie and his academic trajectory. His model system for learning, hungry kittens in a box, became a paradigm for American educational practice. Learning, Thorndike told his readers, was governed by situations not by culture or personality. Certain situations could become technologies for producing effects in the mind. His experiments also shaped the new discipline of comparative psychology. Hunger became a tool for producing psychological knowledge and a model for how to stimulate learning.

Having carried out animal experiments for a year in William James's basement, Thorndike moved to complete his doctorate at Columbia University, which was more accommodating with a graduate stipend and on-campus laboratory space. He wrote to his future wife, Bess, that he was impatient to install his "menagerie" at Columbia; he was, he wrote, "hungry for work" (Jonçich 1968, 118). Thorndike was ambitious and eager to challenge prevailing assumptions about animal intuition and intellect. As the child of a New England traveling minister, he was raised in a culture of self-control and diligence; his prodigious publication record testifies to his professional discipline. He thought of himself as a disrupter, bringing scientific rigor, laboratory experiment, objective measurement, and statistical analysis to a field dominated by anecdote and speculation. His contemporaries praised his thesis on "Animal Intelligence" as a foundational work in the rising field of experimental comparative psychology (Washburn 1908, 11). Senior scholars in his field, however, did not appreciate Thorndike's brash dismissal of work preceding his own (Mills 1899).

Thorndike saw hunger as a solution to psychologists' lack of scientific objectivity. Hunger offered a controllable and quantifiable experimental variable. This variable could be measured using everyday equipment—scale balances (to weigh food) and clocks (to record duration of fasting and speed of activity). Subjected to a standard rate of food deprivation, animals presumably would respond with consistent behaviors. Animals in a state of "utter hunger" could be run repeatedly through a puzzle box and produce coherent results. Such results required no interpretation or subjective judgment: all an experimenter needed, said Thorndike, was a clock. "Facts . . . may be obtained by any observer who can tell time" (Thorndike 1911, 28). Hunger made objective psychology possible. These experiments turned animal psychology into laboratory work. Thorndike had to create his own experimental setup for animals. Just as he repurposed common technologies (clocks, boxes) as experimental instruments, he repurposed domestic animals as experimental subjects. He first installed his menagerie in his Cambridge, Massachusetts, boardinghouse, whose landlady voiced strong objections. From there the animals moved to James's basement then on to New York, to an attic in the new Columbia University psychology building. At various times Thorndike's attic lab housed chicks, kittens, dogs, a monkey, and even a tank of minnows. All were domesticated animals. Chicks, cats, and dogs depended on human food and care, and were accustomed to human infrastructure. Thorndike's experimental schedule must not have differed too much from that of a household pet, locked indoors and fed once each day according to human rhythms of industry, work, and consumption.

Thorndike tested his model for learning and intelligence on "simple" minds: kittens, chicks, children. Simple-minded subjects allowed him, he thought, to observe the operation of learning at its most basic. Before building cat puzzle boxes at Harvard, Thorndike traveled to a mental institution to study unconscious cues in young children. He gave pieces of candy to three-year-olds if they guessed correctly a number or letter he was thinking. When the authorities denied him further access to girls and boys (for reasons unclear), Thorndike turned to animals. Instead of candy, the animal subjects who succeeded in their task received a morsel of food to relieve their hunger. What applied to animals, at the most basic level, applied equally well to humans. To learn was not to think or intuit but to respond to "situations," which connect specific feelings, sensations, and bodily movements (Thorndike 1919, 136). Thorndike's model operated at a basic level, directing simple feelings to aggregate along a particular path. The key to learning, in his mind, was the capacity to form mental connections between ideas, actions, and things.

Thorndike made much of the fact that his kittens only gradually became better at opening the puzzle box's trap door. The smooth curve of their improvement suggested, he thought, that they stumbled across the right solution purely by blind and fumbling chance. He found "no sign of abstraction, or inference, or judgment" in kittens' repeated attempts to open the door (Thorndike 1911, 75). "The cat does not look over the situation, much less think it over, and then decide what to do" (Thorndike 1911, 74). He contemptuously dismissed observers who sought proof of animal intellect, memory, or rationality; such attempts, he scoffed, were as ridiculous as a zoologist looking for claws on a fish (Thorndike 1911, 75). Higher-level learning differed from animal learning by quantity not quality. Complex human intellect was "an extended variation from the general animal sort": intelligent people simply were able to form many more connections than animals or simple-minded folk. "[The] intellectual evolution of the race consists in an increase in the number and speed of formation of such associations" (Thorndike 1911, 294). He thought that the human capacity to form connections was inheritable, and he hoped to subject it to eugenic breeding.

Thorndike was a committed eugenicist and insisted on hereditary difference: "in the same way and for the same reason that tall parents have tall children or dark-haired parents dark-haired children, so also stupid parents have stupid children, hot-tempered parents have hot-tempered children, and musical parents, musical children" (Thorndike 1907, 195). One wonders how many families he actually observed. Inherited qualities determined children's capacities to make associations and learn. Thorndike did not hesitate to draw racist conclusions from this premise: he reportedly told a popular audience that psychology's first task following the World War I would be to investigate "the problem of the mental and moral qualities of the different elements of the population of the United States. What does this country get in the million or more Mexican immigrants from the last four years. What has it got from Italy, from Russia, from Scotland and Ireland?" (Jonçich 1968, 375). Late in his career, Thorndike sat on the board of the American Eugenics Association and the Subcommittee on Psychometry of the Eugenics

Research Association ("Sub-Committee on Psychometry" 1928). The kittens' simple minds modeled "feeble-minded" victims of eugenic segregation and violence.

Thorndike's cats left a long-lasting imprint on the American educational system (Tomlinson 1997, 367). In 1899 he was hired to bring his scientific, experimental rigor to the newly affiliated Columbia Teachers College, where he went on to train generations of American educational leaders. His textbooks, dictionaries, teaching, and testing materials extended his influence far wider. His *Thorndike-Barnhardt Junior* and *Intermediate Dictionaries*, containing selections of frequently used words, still remain in publication in the early twenty-first century. Education scholar Ellen Condliffe Lagemann (1989, 185), exaggerating somewhat on purpose, wrote: "One cannot understand the history of education in the United States during the twentieth century unless one realizes that Edward L. Thorndike won and John Dewey lost."

Teaching tools based on this educational model, many designed by Thorndike, spread across the United States. Thorndike "devised rating scales to standardize and measure children's proficiency in hand-writing, spelling, drawing, history and English comprehension, and sold millions of arithmetic textbooks that stressed drill, repetition and the 'overlearning' of basic skills" (Tomlinson 1997, 363). He was deeply involved in designing the Army Alpha and Beta tests for incoming recruits during World War I (Carson 2007, 206). He applied the same analytic zeal to children's education, disaggregating each skill into its smallest component tasks and exercising them one by one. The cat experiment showed, Thorndike claimed, that learning was cumulative not holistic. Teaching must focus exclusively on tasks with future use-value.

Thorndike excoriated classical humanistic education. He had no time for nebulous claims on behalf of general culture (Tomlinson 1997, 373). He single-handedly scoured word frequencies in a library of core English books, beginning with the Bible, so that his dictionaries would present only words that children were most likely to encounter every day. And encounter they did, through the laborious exercises that many American students today still undergo, as they copy vocabulary words five or ten times in a row. Thorndike's teaching technologies were to education what Frank Gilbreth's (1911) motion studies and the sciences of work were to industrial labor. Use-value guided both content and method: exercise, repetition, and reward. When schoolchildren rewrite their multiplication tables twenty times for a teacher's treat, when policy makers disparage humanist claims for the richness of general education, when education is sold as a set of transferrable skills, we have entered the cat box. We become part of Thorndike's model system.

. . .

Thorndike's cat work stimulated a consequential and long-lasting debate over punishment and reward. Was it better to prevent and punish, or to reinforce and reward? Which made animals (or children) learn best? Which was more efficacious, or more humane? In animal psychology punishment came to mean electric shocks, and reward meant to give some food to the deprived and hungry. Harvard psychologist Robert Yerkes wrote a scathing critique of Thorndike's method, which was by then (1907) the dominant paradigm in animal behavior study. "Usually in experiments with mammals hunger has been the motive depended upon," Yerkes wrote. "The animals have been required to follow a certain devious path, to escape from a box by working a button, a bolt, a lever, or to gain entrance to a box by the use of teeth, claws, hands, or body weight and thus obtain food as a reward." Yerkes objected to this method as both inconsistent and cruel. Experimenters could not be certain that their animals felt as hungry at the beginning of a test run as at its end; nor could they know if one animal's hunger was equivalent to another's. For hunger to function as a consistent motive, it would have to be so strong as to damage the animal and its abilities. For these reasons "the use of the desire for food as a motive in animal behavior experiments . . . [is] almost worthless in the case of many mammals" (Yerkes 1907, 98).

An animal in a state of "utter hunger" (like Thorndike's cat) would be constitutionally unable to perform complex acts. The experiment itself produced an incapable subject. More than this, Yerkes strenuously objected to hunger on moral grounds. It was "inhumane." Hunger only works, he argued, when an experimental animal is so hungry that it exerts its strongest efforts continuously and repeatedly. Yerkes complained that "is not pleasant to think of subjecting [an animal] to extreme hunger in the laboratory for the sake of finding out what it can do to obtain food" (Yerkes 1907, 99). Yerkes proposed that electric shocks were superior to food deprivation on grounds of consistency and humanity. He exercised his animal subjects, dancing mice, in a "discrimination box" designed to test visual ability. In order to escape a narrow, confining corridor, the mouse had to pass through one of two white, gray, or black boxes. When it entered the "wrong" box, the mouse received an electric shock of a voltage "disagreeable but not injurious" to the animal. Over repeated tests, the mouse gradually came to choose the correct box more often than not.

Yerkes (1907, 99) vaunted the reliability of electric punishments as compared to food rewards: "The experimenter cannot force his subject to desire food; he can, however, force it to discriminate between conditions . . . by giving it a disagreeable stimulus every time it makes a mistake." He took pains to justify the "humaneness" of this practice: he regulated the current carefully, so as to prevent injury; the shocks were brief and went off at intervals; his mice remained in perfect health for months (Yerkes 1907, 100). As strange as it may appear to a reader today, Yerkes weighed food deprivation against painful electric shocks and judged the latter best. He translated these experimental methods into the language of utilitarian psychology. Electric shocks were "punishment"; food was a "reward" for hungry animals. These terms became common shorthand in the field. Yerkes (1907, 99) himself considered "the method of punishment . . . more satisfactory than the method of reward, because it can be controlled to a greater extent."

Decades and dozens of papers in the *Journal of Animal Behavior* (which Yerkes edited) tested the relative merits of punishment and reward. Mildred Hoge and Ruth Stocking of Johns Hopkins ran rats through a visual discrimination box. Some rats were hungry, and others were not. Their "punishment was a light electric shock; the reward, milk-soaked bread. The rapidity of learning in the two cases was taken as an indication of the value of the method" (Hoge and Stocking 1912, 42). Rats punished by shocks made correct choices somewhat more quickly than hungry rats incentivized by food. Hoge and Stocking recommended both punishment and reward for rapid learning.

Yerkes's student John D. Dodson compared the two tools, hunger and electric current, at various levels of intensity to determine the optimal setup for learning. He ran rats through a discrimination box under varied conditions of duress. As they became hungrier, the animals got faster and more accurate. Past forty-one hours without food, though, their performance declined. They appeared disturbed and "assumed the hump of a starving animal" (Dodson 1917, 265). Likewise, animals improved their performance when subjected to increasingly strong shocks, up to a point of severity beyond which their performance fell off. This curve of optimal drive strength became known as the Yerkes-Dodson Law (Yerkes and Dodson 1908). Dodson (1917, 237) compared "a curve of relative values of different degrees of hunger and a curve of the relative values of different strengths of electrical shock." He found that electric shocks produced the fastest learning times. Dodson wondered whether this had to do with the difference between pleasure and pain, or whether rats simply were primed to flee a dangerous situation more quickly than to seek out food. In any case, punishment trounced reward (Dodson 1917, 276).

As a group, psychologists decided in favor of both punishment and reward. No sooner had Yerkes published *The Dancing Mouse: A Study of Animal Behavior* (1907) than nearly every animal apparatus began to employ both methods.[1] Hunger and electricity, alongside the puzzle maze, became standard equipment for behavioral psychologists from John B. Watson to B. F. Skinner, from the 1910s to the 1950s and still to this day. Punishment and reward. I am stuck considering how the relief of hunger came to represent a reward. Animals deprived of food for one, two, or three days, running and digging and swiping at levers to relieve their discomfort: these were psychological models for pleasure. Even Yerkes, who considered starvation unpleasant and inhumane, called food incentives for deprived animals "the method of reward." Both hunger and electric shocks imposed pain and discomfort. In one case, relief was quick (the shock ceased); in the other, relief (in the form of food) appeared only after animals solved a maze or puzzle. What kind of reward was this? Work hard, driven by hunger, and you will earn a small taste of pleasure—only to be pulled away to work again. Reward, in this utilitarian psychology, meant just a little less suffering, contingent on successful work, lasting only for a short while.

. . .

Thorndike's psychology hung on utilitarian claims about the power of satisfaction, "exercise and reward." The cat's pleasurable feelings, when it opened the door and reached its fishy prize, imprinted upon patterns of movement. The cat, like a child in a classroom, learned by exercise and reward. But thinking with the animals leads me to believe that Thorndike's narrative was misleading. *His cats, in fact, were never satisfied.*[2] When Thorndike reprinted his doctoral dissertation a dozen years after the fact, he added a telling footnote. The original publication had made much of the usefulness of "utter hunger" as an experimental tool. By 1911, however, he felt a need to defend it: "I have been accused of experimenting with starving or half-starved animals" (Thorndike 1911, 27). To demonstrate his probity, Thorndike revealed in that footnote, what the cats ate and when. This is how we know that the same cats repeated multiple iterations of the problem-box experiment. The cats experienced hunger and discomfort, then relief, over and over.

But this seems like a contradiction: if the cat's hunger gets satisfied when it opens the box, how would it still be hungry on the next round? Experimental consistency required that "the animal should be as hungry at the tenth or twentieth trial as at the first." Thorndike explained his solution: "to attain this [consistency,] the animal was given after each 'success' only a very small bit of food as a reward (say, for a young cat, one quarter of a cubic centimeter of fish or meat)" (Thorndike 1911, 27). That quarter-centimeter cube was the reward, the relief, the satisfaction that was meant to produce learning. In fact, it was also a prerequisite for further experimental work. *The "reward" was not one.* Thorndike designed the cat's reward so as to maintain its hunger. What kind of satisfaction was this?

Willard Small picked up this question while elaborating on Thorndike's experiments in 1898–1899 as a graduate student at Clark University. Small built puzzle boxes for hungry rats to break into. Later, he introduced his animals to the Hampton maze. Hunger was their "motive"; food inside the box their reward. An early series of his tests failed catastrophically. One of Small's rats died and the other refused to move. This, he believed, was above all a "pedagogical failure": he had not brought the animals to full satisfaction before starting up the test again. "The quick succession of experiments, followed in each case by deprivation of the fruits of their labor, was bad method," Small concluded. "Nothing could be worse pedagogically, at least from a human standpoint." The failed rats were not able to form strong mental connections between hunger, puzzle solving and pleasure. "To establish an association train of which the motive and first term is hunger, and the end and last term is satisfaction of hunger," he wrote, "the train ought to be fully realized each time" (Small 1900, 139). In other words, for food to truly be a reward, the hungry rats should feed until they are fully satisfied. They had to feel real pleasure at the end of their work.

John B. Watson (1903, 9) disagreed: "The rat does not reason, 'I was not allowed fully to satisfy my hunger when I went to the food just now; therefore I really do not care to make the effort a second time.'" Watson repeated Small's experiments as a graduate student at the University of Chicago. He set test boxes containing bread before hungry rats and observed how quickly they managed to enter. Like Thorndike, Watson allowed successful rats to taste only a small amount of food "for an instant" before immediately starting another test run. He saw no reason to allow the animals to sate their hunger. "Small is possibly applying here somewhat too much of his own conscious processes to the associative powers of the rat," Watson (1903, 9) concluded. "If the rat is successful in overcoming the difficulties keeping it from the food, and is allowed to eat of the food for a short time, both terms of the 'association train' are completed and the rat is instantly ready to repeat the same procedure until his hunger is fully satisfied. Such was certainly the case with my rat." In other words, one could trick the rat into going back to work by giving it the slightest hint of satisfaction. Watson (1914, 58) complained that some psychologists (namely, Yerkes) had maligned the hunger method: "It is not fair to talk of the cruelty and inhumanity of keeping the animal hungry, as has been done by several writers. . . . There is not the slightest difficulty in keeping the animal in perfect condition and at the same time hungry enough to work properly."

Satisfaction and reward therefore did not have to be fulfilled to motivate animals to work. Even a promise, a taste, was enough. It may be worth mentioning that Watson spent most of his subsequent career in advertising, a field dedicated to stimulating desire for delayed gratification (Lemov 2005, 30). B. F. Skinner (1953) eventually would carry delayed gratification to an absurd level. Skinner trained hungry pigeons in the 1950s to press a lever hundreds of times to receive a single small pellet of food (Meehl 1992). The longer the delay, he claimed, the more his animals grew "increasingly compulsive" in their activity (Gere 2017, 174). In this way Skinner made explicit Thorndike's deferral of animals' satisfaction. Skinner conditioned his pigeons to work indefinitely toward a deferred reward. Thorndike's cats, like Watson's rats and Skinner's pigeons, were always hungry. They were meant to feel neither relief nor reward but rather a fleeting promise of future satisfaction: the odor of fish, tiny pieces, incomplete meals.

Even at the close of their workday, the cats were not given what they hungered for. "After the experiments for the day were done, the cats received abundant food to maintain health, growth and spirits, but commonly some what [sic] less than they would of their own accord have taken" (Thorndike 1911, 27). Thorndike designed the cat's feeding schedule to replicate the industrial time clock of working hours and meals. (How did Thorndike know what the cats would have eaten of their own accord? Were they his pets before becoming his subjects? Watson later weighed his animals to establish a baseline "maintenance ration.") In any case, Thorndike then left them, still hungry, without food for fourteen hours in preparation for the following day's work.

What does this tell us about the utilitarian promise of hunger and about the parameters of the cats' situation? Thorndike presented the cat's experience as a closed circle of discomfort, movement, and relief. When one of the cat's random clawings and squeezings flipped the latch and the same action led, over repeated trials, to similar success, the cat came to associate that action with the satisfaction of a small piece of fish. The action connected to pleasurable feelings (clawing the latch and eating fish) was strengthened; other actions connected to discomfort or annoyance (like the continuing sensation of hunger) were weakened. Thorndike called this relationship between satisfaction, discomfort, and learning through repeated experiences the Laws of Effect and Exercise. His advice to teachers sums it up: "Exercise and reward desirable connections; prevent or punish undesirable connections" (Thorndike 1919, 142). Yet this narrative was undermined by his own cats' experience. They lived in a constant state of low-level hunger and dissatisfaction, primed to perform experimental work for the future promise of a taste or a smell.

As historian Cathy Gere (2017, 169) has demonstrated, Thorndike established utilitarianism as a founding principle of modern American psychology. Utilitarian philosophers held up hunger as a tool for learning—specifically a tool for impressing laborious and thrifty behaviors upon spendthrift and shiftless people. Hunger was their whip. Ideologies of hunger, learning, and capitalism formed an implicit part of Thorndike's experimental situation. In effect, he turned utilitarianism into an experimental science. Hunger's discomfort was supposed to push one toward civilization. This was the situation: hard work for meager returns, the promise of a reward deferred. Hunger drives people—and animals—to work for food. Hunger appeared as an original, natural, basic feeling, a low entry in the hierarchy of mental functions.[3] Thorndike referred to possessiveness as one of the "original tendencies concerned with food getting," to "pounce," "grab," and "seize" at things (Thorndike 1919, 17). The desire for property appears as a logical, evolutionary outgrowth of hunger. There is no more powerful natural justification for human labor. Hunger models the nature of life under capitalism. But Thorndike's own experimental situation belies this claim.

Utilitarian tales about desire, work, and reward were belied by these experimental cats, who were lured to work by false promises of a future satisfaction that never arrived. The cats' experience suggests that to understand this experiment, we need to open that frame. We know that the cats' hunger was not contained within the problem box. Their hunger was perpetuated by the very "reward" that was meant to represent satisfaction due to a job well done. The promise of a reward was always deferred.

. . .

FIGURE 2. "Motivation and Reward in Learning." *Source*: Miller, Hart, and Yale University Institute for Human Relations 1948.

A blocky sans-serif font on a slightly shaky black background announces the genre of a mid-twentieth-century educational film: *Motivation and Reward in Learning.* "Two pale albino rats," intones a tenor voice. "What do you think is the reason for the difference in their behavior?—The one on the left is hungry" (Miller, Hart, and Yale University Institute of Human Relations 1948, 0:18). We see two rats set on a table in cylindrical wire baskets, one empty and one lined with pet food. One rat climbs up the basket wire, pokes his nose through the open mesh, pushes the latch with his head, and climbs out as soon as an opportunity presents itself. The other raises his head in acknowledgment of a human opening his basket and continues eating. (Here I follow the usage of the film, which genders both rats male.) Two human arms enter the frame: a masculine hand with a light-colored sleeve seizes the escaping rat, and a feminine hand with black sleeve picks up the eating one.[4] They place the rats in a wood and Plexiglas box, divided into two chambers labelled "VERY HUNGRY" and "NOT HUNGRY."

Human hands disappear from the frame. On the far wall of each compartment are affixed a metal stirrup and a tin dish. The box's floor appears at first to be striped; closer examination reveals that the stripes are regularly-spaced metal bars, which open to a compartment underneath. The box has more depth than we can see: the rats are balancing on a metal grid above empty air. The slats are wide enough to allow food pellets to fall through. (Later scientists will use a platform suspended in the air like this to produce the rodent equivalent of human stress.)

Noses flaring, the rats case the joint. They sniff each corner and wall, stretching upward toward the open box top and bright bulb. After some minutes, having investigated all possible escape routes, Not-Hungry turns away, presses his back against the Plexiglas barrier and hides his head in the shadow of the suspended tin dish. He remains there, immobile, availing of some privacy. Very-Hungry continues to sniff and climb. His nose flutters rapidly; his eyes, intense and black, reflect the strong light above. What can he see and smell, to his sides and below, that the viewer cannot? Can he smell his neighbor across the wood and Plexiglas divide?

Very-Hungry stands high on two legs, sniffs the air, descends. One such descent activates the metal stirrup, and a food pellet falls into the tin dish. When Very-Hungry discovers it, he crouches, folded over his belly as if he would hide the pellet in a pouch, and eats from his front paws. He leans one paw on the dish and licks the other. The tenor voice tells us: "Food would not be a reward without the drive of hunger." A montage shows Very-Hungry sniffing ever more insistently around the dish and stirrup, moving ever more directly to activate the lever. The voice: "After several more trials, which are not shown, . . . the animal has eliminated irrelevant responses. He has *learned* to press the bar efficiently." The camera pans to the right. Not-Hungry is still hiding, immobile, in a corner beneath the tin dish. "Now, what do you think the satiated animal has learned to do?" (7:21).

A text slide appears: "Will the satiated animal learn if we give him a drive?" At this point the viewer encounters Robert Yerkes's contribution to the hunger-electricity-puzzle apparatus.[5] A feminine hand enters the frame, turning the knob of a potentiometer until, the tenor voice tells us, "the shock is adjusted to be annoying, but not painful." A tone sounds. Not-Hungry bristles like a scared cat and repeatedly leaps off the electrified metal floor, high enough to leave the camera frame. On one landing, he hits the stirrup bar and the shock cuts off. He buries his head under the tin dish, and the voice tells us that he has been "rewarded," although his fur remains visibly stiff and bristled (7:55). And so the experiment repeats. We are told that Not-Hungry "learns even more rapidly than the hungry one, . . . because the drive produced by the electric shock is stronger than hunger" (8:52). To belabor their point well beyond any threshold of cruelty, the producers show us rats biting through rubber tubing, turning exercise wheels, and even fighting other rats in response to repeated electric shocks. "We have demonstrated," intones the tenor voice, "that the satiated animal is neither stupid nor lazy. All he needs is a little motivation" (9:13).

*Motivation and Reward in Learning* was produced in 1948 by psychologist Neal E. Miller and the Yale Institute of Human Relations to illustrate the drive-reduction theory of learning. "Rat learning," writes Rebecca Lemov (2005, 92), "lay at the heart of the [Yale] institute's hopes for a grand theory that would explain the full range of human behavior." Hungry rats, being experimentally available and manipulable, served as laboratory models for the general categories of animal drives and human motivation. Traces of Thorndike's setup appear throughout the film: a problem box, domesticated animals, hunger, learning, reflex-reward, pain and pleasure, stimulus-response, rates of activity over time—all of which constituted a model apparatus for human psychology.

What of Very-Hungry and Not-Hungry? On a first viewing of *Motivation and Reward in Learning*, the rats play the roles that they are assigned by the film's producers. They react predictably to stimulation, and their rates of activity seem to vary in response to different kinds of "drive." As primatologist Harry Harlow (1953, 28) remarked in a blistering critique, the rats seem to respond as though they have no minds of their own: "The kinds of learning problems which can be efficiently measured in these apparatus represent a challenge only to the decorticate animal. It is a constant source of bewilderment to me that the neobehaviorists . . . should choose apparatus which, in effect, experimentally decorticate their subjects." On closer view, however, the film does not show us dumb animals. The rats explore every corner of the box, leading with their very active noses. They offer some support for Harlow's and others' claims that mammals are moved by curiosity and exploration, even more than by hunger. The rats seek shelter and privacy to rest and eat. Their eager noses point us to chemosensory avenues of research that were beginning to develop in the 1940s. While researchers were counting lever presses, the rats' flaring nostrils were mediating a chemosensory encounter with metal, air, wood, lightbulbs, and Plexiglas as well as human and animal scents.

I catch myself here, trying to prove to Harlow that the rats are not as brainless as he thought and that they show signs of intelligence and inner feeling. In so doing, I am replicating the same hierarchy from simple to complex, from brainless to intelligent, that Harlow, Thorndike, and others promoted. Hunger and other "visceral" feelings appear on the lowest rung of the developmental ladder. Higher up on the evolutionary scale, simple feelings become complex emotions. "As we go up the phylogenetic scale," suggested psychologist Abraham Maslow (1943, 90), "appetites become more and more important and hungers less and less important. . . . As we go up the phylogenetic scale and as the instincts drop away there is more and more dependence upon the culture as an adaptive tool." This hierarchy assigns hunger and simple motivations to the "lower" organisms and associates "higher" needs with more developed beings.

Harlow's scales of drive were also social scales. Some people were bound, by nature or society, to pursue simple bodily hungers; others were free to seek complex feeling, culture, and self-actualization. Maslow opined that society ought to provide for everyone's basic needs and allow them to reach for higher ends. Yet, he hedged, some people were bound by circumstance to a simple ("decorticate," in Harlow's terms) state of mind (Maslow 1970; Weidman 2016). Still today, motivation discourse pops up everywhere in discussions of underserved and underrepresented children: how to motivate them to learn? Young people in classrooms circa 1948 must have encountered a doubling or entangling effect in this educational film. The soundtrack, that authoritative tenor voice, narrates the rats' and the viewers' own learning experiences, both at once. The voice tells students what they are learning (the content of their lesson) and how they are learning (like the rats on the screen).

"Now, what do you think the satiated rat has learned to do?" With which rat were students meant to identify? The Very-Hungry rat, driven by hunger and active in pursuit of efficiency? The Not-Hungry rat, who at first appears stupid or lazy but is shocked by low-level pain into rapid learning? How well they learned, young viewers were told, depended on the strength and nature of their motivation (Luissier 2018). The "reward" in *Motivation and Reward* was not much of one. A reward, like a small piece of fish or a pellet of rat food, only temporarily relieved the deprivation of the hungry animal. These so-called rewards did not necessarily bring pleasure—that was not their goal. They only partly alleviated a need, a drive, a lack, that experimenters caused by depriving their subjects of food. Need-drive experiments, as Otniel Dror (2016, 230) put it, reflected an "implied scarcity economy . . . inside the laboratory" and well beyond, in midcentury classrooms and workplaces.

Thorndike's kittens and the other experimental animals were paid for their labor with starvation wages, tiny bits of food. Experimenters kept the animals in a state of insufficiency, driven to complete units of instrumental labor for unsatisfying tokens of reward. The experimental animals shared this condition with many workers in the early twentieth-century. Workers received starvation wages in coal mines, textile mills, plantations, domestic work, charity workplaces, and other sites of labor extraction. Chapter 3 records workers' struggles in the 1930s against starvation wages, labor, debt, and welfare regimes designed to keep them hungry.

# Fight—Don't Starve

"Us workers have got to do something or we will starve to death while working." A weaver at the Schoolfield textile mill in Danville, Virginia, and "Hopeless Mother of Five," wrote in late 1931 to the Communist Party weekly *Southern Worker*. She had a baby at home but was obliged to work, as her husband had been black-listed for union organizing. Mill owners had put him and other activist workers out "to starve." The writer fervently hoped that the union soon would force the mill to "pay decent wages" ("Mill Slavery" 1931). Another letter from "A Farmer" in Lancaster, South Carolina, reported that the white landlord there fraudulently indebted his Black tenants. "When we buy flour and pay for it, he waits until we get home and then tells us it is his flour and makes us give it back to him. Now we tenant farmers and young farmers are going to organize together and stop this robbery and starvation" ("Tenant Organization" 1931). A coal miner from Harlan, Kentucky, wrote: "We all work like hell, winter is coming on, no food, no clothing, no shelter. Are we going to freeze and starve our families to death? Hell, no! We will fight" ("Too Many Thugs" 1931).

During the Great Depression thousands of workers, sharecroppers, and unemployed people developed a common identity around their hunger. Author Richard Wright experienced the dawning of this collective of the hungry while waiting in line in 1930 or 1931 at the Chicago Public Relief Office. Wright "felt as if I were making a public confession of my hunger" alongside all the others waiting for city relief. "The mass of hungry people around me" joined in a common realization. "The black men and women were mumbling quietly among themselves; they had not known one another before they had come here, but now their timidity and shame were wearing off and they were sharing experiences. . . . Their talking was enabling them to see the collectivity of their lives. . . . These people now knew that

FIGURE 3. Demonstrators gather at a Communist Party meeting hall in Washington, DC, 1930. One holds a sign reading "Fight Or Starve." Photograph by Harris & Ewing, LC-DIG-hec-35732. *Source*: Library of Congress, Prints & Photographs Division.

the past had betrayed them, had cast them out" (Wright 2005, 300). Wright saw them understand their hunger as a product of history.

Low-wage workers, unemployed people, and tenant farmers articulated hunger as a common identity on breadlines, in Unemployed Councils, Communist newspapers, and in hundreds of local and national "hunger marches." Communist Party leaders recognized this emergent collective as an opportunity to organize Black workers and farmers, women, youth, and unemployed people, who had been neglected by traditional labor unions and who were most harshly impacted by the Depression. Black and white women, men, and young people formed local Unemployed Councils and led demonstrations to demand unemployment insurance, cash relief, and food for their families (Leab 1967, 303; Harris 2009; Orleck 1993).

These three writers to the *Southern Worker* all experienced starvation as a direct consequence of their labor. They accused employers and landlords of creating hunger conditions to suppress dissent and to extract more work for less pay. Plantation, mill, and mine owners tightly controlled access to cash and food commodities.

The situation of workers in "base industries" and agriculture grew increasingly perilous from the late 1920s through the Depression, though the underlying relations were present well before then. "Starvationist" tactics were most visible in extractive settings, mines and plantations.[1] Miners and tenant farmers went into debt to their employers for the commodities that they needed to live. Mine and plantation owners furnished advances or company scrip, which forced workers to buy food and necessary goods from the owners themselves. Workers often found themselves without cash and in debt at the end of the pay period or crop reckoning. Charity agencies like the Red Cross and local welfare relief offices were managed by mine and plantation allies, who cut aid from any worker who organized for unions or who refused to accept poor working conditions. Striking workers' self-help kitchens and settlements were bombed and destroyed. Closed circuits of work and consumption allowed for capital to control labor through hunger, debt, and relief.

Social welfare and relief aid were often tightly, even forcibly, integrated into the starvation wage complex. With low wages and conditional access to aid, employers and welfare officials directed labor to specific sites and imposed controls on the time and pace of work and output. When labor was no longer required or when workers went on strike, employers and local authorities withheld food completely to force workers and their families to move elsewhere. This dynamic impacted both wages and welfare: "starvation wages" for employed workers, and conditional access for those seeking charity and unemployment relief. Welfare relief and food advances sustained the potential value and quiescence of unemployed or low-wage workers. The result was a "state of organized debility," which suspended workers' liveliness and their capacity for protest (Kalina 2019, 60, 69). Starvation and relief, withdrawals and advances, punishments and rewards were facets of this same cycle.

Hunger marchers during the Great Depression accused employers, charity organizations, and local, state, and federal welfare authorities of collaborating in a total campaign of starvation. A "poor widow" from Danville, out of work, wrote to the *Southern Worker* to accuse the government and "charity bosses" of "try[ing] to starve us." She saw herself as part of a collective "organizing and fighting for food to keep from starving" ("Charity Grafters" 1931). Thousands of people responded to summons in the *Southern Worker* and *Daily Worker* to march on city halls and relief centers across the country and on the Capitol. Hunger marches brought together poor and unemployed people, workers, and recipients of charity and welfare relief under the banner: "Fight—Don't Starve!" In the era of the hunger marches, Black sharecroppers, Appalachian miners, and urban Black and immigrant women became standard bearers against starvation wages. By the early 1930s the *Daily Worker*, the *Southern Worker*, and other more mainstream publications were full of reports on miners' and sharecroppers' struggles against starvation. Coal and cotton workers spoke out, struck, and demonstrated against landowners, mine owners, and their allies. Urban Black and immigrant women organized boycotts and demonstrations. Their fight against debt, dependence, violence, and hunger served as a standard for hunger marchers across the country.

The hunger marchers' slogan "Fight—Don't Starve" linked together the biological time of hunger (starvation) and the historical time of class struggle (the fight). The marchers' hungry bodies were themselves evidence of historical violence against the working class. The biological fact of hunger may have led marchers to experience, physically and corporeally, historical dynamics of class-based violence and struggle. Anthropologist Alan Feldman (1991, 225, 230) described "the political efficacy of the signifying body" with which hunger strikers challenge the usual unfolding of historical time and impose the "directional biological time" of hunger. Perhaps the 1930s hunger marchers felt a similar collapsing of the biological and the political. Perhaps they came "to experience, or at least [to] theorize, the political manipulation of their bodies as a managed project" (Feldman 1991, 230). The imperative to live, to survive, led marchers to struggle in a collective, historical, social, and political arena. Hunger marchers fought because they refused to be made to starve.

· · ·

In the early years of the Great Depression the "starvation wage" became a site of struggle. Hunger marchers, catalyzed by Unemployed Councils and Communist dailies, denounced starvation wages as capitalist exploitation. The *Southern Worker* explained in October 1931 that "the policy of the capitalists in this country is to make the workers starve" ("National Hunger March to Washington" 1931). The Communist *Daily Worker* declared, on the day of the national Hunger March on Washington, DC, in December 1931, that American workers lived "in wage-slavery, in misery and starvation. . . . The suffering and starvation of millions of unemployed is an essential part of [a] general plan of still sharper exploitation of the working class" ("National Hunger March Parades" 1931). Despite the wooden and bombastic language of Party declarations such as these, there are signs that the message resonated with readers. A young Party member from Charlotte, North Carolina, wrote: "Why are these young workers starving? Because the dirty boss class wants them to starve so that they will work cheaper" ("Youth Starving" 1931).

"Starvation wages," in the early twentieth century, signified social exclusion, Blackness, foreignness, and femininity. Traditional labor unions and their allies often blamed impoverished workers for their own low wages. Labor leaders repeatedly accused immigrants and Black people of threatening the wages of whiteness. The American Federation of Labor fought to defend a "living wage" for male, white, nonimmigrant union members, against others—Black, foreign, and female—who accepted pay below that standard (Glickman 1997, 78–86). "Starvation wages, when encountered," wrote minimum wage advocate Henry Seager (1913, 87), "are due to exceptional circumstances . . . [that] usually reduce to

FIGURE 4. "Fight or Starve! Demonstrate Mar. 6th." *Source*: Ellis 1930.

characteristics of the workers which greatly limit the range of occupations open to them (such as, ignorance of English, in the case of immigrants; inability to leave the home, in the case of women and children doing home work)." Chinese workers in particular were singled out for "low standard of living" and "degradation of labor" (Glickman 1997, 85).

Others, like Grace Burnham and the Labor Research Association (1930, 4), accused employers of purposefully suppressing wages by recruiting marginalized workers: "Women and children are hired to replace the more highly paid men workers. Negro, Chinese, Filipino, and Mexican workers are drawn on to repress wages. Advertisements in Southern papers are made use of to get unskilled labor to come North and flood the labor market." Hunger marchers during the Great Depression sometimes echoed this rhetoric and even took it on as a common identity: "Refuse to starve! . . . Let all workers understand the capitalist plot to cut the standard of living to coolie level!" ("Hunger Marchers Speak" 1931). Rather than fighting to differentiate and rise above a racialized, impoverished, abnormal human other, many hunger marchers embraced and generalized this alterity. Hunger marches were often led by people identified as Black, foreign, and women.

Hunger marches grew out of long-standing struggles against starvation wages in two of the most exploitative and marginalized areas in the country: plantations and coal mines. Those workers received literal starvation wages. Employers used hunger as a technology of labor control, and workers' resistance movements centered around food, hunger, and survival. Plantation landlords maintained tight control over sharecroppers' access to food. During growing season, landlords furnished food advances to tenants, and after harvest these advances were subtracted from their payment for the crop. Landlords chose what food to hand out and under which conditions. They rarely quoted a price or gave a receipt, with which croppers could calculate their debt against anticipated earnings (Ownby 1999, 71).

The *Southern Worker* interviewed a sharecropper who complained that his landlord refused to give croppers advance furnish of lard, only flour. "We can never check up on the cost of the food we get, as the landlord, is the one who gets it and brings it out. By the end of the season the landlord takes the whole crop and we are left to starve the rest of the months until the work on the new crop begins" (cited in Carson 1931, 4). The cycle of debt was continuous and inescapable. "Advances for food and sometimes railfare to the plantation place the worker in 'debt' to the planter at first—and he never gets out of debt. Attempts to escape result in arrest for various 'crimes' and the chain gang" ("Red Cross, Police" 1931, 4). White planters used Black croppers' debt for subsistence goods, alongside vigilante violence, to "maintain power relations" (Ownby 1999, 68). Food advances were similarly tools of power. The Croppers and Farm Workers Union (later renamed the Share Croppers Union) took root in Alabama through a struggle with plantation landlords over control of food advances. As Robin D. G. Kelley has recorded, just after the cotton in rural Tallapoosa had been planted and weeded in spring 1931, landlords cut off sharecroppers' access to food advances. This was "a calculated effort to generate labor for the newly built Russell Saw Mill," which paid exactly the same daily wage as plantation owners paid to farm workers (Kelley 1991, 40). Croppers were forced by hunger to work at the mill during the off-season. The newly formed union demanded that food advances be restored and that farm workers be given access to small subsistence gardens. Plantation owners met organizers of movements like this one with murders, beatings, arrests, and expulsions; and nevertheless croppers persisted.

A similar story played out in Appalachian coal mines. Coal company scrip served the same function in the mines as food advances did on the plantation, binding miners to their employers through debt. "[In] Harlan County and elsewhere," for example, "men complain that the system of payment by scrip, with cash once in two weeks, keeps them in perpetual debt to the company" (Stark 1931a). Scrip—usually brass tokens stamped and numbered by the mine—served as advances on cash wages. Coal miners could use their scrip only in company stores or commissaries, which were adjacent to their worksite, often overlooking a "hundred or two hundred miners' shacks, scattered haphazardly" (Dreiser et al. 2008 [1932], 8). If a miner purchased cheaper goods at independent shops in town, he was liable to receive a letter threatening dismissal from his job (29). When Harlan County miners went on strike in spring 1931, mine commissaries and access to food were "at the center of the troubles" (28).

*New York Times* reporter Louis Stark (1931a) found that "those who live in company coal camps say they are compelled to trade in the commissaries." At the commissary miners had to buy not only subsistence goods but also carbide, fuse, and powder to perform their work. Mrs. Jim Smith, wife of a striking mine worker at Straight Creek, Kentucky, wrote to the *Southern Worker*: "If I can't get food and clothing for my children I can't send them to school this winter." She reported that the commissary gave her half a pound of lard for the price of one pound and set higher prices than elsewhere. Others reported prices twice as high as prices at outside stores. With all of the required expenses for her husband and sons just to do their work, Smith "had to trade at a company store for it was impossible to get a pay day so we could trade elsewhere" (Smith 1931). Union activist "Sudy" Gates complained that "we . . . the miners' wives have to go to the stores to draw the scrip what their husbands made the day before, probably they could get some and probably not." Mine owners "give [a worker] a scrip and get him into debt and then he works and works and pays the debt. And then if he refuses to get in debt then they won't let him work" (Dreiser et al. 2008 [1932], 289).[2]

The coal industry contracted after World War I, and mine owners implemented measures to limit the cost and power of labor. Operators tightened social control by all available means, as John Hennen (2008, 9) has described: "company stores, company housing, payments in scrip, 'yellow-dog' contracts, blacklisting, private police forces, and influence over county government and law enforcement agencies." The Great Depression brought even more tightening and wage cuts. When miners went on strike in spring 1931 to protest the cuts, owners responded by firing and evicting masses of workers, with the support of the Kentucky National Guard. The Communist-affiliated National Miners Union (NMU) stepped in to support striking miners with food relief (Hennen 2008, 13–16). The strike and the miners' desperate conditions attracted the attention of left-leaning intellectuals including Theodore Dreiser and John Dos Passos, who traveled to Harlan to report on the situation there. Writer Waldo Frank viewed the Harlan mines as a bellwether for American workers, "a situation which very well may become national." He described the workers' condition: "Here are a group of men who are literally being starved. Their resistance is being killed by terror and starvation" (in Dreiser et al. 2008 [1932], 325, 323).

My grandmother's parents, cousins, and uncles worked the Harlan coal field. My great-grandfather Thomas Whitfield survived a Bell County mine explosion that killed a close relative. A different branch of the Whitfield family moved to Harlan County at the beginning of the 1910s coal boom and owned at least two mines there. According to a local historical website, those Whitfields were known as the most ferociously antiunion of all the Harlan County operators (Ruth n.d.). Their Clover Fork Mine was the last mine to open to unionization under federal mandate in the late 1930s; two decades later, Jack Whitfield chose to close the whole mine down rather than accede to union demands. The Clover Fork commissary apparently still remains almost exactly as it was back then, a monument to labor control and exploitation (East 2016). My grandmother moved to Chicago to train as a nurse during World War II and never spoke of Kentucky. I wish that I could have asked her how she and her family experienced the strike of 1931.

Some of the worst violence during the strike took place at sites of food aid. One National Miners Union soup kitchen was destroyed by dynamite. Two men working at another NMU soup kitchen were shot right outside the kitchen—one dead—by private police deputies hired by mine owners. Other men were arrested and jailed for helping at the union soup kitchens. Miner Caleb Powers was arrested and released on condition of no longer distributing food to strikers (Dreiser et al. 2008 [1932], 144–168). Area shopkeepers who provided food aid to striking workers were forced to close shop and leave town (Dreiser et al. 2008 [1932], 33, 35). Writer Waldo Frank was arrested, beaten, and expelled from Harlan County because he led a delivery of food for strikers. Adelaide Walker reported that mine operators sought to "break the strike by starvation," going so far as to shoot feral pigs "to prevent the hungry strikers using them for food" (in Dreiser et al. 2008 [1932], 90).

Despite the threat of violence against anyone who fed striking workers' families, the soup kitchens continued to operate. Aunt Molly Jackson, a midwife, folk singer, and community leader, recalled how she and other miners' families created a soup kitchen "where we had emptied, in Spring, in April [1931], all of our canned stuff that we had canned up and the food we had, we had all throwed it together in order to make soup and to save the lives of the children when the miners was blacklisted." The strikers' soup kitchen functioned on the principle of mutual aid: "We all put the last teaspoon full of salt in so even. . . . If we have anything in that soup kitchen it's for everybody" (Jackson 1961, Track 10). Jackson relied on the soup kitchen to provide for her sick husband and family. She recounted that once she held up a mine commissary at gunpoint to get food for starving families of striking miners. "I said, 'I have to feed some children, they're starving, they can't wait for me to go around and try to collect by nickels and dimes, enough to get 'em something to eat. They need to eat now'" (Jackson 1961, Track 5). While sitting at the soup kitchen table on a cold day in fall 1931, Jackson wrote the strikers' anthem and folk classic "Hungry Ragged Blues."

> I'm sad and weary; I've got the hungry ragged blues;
> I'm sad and weary; I've got the hungry ragged blues;
> Not a penny in my pocket to buy the thing I need to use.
> No food, no clothes for our children, I'm sure this ain't no lie,
> No food, no clothes for our children, I'm sure this ain't no lie,
> If we can't git more for our labor, we will starve to death and die.
> . . .
> Ragged and hungry, no slippers on our feet,
> Ragged and hungry, no slippers on our feet,
> We're bumming around from place to place to get a little bite to eat.
> All a-going round from place to place bumming for a little food to eat.
> Listen, my friends and comrades, please take a friend's advice,
> Don't put out no more of your labor, till you get a living price.
> Some coal operators might tell you the hungry blues are not bad;
> Some coal operators might tell you the hungry blues are not bad;
> They are the worst blues this poor woman ever had. (In Dreiser et al. 2008 [1932], v)

Charity and welfare organizations allied with the mine owners. Dreiser and Dos Passos charged the Harlan County Red Cross with "aiding and abetting starvation" ("Red Cross Held" 1931, 3). Red Cross agents refused to aid the families of striking workers: "They won't give anything to a man unless he does what the operators want him to." Stark (1931b) reported that "the Red Cross will not take part in an industrial dispute. Feeding a hungry miner's family, one who is in the bad graces of the operators, is considered meddling in an industrial dispute. Miners considered loyal to the company will be fed by the operators." Red Cross agents told Aunt Molly Jackson: "'We are not responsible for those men out on strike. They should go back to work and work for any price that they will take them for'" (in Dreiser et al. 2008 [1932], 280). In Harlan County and elsewhere, charity and welfare often functioned like company scrip and food advances, to maintain wages and working conditions to employers' advantage. Violence at Harlan miners' soup kitchens points to the role of food aid and welfare relief in the starvation wage complex.

. . .

Welfare and food aid often served to perpetuate starvation wage relations. Welfare relief kept death at bay, maintaining workers' "virtual value as perpetually unrealized" (Kalina 2019, 60). Conditional charity enforced discipline, exchanging aid against quiescence and labor. Commodity distributions of flour and other goods were designed foremost as price supports for agriculture, not to serve the needs of the hungry (Poppendieck 2014, 177). Relief and food aid could be withdrawn or redirected to serve the needs of food producers and employers. Welfare could be used to create or reinforce hunger.

A worker in Birmingham, Alabama, wrote in October 1931 to the *Southern Worker*: "The Red Cross outfit here is conducting a regular campaign of terror against workers, white and black, appealing for aid." Birmingham Red Cross agents sent unemployed workers to pick cotton on the Mississippi Delta for starvation wages. "For refusing to accept such slavery the workers are threatened by the Red Cross with having their 'relief' cut off. The 'relief' amounts to exactly 50 cents a week" ("Red Cross in Vile Plot" 1931). Another Birmingham worker reported that armed Red Cross agents stood over relief workers as if they were a prison gang (Kelley 1991, 20). The *Southern Worker* called for workers to reject charity and "fight for compulsory unemployed insurance" self-administered by workers. "Down with this fake relief" ("Red Cross in Vile Plot" 1931). In many places workers with jobs were subject to compulsory pay deductions for the local charity fund, which was administered by the Red Cross and similar organizations. Aid was often conditional on cheap or free labor. In Henryetta, Oklahoma, relief officials adopted the motto "no work, no eat" ("Hunger March Spurs" 1931).

Hunger marchers rarely targeted employers. They marched instead on local relief offices, charities, and government agencies. Organizers recruited marchers on breadlines and unemployment lines. The downtown New York City Unemployed Council led a thousand jobless and homeless men on a demonstration to the call of "smash the breadlines" ("Reds Lead Jobless" 1931). Seven hundred people gathered in May 1930 at Capitol Park in Birmingham to demand aid for the unemployed; a few months later, twenty-five hundred unemployed metal workers rallied there for unemployment insurance under the slogan "Organize and Fight! Don't Starve" (Kelley 1991, 15, 18). Hunger marchers rode through New York City under banners reading "Hoover's Relief Program Means Death for the Workers" and "To Hell with Charity—We Want Relief" ("Hunger Hikers' Halt" 1931). In Denver, Colorado, a "bloody riot" occurred when "a mob of about 300 attempted to halt work on a relief project" ("FBI Probes Clash" 1934). The Harlem Unemployed Council held an open hearing on unemployment, where they elected a mass delegation that marched on the local Charity Organization branch and demanded relief for the most needy families ("Open Hearing in Harlem" 1931). On the steps of the Saint Louis City Hall, organizer Verna Mason told demonstrators: "If the unemployed could not get food otherwise, they would take it." Marchers carried slogans against inadequate and abusive relief: "'Free milk for babies of the unemployed" and "Give charity garbage to the pigs: we want food" ("Hunger March in St. Louis" 1931).

At a Youth Hunger Hearing held in late 1931 in the Charlotte, North Carolina, Workers' Hall, workers accused the city mayor of "starving the unemployed youth of Charlotte and refusing relief." Children and young people testified to their hunger. "Eunice Broadway, eleven years old, daughter of a textile worker, told of her father working twelve hours each day, received only one dollar. She . . . must go to school often without eating. Elliott Phillips, a young Negro worker, testified how he was turned down by the Associated Charities after being out of work six months" ("Mayor Evades Hunger" 1931). The same charity sent another young worker to cut cordwood for two ten-hour days and in return paid him only two bags of groceries. A "young Negro girl" testified that city officials arrested and held youth on false charges of stealing. By its end "the trial . . . convinced every worker in the hall of the great need for struggle against the bosses' system as the only guarantee for securing cash relief. Every one present pledged to support the Hunger March to Washington" ("Mayor Evades Hunger" 1931). Public hearings on hunger and welfare also took place elsewhere. In Newark, New Jersey, a "jury of workers" heard "cases of destitution" and delivered "a verdict against the system that starves the working class children" ("Newark Hunger Hearing" 1931).[3]

By extending life at a minimum level, welfare and charity reinforced the starvation wage. Relief replaced wages and food advances during slack times. Relief kept workers in place and available to labor; for Southern plantation owners, food aid served as an extension of their own food advances. Welfare relief provided plantation workers with a source of food during the fallow winter months, thus relieving planters of the need to provide food or wages (Poppendieck 2017, 229). Aid was often made conditional on working the fields. Little Rock, Arkansas, Red Cross agents informed destitute families that anyone who did not pick cotton in fall would receive no aid in winter ("Forced Labor in Arkansas" 1931). The *Southern Worker* called the Red Cross "a weapon of the ruling class against the [farm] workers and [tenant] farmers": "'Stay on the plantations as serfs and starve!' That is the slave decree of the Red Cross to the croppers and tenants in the cotton belt of the South" ("Red Cross, Police" 1931).

When federally funded relief replaced charity aid under the New Deal, this dynamic continued. Welfare agents in Palm Beach County, Florida, made Black families work for "starvation wages" to receive federal distributions of flour, while white families received the distributions for free ("Forced Negroes to Work" 1932). On Southern plantations federal farm relief further weakened Black sharecroppers' power. Owners pocketed federal funds meant to be shared with tenants and forced tenants to close down their subsistence gardens. Black sharecroppers were massively displaced by the federal Farm Security Administration (Adams and Gorton 2009, 330; De Jong 2000, 110). Local county welfare administrators, allied with employers and plantation owners, assured that access to federal welfare and food aid remained conditional on obedience. In these cases welfare relief bound workers to the starvation wage complex.

Federal welfare relief did not disrupt the power relations underlying starvation wages. Some proponents of federal food aid, like far-right extremist Congressman Hamilton Fish, hoped that relief might weaken Communist influence and silence hunger marchers' demands: "I know of no better way to fight communism than to see that American people do not starve" (*Hearing before the Committee on Agriculture* 1931, 79). However, New Deal welfare programs prioritized business and agricultural interests over those of the poor. Federal commodity distributions were ironically designed to prop up agricultural prices, which actually made it harder overall for poor families to purchase food (Poppendieck 2017, 127). Farmers insisted that food aid should be made difficult to access so as not to decrease consumer demand for full-priced goods (Poppendieck 2017, 147). Food stamps, first implemented in 1939, required recipients to purchase a subsidized booklet of stamps, making them inaccessible to very poor people (Moran 2011, 1004). Food aid, in the hands of local administrators, could serve as a form of political violence, an extension of the plantation furnishes and the coal miners' scrip.

The starvation wage complex was a totalizing relation that involved wages, political power, and access to aid. Workers writing to Communist Party papers in the early 1930s saw all three of these as causes of their starvation. Each one of those elements served to reinforce the others. One worker wrote that since the Red Cross required him to pick cotton to get aid, "he who does not pick cotton at starvation wages will starve anyway" ("Forced Labor in Arkansas" 1931). Localized relief efforts "keep [unemployed workers] quiet while they starve," and "charity-mongers" serve only "to prolong the starvation a while" ("Organize for National Hunger March" 1931).

. . .

A branch of the National Hunger March rolled through New York City in early December 1932. At the head of the procession through Union Square was a "high-stepping man from Georgia in a rainbow-colored beret, with scarf to match. . . . Behind him trudged a brown-skinned woman [actress and writer Louise Thompson], a coon-skin coat flapping about her ankles and a happy smile on her face." Two trucks in the lead carried sixty unemployed sailors and longshoremen; they were followed by young textile workers from New England, "Filipinos from the cities, metal workers from Massachusetts, men and women from the needle trades of New York's garment center." Twenty-three nurses wearing green crosses for workers' first aid followed behind. A reporter for the African American newspaper *Chicago Defender* noted a "goodly sprinkling of black faces among the white, and yet there was no specialization or segregation of the races." A "Red Band" dressed in gray uniforms blared music in between chants, songs, and speeches. As the procession ended, the caravan of seventeen trucks carrying six hundred marchers drove down Broadway on its way to Washington, DC (Bearden 1932).

A few days later, the caravan joined three thousand hunger marchers in a demonstration across the capital city. "Negroes, women, a few veterans in service caps, and boys still in their teens were in the parade, as it stretched for eight blocks. They appeared in bedraggled sweaters, worn coats and dirt-smeared windbreakers." Demonstrators carried placards: "Fight—Don't Starve"; "Against wage cuts for unemployment insurance"; "Against forced labor, make the rich pay"; and "No discrimination against the Negroes and the foreign-born in giving out relief." As they walked the marchers chanted, "Stand them on their heads, stand them on their feet: comrades, comrades, when do we eat?" ("Curtis Silences" 1932).[4]

Hundreds of hunger marches took place across the country during the early years of the Great Depression: in Albany, Annapolis, Birmingham, Boston, Charleston (West Virginia), Chicago, Cleveland, Denver, Detroit, Hartford, Henryetta (Oklahoma), Los Angeles, Newark, New York City, Poughkeepsie, Sacramento, Saint Louis, Sioux City, Springfield, Trenton, and Wilmington, among other places and in addition to annual national marches. Hunger marches took place in England and elsewhere around the world (Vernon 2007, 245–256). In Los Angeles and Saint Louis women took the lead in exhorting the demonstrators ("Hunger March Squelched" 1932; "Hunger March in St. Louis" 1931). In Denver, Saint Louis, and Wilmington clashes with police left many marchers injured ("Color Line Missing" 1932; "FBI Probes" 1934). Several marches and parades were broken up with tear gas and beatings. In Virginia the Ku Klux Klan mobilized to block marchers' passage to Washington, DC ("Klan Rides" 1932). The sheriff of Imperial Valley, California, blocked a caravan of food for a hunger march of striking farm workers ("Sheriff Drives" 1930). In other places marches were festive occasions with music, speeches, and mutual aid collections.

Many of the national hunger marchers were elected and supported by local Unemployed Councils. Following the financial crash of late 1929, the American Communist Party directed its organizing efforts toward the jobless, and Party-affiliated Unemployed Councils grew rapidly across the country. Party organizers visited towns and cities and encouraged jobless workers to form or elect a Committee of Action, from which the Unemployed Councils grew. One Party operative, for example, inspired a group of housewives to organize "empty pot and pan demonstrations" (Leab 1967, 303). By spring 1930 the city of Chicago alone had twelve local councils with more than a thousand members. Philadelphia had seven locals, the Minneapolis local enrolled 375 people, and councils were set up in Duluth, Indianapolis, Milwaukee, and elsewhere (Leab 1967, 313). One contemporary estimate set total Unemployed Council membership at 300,000 people across 340 locales (Weyl 1932, 118). Secret Service sources to the *New York Times* called the councils "the best organized and most ambitious Communist effort so far discovered in this country." Councils were known to "draw in 'Negro women and youth' and persons who have been employed in base industries" ("Communists Behind" 1931, 1, 13).

In the early phase of the Depression, local Unemployed Councils operated fairly autonomously with little Party coordination. Councils formed committees by block or tenement house to help workers resist evictions, receive relief, and find food; and they set up "listening posts" where workers could share their grievances (Leab 1967, 311). Breadline, flophouse, and relief-center committees sent delegations to support individual grievances and to demand better treatment. In Chicago the flophouse committee persuaded officials to provide clean sheets and more space between beds (Weyl 1932, 118). Unemployed Councils participated in the 1930s "housewives revolt," organizing demonstrations against evictions and consumer boycotts to protest high food prices. In Harlem and Chicago women picketed butcher shops over the high price of meat. Women marched on meat-packing plants in Detroit, overturned meat trucks, and set fire to stores of meat (Orleck 1993, 163). As historian Annelise Orleck has suggested, actions like these drew together a diverse coalition of Black and Jewish women in the big cities, and Polish and Scandinavian immigrants in the Midwest and the Northwest. The coalition began to break apart in later years of the Depression, when Communist influence became more direct, visible, and contested (Orleck 1993, 156–166).[5]

In preparation for the National Hunger Marches, Unemployed Councils held public hearings on hunger and poverty, elected delegates, and took up collections to support them. Local councils rented trucks to drive their delegates to Washington, DC. Trucks were not segregated by race or gender, and many truck "captains" were Black. Marchers rode toward Washington, DC, to the "strains of 'Onward Christian Solider' and the 'Red Internationale.'" The sides and back of each truck were festooned with placards: "Fight for Unemployment Insurance"; "A Dollar a day for each unemployed Seaman"; and "We demand $50 cash winter relief for each jobless worker as a supplement to local relief" ("Color Line Missing" 1932). As the trucks stopped in towns along their way, local Unemployed Councils organized processions, meals, and an overnight stay at the town Workers' Hall. They invited newspaper reporters to cover the events. En route to the 1931 national march, two trucks of delegates from New England towns stopped on a late December afternoon in Hartford, Connecticut. They were greeted with a "a brief street demonstration, a hot lunch and a supply of food, clothing and cigarettes provided by local sympathizers" ("55 Stop Here" 1931). In other locales the reception was less warm, sometimes violent, and caravans were forced to stop overnight by the road outside of town. Police in Washington, DC, grounded the 1932 caravan on a barren side street far from the planned demonstration site. After some days of standoff the marchers' "mile-long motorcade of white and colored men and women" was eventually allowed to enter and carry out their planned parade near the Capitol ("Hunger Parade Today" 1932).

Hunger marchers claimed a right to survive, a right to welfare. The history of welfare rights goes back to Depression-era struggles over food advances and unemployment relief. Karen Tani (2016, 11) has traced the idea of welfare rights to the Great Depression and the New Deal: "To speak of welfare in terms of rights . . . was, and is, about poor people's relationship to the governing authorities around them—about the meaning of citizenship in a divided polity." Even before the New Deal was enacted, hunger marchers and Unemployed Council members made claims to welfare rights. In Chicago, in winter 1931, three thousand unemployed people marched through the South Side to "fight for [the] right to live" ("Unemployed March on Chicago" 1931). Marchers' demand for a right to life echoed across the twentieth century and beyond, in the welfare rights movement of the 1960s and 1970s and in the contemporary Poor People's Campaign. Marchers claimed a right to life in the broadest sense, meaning survival, health, autonomy, and well-being.

Hunger marchers made hunger their political identity and their battlefield. In response, commentators and experts challenged the reality of their hunger. "The hunger marcher, in this year of depression, is getting to be a well-known individual," the *Austin Statesman* snarked, suggesting that marchers cared more for public attention than for a bite to eat. The newspaper disapprovingly reproduced a photograph of a Toledo, Ohio, hunger marcher grimacing at the bad taste of a free meal ("Hunger Marcher?" 1932). The *Daily Boston Globe* claimed that "very few" of the hunger marchers "show signs of having been hungry of late or of having suffered greatly." The *Boston Globe* cared little for the "diversified group of white and colored men, schoolboys and schoolgirls, jobless workers and half-educated idlers" marching through Washington, DC, and was particularly offended by marchers' singing, snake-dancing, and "noisy flirtation" ("Police Meeting" 1932). The *Chicago Defender* noted suspiciously that hunger marchers in New York City "seemed to be in fine condition" and even had just eaten a free breakfast (Bearden 1932).

"You don't look hungry," one reporter told eleven-year-old Grace Chiaramadi, daughter of two unemployed Lawrence textile workers. "Oh, don't I though! Don't I though!" she retorted. "Sometimes we go for days without eating anything. There's a little baby in our family. He's two months old, and he keeps us worried. He faints all the time. We never have milk to feed him with. We're afraid he'll die on us any day." Chiaramadi came to Washington, DC, on Thanksgiving 1932 as a delegate to the Party-led Children's Hunger March. "I came here to fight," she told the reporter, "I have seven in my family, and I want to tell you we know what it means to be hungry" (Kay 1932). Chiaramadi stood her ground; she knew hunger, she had experience of hunger, and she was prepared to fight for redress and relief.

The hunger march was a specific form of political action centered on the politics of life, health, and survival. Marchers named their hunger as an instrument of class violence against poor people, Black people, women and immigrants. As Richard Wright observed in the Chicago relief office, many participants in hunger marches, Unemployed Councils, and breadlines came to experience their hunger collectively. Hunger was systemic, more than an individual affliction or ill fortune. New forms of coalition between unemployed workers, coal miners, sharecroppers, and urban housewives could emerge around a common experience of subjection. Hunger marchers called out employers, landowners, and relief officials for carrying out a deliberate program of starvation. In response, hunger marchers were called to fight. As one placard put it: "Only fools starve, while real men fight" ("Unemployed March on Chicago" 1931).

"Fight or starve" suggests that survival, life itself, requires political struggle. Whether working or unemployed, poor people were subject to death by starvation. Working for starvation wages, as one miner explained, "simply means you starve a little more slowly than when you are out of work or on strike" (Gannes 1931). The fight against starvation was not only about work and wages; the starvation wage complex included various forms of rehabilitation and relief, food advances, scrip, charity, and state welfare. "Fight or starve" set up a stark choice: class struggle or death.

. . .

President Herbert Hoover disagreed with the hunger marchers: "There is no question of doubt that nobody will starve or go hungry in the United States" (Hoover 1931b, 419). One day after the 1931 National Hunger March to Washington, DC, Hoover delivered his State of the Union speech. He cited US Public Health Service statistics to suggest that Americans' diet and well-being remained intact. Since sickness and mortality rates were lower in 1931 than in previous years, Hoover (1931b, 419) concluded that "our people have been protected from hunger and cold." He complained that the public had been disturbed by "over-exaggerated" reports of mass destitution; he suggested that private charity remained the most effective response to economic crisis and refused to sanction a "government dole" (Hoover 1931b, 417, 419). The Red Cross, he insisted, had the situation under control. Hoover's flat statement that no one went hungry in the United States negated the hunger marchers' collective experience and their political claims. Citing the Public Health Service, he implicitly defined hunger as a medical category rather than a political one. At that very moment, in the early 1930s, a debate roiled in the medical field over how to describe and measure malnutrition. Public health experts had warned for decades that American children were at risk for malnutrition. Ironically, this consensus broke apart just as the Depression hit.[6]

Some prominent doctors believed, like Hoover, that reports of malnutrition in the United States were overexaggerated. In the early twentieth century a two-part consensus emerged among public health and child welfare experts: First, malnutrition was rampant in the United States. Second, malnutrition was caused mostly by poor parenting rather than poverty. Malnutrition or "hidden hunger," in early twentieth-century public health literature, was not equivalent to hunger caused by lack of food (Biltekoff 2013, 49). In fact, a lack of appetite appeared on lists of possible signs of malnutrition, alongside sallow skin, flabby muscle tone, rough hair, a stooped posture, chronic fatigue, bad teeth, and poor concentration (Roberts 1927, 1). Concerns about malnutrition peaked in the aftermath of World War I, when the US Army rejected some forty thousand draftees due to poor weight, height, muscle tone, or other physical insufficiencies (Clark 1921, 924).[7] Public health nurses in schools and charities mobilized to weigh and measure their charges. Nurses compared children's weight-to-height ratios against standard norms and labeled those falling below 7 percent or 10 percent of the norm as malnourished (Brown 1920). Standardized charts of height and weight allowed public health workers to measure massive numbers of children and to build large data-sets (Brosco 2001, 1386). By 1927 the US Children's Bureau claimed with confidence that "from one-fourth to one-third of the children in the United States are definitely malnourished" (Roberts 1927, 8).

Experts blamed malnutrition on parents rather than poverty. "Abundant evidence has found that ignorance and lack of parental control are more important causes of malnutrition in children than poverty" (Roberts 1927, 8). The Children's Bureau complained that parents were unaware of nutrition guidelines and incapable of using their food money wisely to follow them. American parents fed their children poorly, failed to monitor and discipline their habits, and did not understand how to provide the correct amounts of calories and vitamins (both of which had fairly recently emerged as units of nutrition). Popular magazines and public health materials conveyed warnings to parents: "Is your child malnourished?" (Clark 1921, 924).

The Depression sharpened the politics of malnutrition. From 1929 to 1933 health authorities and charities examined overall health, height, and weight of their local schoolchildren. The US Public Health Service carried out a survey of children's nutritional health, as part of a global data collection by the International Health branch of the League of Nations. The Public Health surveys found that the sharpest declines in health and nutrition happened in families that had experienced a recent drop in income (Sydenstricker 1933, 278). Worst off were Kentucky coal miners' children, nine-tenths of whom the Children's Bureau defined as malnourished (Abbott 1932). At the same time, physicians challenged the validity of such statistics. Doctors argued that malnutrition should only be diagnosed after a full physical examination by a medical professional. Mere measurements of height and weight were meaningless, they claimed, particularly if performed by "unsupervised" (female) nurses and teachers. By insisting on individual professional diagnoses, doctors invalidated attempts to gather mass statistics and undermined claims of widespread malnutrition (Brosco 2001, 1387). An editorial in the *Journal of the American Medical Association* insisted that no evidence could be found that poor nutrition was on the rise. Like Hoover, the editorialist denounced "hysteria about the increase of malnutrition as a result of the depression" ("Economic Trends" 1933, 1804).

Hunger marchers also mobilized the medical language of malnutrition. "Capitalism Kills Children," wrote the Communist Party–affiliated Labor Research Association. The Association cited public health surveys of malnutrition and warned that "workers' and farmers' children are dying of slow starvation" (Labor Research Association 1931, 4). An investigation by the Newark Unemployed Council found that "babies and children of unemployed workers are actually dying from hunger and malnourishment" ("Newark Hunger Hearing" 1931). Pediatrician Dr. Emil Conasson accompanied Grace Chiaramadi and the Children's Hunger March delegates to the Capitol in November 1932. He testified to the "malnourished state of the children, many of whom right within the delegation suffer from rickets, scurvy, and just plain starvation" (Kay 1932). Aunt Molly Jackson told of burying four to seven Harlan County babies every week in summer 1931 "on account of cholera, famine, flux, stomach trouble brought on by undernourishment" (quoted in Dreiser et al. 2008 [1932], 85, 279). Hunger, wrote an organizer in the *Daily Worker*, "saps the vitality and life of the women workers" (Damon 1931).

. . .

Hunger marches opened up forms of political identification across race, gender, and geography, based on starvation wages. Starvation relations pointed to long-standing historical forms of labor exploitation and linked work, wages, and household consumption as interconnected sites of power. The American Communist Party recognized the potential for mass mobilization around the common cause of hunger. State and local officials also recognized this potential and worked to contain it. They branded hunger marches, neighborhood committees, and mutual aid groups as Communist, cleaving apart their potential for unification. Within a few years many neighborhood groups had broken up over allegations of communism (Orleck 1993, 165). Still today, histories of the Depression hunger marches treat them as a subplot in the history of the American Communist Party.[8] Certainly that history is not inaccurate. But there are also many other stories to tell of marginalized people mobilizing to fight historical relations of starvation.

New Deal welfare contributed to breaking up hunger marchers' solidarity. New Deal policies reinforced racist and gendered divides, especially between urban industrial workers, domestic workers, and rural agricultural workers. The National Labor Relations Act of 1935 outlawed payment in scrip and opened mines and other extractive sites to unionization. But domestic and agricultural workers were excluded from New Deal reforms. Commodity distributions worsened gender and racial disparities; in some areas of the South, welfare rules made hunger worse rather than better (DeVault and Pitts 1984, 548). For white, urban industrial workers the New Deal introduced a language of security, rehabilitation, and self-government, which promised an end to starvation wages. The New Deal depoliticized hunger while reinforcing some of the underlying relations of starvation. World War II and international relief programs soon overshadowed hunger activism within the United States. Hunger appeared to be elsewhere, outside of the United States. Hungry people, it seemed, were to be found in distant Europe and Asia, teeming masses, passive and suffering, awaiting rescue. International relief agencies and social scientists described a psychological, physical, and political type: "the hungry." Hunger appeared as a distant abnormality to be treated and reformed, not as a site of common identification.

4

---

# Food Aid and the Starved Personality

"The hungry" are always plural. They have no past; if they had one, they have forgotten it. They have no politics. They cannot make decisions for themselves. They are animals. They are asocial, aggressive, irritable, lawless, or apathetic and listless. They are not as well tied together as they once were. They are recognizable—hard stare, emaciated frame, swollen limbs, or distended belly. They are dangerous, deprived, dependent. They risk falling into political extremism. They cannot participate in democracy. They require rescue. They are suffering. The hungry are a population, a multitude, a quantity (thousands, millions). There are too many of them. They have outstripped carrying capacity; their supplies do not meet their demands. They are unproductive. They need to be prevented. The hungry are always elsewhere.

All of these statements are derived from mid-twentieth-century memos, studies, news articles, and agency directives for hunger relief. It is so common these days to see a reference to "the hungry" and their numbers—850 million, 10 percent of the world population—that we might not stop to ask how so many people come to be known, first and foremost, by their hunger. That number—so many millions of hungry people—mobilizes money for charity and development aid, and sensitizes the comfortable to the plight of the impoverished. That number gathers together multitudes of individuals with unique histories of wealth and poverty, food and eating, violence, exploitation and deprivation (Yates-Doerr 2015a; Yates-Doerr 2024). Grouped together in one global statistic, "the hungry" appear as passive victims collectively waiting for rescue. There seems to be only one thing to be done: give them food. This chapter is about how hunger and "the hungry" became objects of knowledge and governance in the post–World War II world. Relief operations established in the aftermath of the war set the foundation for eighty years of international aid and development, and would also shape welfare policy at home.

Since World War II, massive charity operations, international organizations, diplomacy, and media productions focused their efforts on feeding the world's hungry. In the closing years of the war, violence by starvation was visited on millions of people worldwide. The United States and its allies implemented a vast program of hunger management and relief. In the process millions came to be identified, first and foremost, as "the hungry." They were counted and classified in various stages of deprivation. In the eyes of the Allied relief workers and experts, hunger determined their attitudes, emotions, hopes, and social status. Relief workers and policy makers looked at refugees, displaced persons, peasants in drought-struck or destroyed regions, residents of bombed-out cities, and saw "the hungry." Hunger, in all its guises, threatened the new world order that the United States and Allies sought to establish after the war. At the same time, hunger came to be understood as something "elsewhere," happening outside of the United States.

Three assumptions defined knowledge and governance of hunger beginning in the postwar period. First, "hungry" became known as a type, a set of qualities, a way of being, a mode of human otherness. Physiologists defined the physical symptoms. Anthropologists and psychologists profiled the culture and personality. Policy makers and relief agencies ascribed "the hungry" with a certain kind of politics. To be hungry came to mean much more than to be without food. Above all, *the hungry were characterized by their lack of physical, psychological, and political autonomy.* Hunger had to be governed in a very particular way. The hungry had to be treated and reformed, bodily, mentally and politically. Their fate could not be left to their own judgment. Weak-willed, apolitical, antisocial, they could be easily swayed by a Nazi strongman or a Communist infiltrator. Hungry people were constitutionally unable to make decisions, collaborate with others, or participate in democracy.

Relatedly, hungry people who complained, held hunger strikes, or otherwise made their hunger political were marked as pathological. Protest became pathology. Political grievances appeared as symptoms of psychological regression. The proper subjects for rehabilitation and relief, in the eyes of Americans and their allies, were passive victims awaiting rescue. Those who demanded better conditions, or who protested against prevailing power relations, were dismissed as acting out their psychological fears and insecurities. Hostility and contestation were understood as symptoms of food deprivation, to be treated and cured by a firm and benevolent authority. In the postwar world, *hunger was antidemocratic.*

Finally, and in consequence, *food aid was used to get people, and entire nations, to think, feel, and do things differently.* Rehabilitation measures sought

FIGURE 5. "Amid war-damaged buildings, the American Presbyterian Hospital cooks for the daily lineup of homeless," July 1946. *Source*: S-0801-0006-0004-00029, United Nations Relief and Rehabilitation Administration (UNRRA) Photographs, United Nations Archives.

to modify the psychology and behavior of poor and starving people, to make them more modern and market-oriented. Hunger relief was designed to change people's relations to food and to politics, to accept the advice of technical experts, to shift to industrialized forms of agriculture, to lessen the numbers of their children. American food aid after World War II was most often conditional on specific policy goals. In this sense, food aid served as one of the most powerful instruments of the international development project (Escobar 2011, 72, 122–123).

. . .

In November 1944 a group of thirty-two conscientious objectors were starved, experimentally and on purpose. They were volunteers for a semistarvation experiment at the University of Minnesota Laboratory of Physiological Hygiene. Subjects were kept for six months on strict diets that had been designed to replicate wartime hunger rations and that reduced their body weight by 25 percent. Researchers recorded changes in their physiological, cognitive, emotional, and behavioral abilities. The starved men lost interest in everything but food; hunger eclipsed all other drives and motivations (Guetzkow and Bowman 1946, 23). Men who were once viewed as "sincere and upright" in their commitment to civilian service lost psychological and "ethical control" under starvation. Some of them cheated and stole. They became irritable and "'blew up' at each other on occasion." They were unable to concentrate. They stopped going out with others, and their social lives deteriorated. They passively let themselves be pushed around by crowds in public places. Even though the men knew that the experiment would end and that their own safety was guaranteed, they experienced intense feelings of anxiety and insecurity (Guetzkow and Bowman 1946, 27–32).

The starving Minnesota volunteers embodied human otherness. These hungry men were not the same as other people. After six months of deprivation the volunteers each became a "special kind of person." They lost their passions and interests, their moral standing, their motivation, and their social abilities. Their bodies had changed, their minds were warped, and their self-governance was compromised. In researchers' eyes, the volunteers lost their individuality and particularity. Collectively they embodied a uniform typology: "the hungry." The Minnesota research group published their findings in *Men and Hunger*, a manual to advise relief workers, physicians, dietitians, and volunteers heading to postwar Europe. Laboratory head Ancel Keys explained to relief workers that "the person who has been starved for long is a special kind of person, different from the ordinary patient or relief client back home as well as from you and me" (Guetzkow and Bowman 1946, 11). The manual outlined changes in behavior, sociability, and mental and emotional capacity, relevant to rehabilitating people who had been starved and devastated by the war. Psychologist Harold Guetzkow observed of the Minnesota subjects: "These are men who were being torn apart by stress, and were not as well knit as formerly" (Guetzkow and Bowman 1946, 45).

The Minnesota researchers, alongside social scientists in Europe and Asia during and after the war, defined "the hungry" as a political subject. Hunger, warned physiologist Walter Cannon (1916, 232), "is a sensation so peremptory, so disagreeable, so tormenting, that men have committed crimes in order to assuage it. It has led to cannibalism, even among the civilized. It has resulted in suicide. And it has defeated armies—for the aggressive spirit becomes detached from larger loyalties and becomes personal and selfish as hunger pangs increase in vigor and insistence." Cannon (1941, 9) feared that that hungry people risked falling under the sway of strong-arm dictators who took advantage of "the plasticity of people when they are uneasy and anxious."

The hungry had a specific kind of politics. They lacked the capacity for autonomy, judgment, and self-government. In many ways this politics of the hungry drew directly from assumptions and tropes in colonial government. The hungry could not be trusted to think for themselves. They had to be treated, rehabilitated, and guided toward a state of full autonomy. "The processes of good government, and especially of democracy, are very difficult to organize in starvation situations because of the breakdown in group life" (Guetzkow and Bowman 1946, 69). Paul Bowman, a member of the Minnesota research team with several years' experience in food relief, suggested that relief workers avoid organizing their community democratically. "The starving usually have little interest in government and cannot call up enough energy to participate in self-government" (Guetzkow and Bowman 1946, 69). Hungry people required a specific form of governance: technical expertise, fair management, and firm administration. Information, not decision-making, should be shared with hungry subjects, and discontentment patiently and impartially addressed. These ideas were applied on a massive scale in the decade following World War II.

Hunger and starvation were weaponized during the world wars. Millions suffered from blockades, sieges, wartime restrictions, and starvation campaigns. Starvation caused more devastation than combat in the Netherlands, Greece, and elsewhere in Europe during World War II (Valaoras 1946; *Malnutrition and Starvation* 1948). The Bengal famine of 1943, precipitated by a cyclone and British wartime restrictions, killed between two million and three million Bengalis (Ó Grada 2009, 159). Nazi plans for German colonization of Eastern Europe led to the programmatic mass starvation of "surplus" Slavic and Jewish populations, including a half-million Jews who died of hunger in ghettos, millions who starved in concentration camps, and three million starved Russian prisoners of war (Gerlach 1998, 13; Snyder 2012, xiii). Well over a million residents died of starvation during the German siege of Leningrad in 1941–1942 (Leigh Smith 2015, 214; Manley 2015). Mental hospitals in Germany, and to a lesser extent in France, practiced euthanasia by starvation as a form of racial hygiene (Proctor 1988, 187; Bueltzingsloewen 2005). In Japanese-occupied northern Indochina, a severe famine killed one million to two million people, perhaps up to one-fifth of the population there (Leigh Smith 2015, 218).

After the end of hostilities in Europe and Asia in 1945, hunger grew worse for many people in those regions. Millions were famished in Korea and Java. One hundred thousand people starved to death in Tokyo in fall 1945 (Collingham 2011, 467).

Rations fell across Western Europe. A drought in 1946 impacted almost the entire globe, with the exception of North America. The monsoon failed in India. The United Nations estimated in 1946 that seven million Chinese people risked starvation, and one-third of the world's population was hungry (Collingham 2011, 470, 476). International governance in the wake of the world wars began with hunger relief (Reinisch 2011). In November 1943 leaders of the Allied powers signed into existence an international body destined to manage the hunger of people liberated from German and Japanese occupation: the United Nations Relief and Rehabilitation Administration (UNRRA). UNRRA was the first nonmilitary international organization to emerge during the war. Unlike earlier humanitarian relief, which relied primarily on nongovernmental charities, UNRRA carried out an intergovernmental effort at a scale never before attempted (Riley 2017, 90, 92, 135).

In its brief existence from 1944 until it shut down in 1947, UNRRA administered aid to sixteen countries. In Europe operations focused on Albania, Czechoslovakia, Greece, Poland, and Yugoslavia; in Asia, UNRRA worked primarily in China, Formosa (Taiwan), Korea, and the Philippines. In less than three years, UNRRA delivered more than nine million tons of food, grains, fats, dairy, and fish (Woodbridge 1950, 1:409). In Germany alone UNRRA employed four thousand aid workers, medical personnel, and welfare officers (E.R.O. 1946, 36). UNRRA's work relied on funding and supplies from the United States. The organization collapsed when the US Congress voted to stop that funding and the United States withdrew from multilateral cooperation. After 1947 the United States pursued a more focused program of food aid in service of its own national security objectives (Reinisch 2013, 89).

On the occasion of UNRRA's founding in 1943, President Franklin D. Roosevelt warned that German and Japanese forces had "one purpose in mind: that in the lands they occupy there shall be left only a generation of half-men, undernourished, crushed in body and spirit, without strength or incentive to hope—ready, in fact, to be enslaved and used as beasts of burden by the self-styled master races" ("On the Hunger Front" 1943). In Roosevelt's dark vision hunger would reduce entire nations to a state of brutish and submissive animality. These people would lose forever their humanity and their free will. Denied proper nourishment, passive and broken, they were destined to submit to authoritarian rule. Even as Roosevelt hailed an international effort to relieve wartime hunger, the specter of enslavement by starvation hung heavy. The future of world democracy appeared to hinge on the bodies and minds of hungry civilians.

. . .

Physiologists, psychologists, and anthropologists mobilized to study these weak and potentially dangerous masses. Displaced Persons (DPs) camps and bombed-out cities became "laboratories" where British and American social scientists

FIGURE 6. "Italy—Refugees line up for noon-day meal at the UNRRA camp," 1946–1948. *Source*: S-0801-0006-0004-00029, UNRRA Photographs, United Nations Archives.

tested their "individualist, psychoanalytic, and familialist visions" (Zahra 2011, 40). As Dutch psychiatrist Joost A. M. Meerloo (1952, 352) wrote after the war, "every emergency is a kind of new psycho-pathological experiment, raising new questions and giving new answers." As the war neared its end, Allied authorities turned to psychologists to help manage the ensuing confusion and chaos. In late summer 1944 the UNRRA Welfare Division assembled social scientists attached to military units in London to form an Inter-Allied Psychological Study Group. The group included Meerloo, who was serving as psychiatric advisor to the Royal Netherlands army; American sociologist Edward Shils, who was attached to the US Office of Strategic Services; Canadian social worker Marjorie Bradford; and British military psychiatrists with ties to the Tavistock Clinic. The Study Group produced a white paper on "Psychological Problems of Displaced Persons" for use by UNRRA relief workers (UNRRA 1945). Their report examined a range of issues related to displacement, forced labor, and subservience; first among them was hunger.

The Inter-Allied Study Group drew from prior experiences working with hungry and displaced people in Europe and the UK. Meerloo had lived in occupied Holland from 1942 through 1944, masking his Jewish identity, until he was arrested for resistance. At his Amsterdam psychiatric clinic he saw patients from across the social spectrum, "to give not only medical advice, but counsel on every type of difficulty" (Meerloo 1945, 17). Food rations at that time only provided for about

60 percent of residents' physical needs. Meerloo described advising a mother how to cook with nettles, and consoling a Jewish man who lost half his family to bombing and the other half to concentration camps. Arrested, tortured, and interrogated, Meerloo managed to escape from a German transport train and walked across France and Spain to finally reach Great Britain (Woody 2022, 3–4). He drew the lesson from his years living under occupation that "the cave-man has appeared once more, and stands scowling outside his cave, club in hand, ready to defend himself against any danger. The elements, hunger, cold, his fellow-men" (Meerloo 1945, 76). Meerloo's ideas about regression and primitivity strongly influenced the Study Group report.

The Study Group sought to summarize the state of knowledge about the impacts of starvation and displacement. They asked military authorities permission to visit and investigate Displaced Person camps on the continent, but their superiors denied them access (Meerloo 1952, 354). Instead, the group gathered reports from European contacts, including a Dutch physician who had escaped from a German concentration camp. British Study Group members drew from their experience with the Tavistock Clinic rehabilitating British prisoners of war. As clinicians in Civil Resettlement Units, they sought to cure POWs' individual personality defects, such as apathy and irritability (Roberts-Pederson 2021, 103). The Inter-Allied Study Group's desk report therefore reflects experts' assumptions and prior experiences, rather than direct observations in Europe or Asia after the war. That said, these assumptions continued to replicate long after the initial postwar period. The Study Group report illustrates a prevailing view of a hungry person's psychological state. "The Psychology of Displaced Persons" profiled a shattered and infantile personality. In the Study Group's analysis, hunger and displacement caused people to regress to a childlike, primal mental state, "falling back to earlier more primitive and for example infantile habits." Regression was "the most characteristic personality change" of people faced with violence, starvation, and "severe emotional straining." Under starvation conditions "acquired forms of civilization" and "cultural decorum" disappeared. Restraints were cast aside; "the brakes have been taken off" (UNRRA 1945, 18). The Study Group's analysis led to practical conclusions about how best to organize relief; there were also political consequences for future global stability.

Hungry and displaced people, it seemed, were ruled entirely by fears around food. As the Inter-Allied Group remarked, "food is the primal token of security" in human life. "It is quite certain that because food is the most vital of all provisions of security, feeling about it is always likely to run high and to reflect many disturbed social attitudes" (UNRRA 1945, 34–35). The Study Group described a range of emotional consequences of hunger: "rivalry, jealousy and greed . . . emerge in great strength" (UNRRA 1945, 4). Many hungry people responded to the mortal fear of starvation with "primitive behavior" and "heightened aggressiveness." They felt "deep feelings of guilt and hostility toward a world that has starved them and 'let them down.'" Others felt "nausea, poor appetite and even food rejection" (UNRRA 1945, 35). The Study Group predicted that these psychological symptoms would endure long after the physical body returned to health.

Fear of deprivation led the hungry to steal and stuff their pockets with food even after a full meal, "just as a well fed child who feels itself robbed and cheated of love may take to stealing food from its parents." These hungry people felt a "desire for revenge and privilege" and a "greed for affection" (UNRRA 1945, 35). "Such people's demands become insatiable like a greedy baby's" (UNRRA 1945, 4). The report identified mistrust and selfishness as symptoms of infantile regression. In keeping with their individualistic, psychoanalytic orientation, the Study Group focused on dysfunctional personality traits rather than collective trauma or historical injustice. The Study Group dismissed political protests as a psychological pathology. DPs in Allied refugee camps angrily complained about relief distribution, demanding more food and supplies, protesting, and occasionally breaking out in violence. The Study Group report observed that many displaced and hungry people expressed "mistrust and hatred of any gesture from any authority" and "a hostile undervaluation of the purpose, quantity and quality of the food supplies" (UNRRA 1945, 35). The report suggested that DPs' political views were "inevitably colored" by "disturbed attitudes toward authority" (UNRRA 1945, 39).

Hungry people had regressed to an infantile mental state. Political protests therefore should be treated like childish tantrums. Study Group member Edward Shils (1946, 7, 13) warned that hungry DPs were "depoliticized" and risked getting caught up in violent or radical actions: "for one . . . whose capacity for rational judgment has declined and who is motivated by strong anti-authority sentiments, the most radical programs are likely to be attractive." Protests should be treated as expressions of emotional disturbance and "sycophantic, apathetic, guilty, submissive, cynical, rebellious, mistrustful" feelings. The Study Group encouraged UNRRA personnel to establish a strong authority on which these people might "lean" and "feed, as it were, on a tolerant atmosphere" (UNRRA 1945, 39).

If protest was pathology, the Study Group thought that UNRRA administrators should exercise their authority over the DPs as a cure. The report suggested that camp administrators should facilitate a "slow move towards increasing self-government and away from the relatively firm benevolent central authority necessitated by the passive dependence of early days." Each "stage of recovery" from the psychological symptoms of starvation allowed for more autonomy. First and foremost, people in the camp should take on "responsibility for making and cooking food" (UNRRA 1945, 23). This diagnosis was reflected in UNRRA's "Welfare Guide" for displaced people in Germany (UNRRA, Welfare Division 1945). The guide recommended a "democratic organization" for displaced people's camps, but only under certain conditions including length of time spent in the camp (UNRRA, Welfare Division 1945, 19). Shils (1946, 18) suggested that "camps must be operated as experiments in group therapy."

By the same logic, hunger depoliticized the Allies' former enemies. The suffering of hungry Germans and starving Japanese people after the war purged them of agency in the eyes of many Allied officials. These former enemies should not be allowed to go hungry, experts argued, lest starvation dissuade them from moving toward democracy (Weinreb 2012, 52, 70). When the United States entered Japan, American policy prohibited relief aid for Japanese civilians except in the case of famine. Japanese officials (and later, occupying American forces) gathered evidence to establish that the country did in fact suffer from famine, opening the door to relief. Jenny Leigh Smith (2015) has suggested that this moment marked a new era of hunger relief, in which an outside authority was empowered to validate a state of famine and release food aid. According to Leigh Smith (2015, 213), General MacArthur shared his concern with US officials "that chronic hunger would erode the psychological well-being and democratic impulses of the new Japan."

It is not clear how much influence the Psychological Study Group's report or the UNRRA Welfare Division had at the ground level of UNRRA's relief operations. Meerloo (1952, 353–354) complained that authorities dismissed the Study Group's focus on individual therapy in favor of "mass regulations" and the "administrative machine." UNRRA's directorate and technical divisions remained suspicious of the Welfare Division and its project of psychological rehabilitation, in contrast to the massive effort and infrastructure needed to acquire, transport, and distribute supplies. The number of psychologically trained UNRRA welfare workers on the ground was relatively small compared with technical staff (Woodbridge 1950, 2:26–28). Thomas Davidson (1947, 14), UNRRA team director of DP Operations in Germany, complained that welfare officers were useless and "pathetic." Nevertheless, the Interallied Study Group was one component of a far-reaching "psychological Marshall Plan" that, in Tara Zahra's (2011, 52) words, "linked psychoanalytic methods to both individualism and democratization."

Social scientists mobilized by the Allies published multiple studies along the same lines. UNRRA relief workers were particularly drawn to cultural anthropologists, given their exposure to cultural relativism while serving abroad (Reinisch 2013, 78). Anthropologists of the "modal personality" and "culture and personality" schools applied psychoanalytic methods to study food habits and cultures. Cora Du Bois (1944) studied culture, personality, and food insecurity among highland residents of the Dutch colony of Alor. Du Bois went on to serve as a high-ranking research officer in the US Office of Strategic Services at Indonesia and Ceylon. Margaret Mead (1943, 50) served during the war as executive secretary of the National Research Council Committee on Food Habits, where she promoted the "application of psychoanalytic theory and techniques to [the problem] . . . of altering American food habits to preserve nutritional standards in the midst of war shortages." This body of social scientific work on hunger had political consequences. Authorities felt justified in guiding hungry people toward autonomy and self-government—but only when they were ready for it. Until then, the hungry were treated as passive victims in need of guidance, treatment, and rescue (Salvatici 2012, 440).

Even as hunger justified the rehabilitation of former enemy peoples, many DPs experienced Allied relief as a loss of bodily and political autonomy. Some DPs went on hunger strike. Despite experts' assumptions about hunger and depoliticization, hungry people in camps, colonies, and occupied areas organized and staged hunger strikes to protest their subjection to Allied authority. Anticolonial fighters in India, Ireland, and British Palestine continued a long tradition of hunger strikes for freedom and independence (Vernon 2007, 60–80). In 1947 thirteen thousand displaced Jewish people in ten DP camps on the island of Cyprus went on a one-hundred-hour hunger strike, to protest the shooting of an escapee from the camp and the lowering of return quotas to Palestine (Guebenlian 1947, 1). Jewish DPs in occupied Germany went on hunger strikes to assert political demands (Holian 2011, 190). Industrial workers in both Japan and Germany also went on hunger strike in 1946 and 1947 to protest their working conditions and lack of food ("Japan Bans Hunger Strike" 1946, 6; "Hunger Strike" 1947, 7). Hunger strikers in the postwar years wielded hunger as a collective weapon of protest ("Hunger Strike Over" 1946, 1).

Hunger, in the wake of World War II, appeared psychologically incompatible with democracy. In a direct echo of colonial discourse about Native peoples, the hungry were deemed incapable of self-government and in need of expert guidance. Their mental and physical state led hungry people to submit to, even require, a strong authority. Their political views were "weak" and "colored" by the ravages of hunger. As William Vogt warned in 1948 (207), "hungry people are not likely to be willing to suffer the slow process of democracy. Freedom seems far less important when one's belly is rubbing one's backbone—and the Man on Horseback, or the man in the red-starred tank, takes on plausibility as a leader out of the wilderness." Only well-nourished people were capable—physically and psychologically—of participating in their own democratic self-determination.

The United States and Allied powers subjected hungry people around the world to regimes of disciplinary control. Hungry and displaced people were kept in camps, even against their will, for their own good. Their fragile mental state required a "firm benevolent" authority. Even as the Allies claimed victory for democracy at the end of the World War, spaces of exception opened up for the hungry, the poor, and the psychologically "underdeveloped." Such spaces of exception would multiply around the globe in the late twentieth and twenty-first centuries (Agamben 1998; Ibrahim 2021). At the same time, hunger became biomedical.

· · ·

The Minnesota Experiment was designed to test and validate the best treatment for mass starvation. To do so, researchers first had to starve the volunteer subjects for six months. As the experiment advanced, the starving men felt a "disconcerting sensation of growing old quickly, as indeed, in effect, they were." "In starving," wrote research leader Ancel Keys (1946, 14), "a person literally begins feeding off his own body." Keys described the gradual process of starvation as a "battle against hunger," from a "slowing down" of pulse and movement to a loss of strength, will, and endurance and defenselessness against disease. Metabolism slows down and circulation decreases by up to half of what it once was. The body no longer heats itself and always feels cold. Brain function and mental abilities remain intact at the cost of energy elsewhere in the body. A starving person's tissues "waste away and are partly replaced by water (edema). Then, without adequate food, he dehydrates and the battle is lost" (Keys 1946, 14). Keys's metaphor of a rapidly and prematurely aging body suggests that it might be difficult or even impossible to regain homeostasis, to return to a stable state. The Minnesota Experiment challenged prevailing assumptions about bodily equilibrium.

When Keys began the refeeding, or rehabilitation, stage of the experiment, he was surprised to discover that many men took a turn for the worse. More calories did not necessarily lead the men to revert back to health. Keys divided the study subjects into three groups, each receiving different amounts of extra calories beyond the starvation rations that they had received during the previous six months. To the researchers' surprise, many subjects' condition deteriorated in response to increased rations. While most of the men began to regain weight, some lost even more than they had under starvation conditions. Hunger edema appeared in subjects who had not had it before. The psychological condition of some subjects took a downward turn. Several felt more hungry, depressed, and irritable than they had under starvation conditions (Keys et al. 1950, 2:837).

Keys was so alarmed by this deterioration that after six weeks of rehabilitation, he decided to increase all the subject's calories significantly (Keys et al. 1950, 2:126). Even after twelve weeks of ample refeeding, study subjects' metabolism was still a good deal lower than it had been before the study began (Keys et al. 1950, 2:330). Vitamin and protein supplements, which some subjects received on top of their increased calories, seemed to have no impact on their rate of recovery (Keys et al. 1950, 2:332). Keys concluded that starvation could not easily be reversed. "Are the processes in rehabilitation merely a reversal, a mirror image, of those of atrophy? There is reason to think that it is more complicated than this" (Keys et al. 1950, 2:296). The balance of water, fat, and muscle tissue of subjects in rehabilitation was not the same as before starvation. In recovery, starved people lost body water and accumulated large quantities of fat, to the point that Keys described a "post-starvation obesity" (Keys et al. 1950, 2:126).

Once subjects were allowed to eat as much as they wished, they gorged themselves and their weights rose even higher than before the study began. Many of the subjects felt hungry all the time, months after the end of the experiment. "Some men reported that at times they had a physical sensation of hunger even after they had eaten a large meal; subject No. 27 commented . . . on having 'an odd sensation of being full yet still hungry'" (Keys et al. 1950, 2:127). Subjects spoke of their fear that their food would not last and there would not be enough to eat. Keys decided that this incessant hunger was not due to any biochemical imbalance and instead was "psychogenic" (Keys et al. 1950, 2:128). Neither the body, the mind, nor the emotions returned completely to their prior state, even after months of refeeding. Keys warned relief workers and Allied officials that "recovery from starvation is not as simple as it might seem." Rebuilding the body was a "slow process" and required long-term, massive supplies. "Starved people cannot be rehabilitated in a few weeks on small hand-outs of vitamin pills and protein concentrates or by a bare subsistence diet." They required "calories—plain cereals in great quantities and all the dried and condensed milk, dried eggs, cheese and meats that we can spare." Even with an abundant diet, formerly starving people would require "probably many months" of care before their muscles and motivation regrew sufficiently to return to a normal and productive life (Keys 1946, 28). Stability appeared far out of reach.

Medical researchers and relief workers in Europe and Asia after the war discovered that recovery came slowly, if ever, to starved civilians. Extreme hunger seemed to require specialized, expert biomedical intervention. Jack Drummond (1950, 13), British biochemist and nutrition specialist, remarked that "it was frightening to realize," as the extent of wartime starvation became apparent, "how little any of us knew about severe starvation." Beyond a certain level of starvation, it took months, if not years, to return to a stable state. As medical workers discovered while caring for starving civilians and concentration camp survivors, starvation disease resisted treatment. Rehabilitation took far longer than medical authorities expected, and required far more calories than they had imagined possible.

Medical work during and after the Second World War established extreme hunger as a distinct disease, also labeled undernutrition, denutrition, famine disease, or starvation disease (Simmons 2008; Moraes 2019). Hunger came to be understood as a biomedical condition, in need of expert surveillance and specialized medical treatment. Most medical research in the period before World War II focused on vitamin deficiency diseases like beriberi or pellagra, whose symptoms could be resolved simply by supplying quantities of that vitamin or mineral. By contrast, extreme hunger was a total illness, impacting every bodily system. In this sense medical research on hunger and starvation disease during World War II formed a precursor to contemporary work on the total effects of metabolic illness. Starvation appeared to profoundly alter the body's ability to regulate itself under strain. It was unclear whether or how a body could recover from it.

Recovery from postwar starvation required massive infusions of calories, grains, milk, and other goods. Yet the world's main supplier of these goods— the United States—refused to curtail domestic consumption or imperil export prices to support starvation relief abroad. The US government eliminated price controls at the war's end and refused to requisition wheat for international aid (Woodbridge 1950, 1:409, 432). In the wake of the global failed harvests of 1946, former president Hoover took to the airwaves to urge Americans to cut home consumption of wheat by 40 percent and fats by 20 percent, to spare supplies for starving nations. Hoover pleaded with listeners to reduce food waste and eat less bread and meat, which together could save twenty-five million European lives (no mention was made of non-European lives). President Truman, speaking alongside Hoover, intoned that "we have a high responsibility, as Americans, to go to their rescue" (Riley 2017, 112–113). But Americans paid little heed to these pleas and rapidly increased their intake of both grains and fats in the postwar years. Instead of reducing and redistributing, the United States entered a crisis of overconsumption.

. . .

"The hungry" were always plural, always too many, and to be eliminated. In the 1950s and 1960s, American farms produced more food than its consumers could absorb. At the same time, the world was full of hungry people. American experts devised strategies to dispose of these excesses. Both food and people were apparently too much, too many, overproduced. The world appeared overfull. The United States implemented policies designed to eliminate surplus, designating both food and people as excessive and expendable. Out of the 1950s and 1960s a regime of hunger management emerged, including modes of knowledge and modes of governance (Escobar 2011, 123). The United States and its allies sought to control hunger not just for humanitarian reasons but also to achieve economic, geopolitical, and ideological ends. American agro-industry dealt with overproduction of food in two ways: by marketing, to get Americans to eat more, and by sending excess production abroad in the form of food aid. Producers viewed food aid as a tool to open world markets to America's excess production. "Surplus disposal" was how Americans in the 1950s called the food aid program.

The United States leveraged international food aid to push for political, psychological, economic, social, and reproductive reforms. Recipient nations were asked to shift from traditional farming to high-input agriculture, open their domestic and export markets, ally with US foreign policy goals, and reduce birth rates. Once again, hunger was employed as a technology. The United States used postwar food aid as a "lever," in the words of one presidential staffer, to "get something done" (Riley 2017, 262). Food aid served as a tool of soft power in the nonaligned world. Soft power operated most impactfully at the level of individual people, their attitudes, economic choices, and personal lives. Technical experts created "infrastructures for experimentalizing populations" (Murphy 2017, 8). They rolled out programs of agricultural modernization and population control designed to change people's everyday acts and feelings. Development programs intruded into the most intimate aspects of their targets' lives (Cullather 2010, 7).

FIGURE 7. "Greece—The first shipload of UNRRA supplies from Brazil is unloaded at Port of Piraeus," 1944–1948. *Source*: S-0800-0006-0001-00055, UNRRA Photographs, United Nations Archives.

The reproductive decisions and possibilities of poor women and families became objects of foreign policy and technoscientific control.

Postwar food aid programs served three goals: anticommunism, economic liberalization, and population control. Each of these priorities operated on several levels, from national leaders to individual citizens, often at contradictory and cross purposes. US policy makers sought to enforce cooperation with their geopolitical objectives, on the one hand; on the other, they sought to "modify the psychology of the peasant," oriented toward free-market, participatory, democratic values (Cullather 2010, 7). Americans made food aid contingent on agricultural "modernization" (Ahlberg 2008, 76). Recipients of American aid were required to promote the use of high-intensity agricultural inputs, chemical fertilizer and pesticides and hybrid seeds, sold by American companies. As a result, countries would remain dependent on US suppliers (Ahlberg 2008, 76–77). Some farmers who had been self-sufficient came to rely on imported fertilizer. Cash crops replaced subsistence foods (Escobar 2011, 123). Large commercial producers benefitted to the detriment of small subsistence farmers (Olsson 2017, 132). Many of these strategies ultimately aggravated hunger among traditional farming communities.

"The hungry" were located in the realm of the underclass, the underdeveloped, the Third World, the formerly enslaved, and the Indigenous. Entire regions, continents, nations, ethnicities, and groups were characterized as hungry, deficient, starved, and dependent (Tappan 2017, 47). A standard imagery congealed around "the hungry," something like Binyavanga Wainaina's (2005, 31) satirical description of the "Starving African": "The Starving African . . . wanders the refugee camp nearly naked, and waits for the benevolence of the West. Her children have flies on their eyelids and pot bellies, and her breasts are flat and empty. She must look utterly helpless." As Wainaina's satire suggests, such imagery strips away individuality, humanity, personal histories, and identities. Arturo Escobar (2011, 123) describes such imagery, of dark and starving bodies, as a form of extreme symbolic violence.

Postwar populationists and foreign policy makers sought to contain this figure of the less than human, the hungry. Neo-Malthusians Joseph Spengler and William Vogt justified population control as a harsh but necessary reality; if policy makers did not reduce the number of people in the world, they warned, hunger and famine would. Vogt (1948, 206, 211) complained that poorer countries had "planted [their] hand firmly in America's dinner pail" and argued that "any aid we give should be made contingent on national programs leading toward population stabilization through voluntary action of the people." Policy makers followed suit. John F. Kennedy, for example, linked population control and hunger relief in a 1963 speech to the World Food Congress (Riley 2017, 224).

After World War II, policy makers justified massive programs of food aid to Europe as an inoculation against communism. House Foreign Affairs Committee chairman Charles Eaton warned that "if the Italian ration falls below what it is, there is no power that can keep the communists from taking over Italy," Greece, Turkey, and others "around the world" (cited in Riley 2017, 132). Aid to Italy was instituted despite the objections of Ethiopia, which had been one of the first countries liberated from Axis occupation but which received almost no aid for recovery (Woodward 1945, 12). In what became a standard policy approach, the United States leveraged food aid in exchange for compliance with American geopolitical objectives. Having abandoned UNRRA, the United States established its own food aid programs, tightly linked to anticommunist and development agendas. Food was used to pull Tito's Yugoslavia away from Soviet influence in the 1950s. Conversely, the United States withdrew food aid when Egypt nationalized the Suez Canal in 1956. In the 1960s, India, Israel, and South Vietnam received significant food aid in the service of foreign policy goals. In the case of Israel, food aid indirectly subsidized defense purchases (Ahlberg 2008, 23, 9).

Lyndon Johnson's Food for Peace program conditioned food aid on agricultural modernization and alliance with American foreign policy priorities. Food for Peace was commonly referred to as a program of "surplus disposal." As Senator George McGovern remarked, "It is acceptable to describe the garbage units in our kitchen sinks as disposal units, it is insensitive, if not insulting, to so describe feeding a child, a mother, or humankind in general" (cited in Ahlberg 2008, 27). Kristin Ahlberg (2008) revealed evidence that Johnson overtly wielded hunger as technology; he used hunger in the wake of the 1965 famine to keep India on a "short tether." Indian grain production fell by 20 percent in two consecutive harvests from 1965 through 1967. In the state of Bihar, food grain harvests were down more than 50 percent compared with harvests earlier in that decade. National food stocks were low, and India relied on imports from the US Food for Peace program to avoid catastrophe. Experts predicted a severe famine (Drèze 1991, 45–49).

Instead of shipping aid to famine regions immediately, however, Johnson made famine aid to India conditional on agricultural modernization and alliance with US foreign policy priorities. If India could "keep this [reform] program going," Johnson told the Indian food minister, "we can help you more." Free-market reforms "permitted" the United States to provide aid (Ahlberg 2008, 124). Johnson privately complained: "I don't know if we got an obligation the rest of our lives just to ship them 10% of what they eat. And not without even having agreement or discussions, or tying in any alliance, or to be sure of serving our national interests" (Ahlberg 2008, 114). Johnson's aide Robert Komer later recalled that Johnson "said, ' . . . you tell that guy to go over there and when he's got a real authenticated case [of starvation], pack up [the] bones and send them back here then I'll believe him.' . . . Well, by God, no Indians starved to our knowledge." Komer lauded Johnson's short tether on Indian famine aid as "a great example of how a master politician can pull the lever and get something done" (Riley 2017, 262).

World leaders, relief organizations, physiologists, and social scientists lay the groundwork for what Sylvia Wynter (2003, 323) has called the "new master code": hunger defined a dividing line between the fully human, the First World; and the underdeveloped, the Third World, the less-than-fully human. "The hungry" became a type: lacking autonomy, incapable of self-government, and subject to technoscientific intervention. The hungry are always elsewhere, never at home. They are found in hungry nations, regions, continents. Yet there is a parallel with American domestic politics, in the ways by which hunger relief became conditional on personal, economic, and psychological reform. Domestic welfare policy, like foreign food aid, was designed to reduce the number of its recipients though work, reproductive restraints, and sometimes through pure violence. Hunger within the United States, as abroad, was used as an instrument of elimination.

5

# Craving and Control

"Nature's 'Hunger Thermostat'" reads the ad copy in *Life Magazine*:

> When your blood sugar level is low you are "hungry as a bear." When it is high the healthy person finds it easier to turn down the extra helpings of food that mean extra pounds. It turns your appetite on and off in much the same way that a thermostat regulates the heating system in your house. If you are watching your weight, this is important news—you can raise your blood sugar level, tame your runaway appetite any time you want to. Just eat or drink something with sugar in it. (Sugar Information Inc. 1953)[1]

Sugar Information, Incorporated, the public-facing branch of the international association of sugar producers, ran this helpful dieting tip in popular magazines—*McCall's, Good Housekeeping, Life, Better Homes and Gardens, National Geographic, Redbook, Time, Reader's Digest*—from the early 1950s through the 1960s. Sugar producers funded this advertisement campaign in response to the rising threat that artificial sweeteners posed to sugar's market share. Sugar Information ads featured young white women in pencil skirts watching their waistline, shirtless white boys chugging soda, and white-collar desk men pouring sugar into their coffee.

Ad copy promised a "New Way to Diet without Hunger . . . by keeping your blood sugar up throughout the day." Beware artificial substitutes, they warned; those sweeteners "can't help curb appetite since they have no effect on your blood sugar level" (Sugar Information Inc. 1954). Only pure sugar works to raise blood sugar level and reset the appestat. "Why not try this the next time you get hungry: Take a little sugar—in coffee, tea, a soft drink, ice cream, pastry or candy. . . . Sugar turns down your appestat, and fast. Sugar satisfies hunger" (Sugar

# Your appestat,* sugar and you.

Do you know you have a hunger switch in your brain?

It's called the "appestat."

When it's turned up, you're hungry. When you're hungry, you overeat.

And overeating makes you fat.

Sugar turns down your appestat–helps you resist overeating.

Sugar is a help when you want to control your weight. Especially when you know these simple facts about hunger. When you're tired and hungry between meals, it's probably because your *blood sugar level* is low. And when that happens, your appestat is turned up, and you're apt to overeat at your next meal.

Why not try this the next time you get hungry: Take a little sugar—in coffee, tea, a soft drink, ice cream, pastry, or candy. Sugar is assimilated into the system faster than any other food. Sugar turns down your appestat, and fast. Sugar satisfies hunger. Artificial sweeteners don't. And even though sugar contains calories (only 18 to a teaspoon), those calories give you quick energy and are readily burned up.

Sugar does things for you no artificial sweetener can do. Sugar gives you energy. Sugar tastes good. Sugar helps diets work.

*"A neutral center in the hypothalamus believed to regulate appetite."— Webster's Third New International Dictionary.

## SUGAR INFORMATION, INC.
P.O. Box 2664, Grand Central Station, New York, N.Y. 10017

FIGURE 8. "Your Appestat, Sugar and You." *Source*: Sugar Information 1968.

Association Inc. and Kelly 1967, 2). Eat a little sugar, and "your hunger switches off" (Sugar Association Inc. and Tatum Jr. 1968, 2).

This image is a relic from the dawn of the neuro era. A pot of sugar reaches up with its handle arm and flips a light switch in a white man's brain. His thin black tie and white-collar shirt flag him as an Average American Man who values self-control but needs help containing his pressing hungers. He wields a sugar bowl like a pocket calculator or a home improvement device, ready to adjust his blood and lessen the strength of his feelings. Feelings are the disruptors in his bodily system.

He becomes "hungry like a bear": animal desires rise up from his blood, overcoming his mental power (Sugar Information Inc. 1953). Such desires are "runaways" and must be "trained," "tamed," "curbed," "turned down." The appestat controls the call of his animal cravings for pleasure and overconsumption. The brain switch functions unconsciously and automatically, like a mechanical feedback and control center. The body is his house, the blood his furnace, and the brain his thermostat. The brain alters feeling levels in response to information about the internal milieu. When blood sugar is low, "you're apt to eat more than you need, without being conscious of overeating before your blood sugar level is raised to the point where it 'shuts off your appestat'" (Sugar Information Inc. 1954). When blood sugar is high, "the healthy person finds it easier to turn down the extra helpings of food" (Sugar Information Inc. 1953). The ads promise their readers that they do not need to work to control their hungers. When the appestat is properly set, "you do not want so much" (Sugar Information Inc. 1954). The appestat effect is instantaneous, like an electrical circuit. The sugar switch turns desires off, "and fast" (Sugar Information Inc. 1954).

It all happens in the brain. The appestat adjusts levels of circulating substances—blood sugar—which changes the body's feeling. The stomach is curiously ignored in this message: stomachs appear incidentally in the ads as the locus for fat and "weight," the inner contents of a slimming waistline. Taste, too, plays no role in this circuit, as the ads depict it. On the contrary, the intense flavor of artificial sweeteners appears a decoy. They may taste sweet, but they cannot flip the brain switch. These Sugar Information ads invoked bodily control, homeostasis, self-regulation, and informed consumer choice guided by expert scientific knowledge, to *sell people more sugar*. Scientific expertise appeared here in service not of public governance but of commerce. The consumer in these ads did not require skills of self-regulation and self-government. No willpower was required; no reflection needed. All one had to do was to follow the advertiser's instructions. The market would govern our desires for our own good.

Sugar, perhaps more than any other foodstuff, materialized the politics of hunger after the Second World War. Sugar is historically implicated in interconnected forms of malnutrition. Sugar began the Plantationocene era; its production engaged forced enslaved labor in one of the first global agro-industrial systems (Mintz 1986; Haraway 2015). Sugar bears a history of enslavement, colonial land occupation, state support of large landowners, and racist marketing strategies (Hatch, Sternlieb, and Gordon 2019, 596). Sugar workers often could not afford food for their own families. In the Philippines province of Negros Occidental, or "Sugarlandia," nearly half of households were judged in the late 1970s to have insufficient food intake, and more than 80 percent of children malnourished (Jones 1979). Sugar sales tactics were, and still are, marked by class and race. The sugar appestat was colored pure white.

Sugar—this sweet, violent, pleasurable, exploitative substance—was flipping switches in our brains. What were these feelings that the sugar-appestat promised to contain? Why were they "running away" and out of control? If the "hunger switch" worked automatically to maintain homeostasis, stability, and balance, as the ads promised, why would consumers need to "take" sugar or anything else to "turn hunger off"? The ads' very premise suggested that hunger was out of whack and required an external intervention. Overweight, diabetes, so-called diseases of overconsumption, appeared in the 1950s as rising threats to life and health. Even as they ran these advertisements, sugar producers already were aware by the mid-1950s that their appestat claims were weak.[2] In these ads sugar works to tamp down excess feeling, not to stimulate it. But already in the 1940s, scientists were asking whether sweetness, sensation, pleasure, and taste could themselves *cause* hunger. Researchers funded by the sugar industry discovered that people preferred to eat more sugar, at higher concentrations, than food processors ever had imagined possible. Taste testers even didn't realize that their preferred samples of canned peaches or tomatoes contained lots of sugar; they just liked the taste better. Researchers identified a "peak preference level," which later came to be called the "bliss point." Consumers, they found, chose products first by taste. They considered nutritive value only later, if they ever did at all (Pangborn 1957; Moss 2013).

Could foods that taste good make us hungrier to eat them, even when those foods do not fulfill our needs? The urge to eat sweet, fatty, or salty foods may even work against our own good health. In other words, scientists discovered that living beings hunger for pleasure. Hunger could be made and could be used as a tool for increasing consumption. This (seemingly obvious) idea caused difficulties for appestats and other theories of homeostasis. If animal bodies were designed to regulate and balance their eating to match the needs of physical activity, body temperature, and nutrient needs, why do we have a sweet tooth? How do pleasure and desire fit in? Do animals learn to desire exactly those things, which their bodies need? Some physiologists, following theories of homeostasis, believed that tastes change over time to attract us to sources of the nutrients we are missing (sugar for energy deficiency, salty foods for a salt deficiency, milk for calcium deficiency, etc.). Why doesn't food taste better when it is good for us? Hedonism and homeostasis were at war with each other. We know very well which side won.

· · ·

Harvard Medical School professor Walter Cannon (1932) popularized the term "homeostasis" in his influential work *Wisdom of the Body*. Cannon imagined the human body as an automatic regulator, a multifunction thermostat. Bodies maintained stable temperature by discharging excess heat. The lungs and digestive organs kept blood sugar, oxygen, and alkalinity at constant levels by eating and breathing. Kidneys acted as "spillways," evacuating "surplus" sugar, salt, water, and other materials. Cannon called these functions homeostasis, meaning a regulatory process that maintains bodily stability. "In the evolution and behavior of living beings," wrote Cannon (1941, 1), "the trend towards security has been one of the outstanding features." Hunger played an important role in homeostasis, because it drove people to seek what they were missing. Bodies got hungry when they needed something to balance their internal state.

By the Second World War, problems were beginning to appear with the homeostatic model. Despite their best efforts at education and administration, wartime experts failed to motivate Americans to follow a scientifically balanced diet. The US Quartermaster designed soldiers' ration packets so that each item contained a durable, portable "quota of vitamins, minerals, proteins and calories." But soldiers threw piles of these perfectly nutritious (and presumably gross) items into garbage dumps across the theaters of the world war (Dove 1946, 187). Attempts to rationalize diets on the home front did not fare much better. Anthropologist Margaret Mead (1943, 43), serving as executive secretary of the Committee on Food Habits of the National Research Council, warned in 1943 that Americans needed to change their diets, because "our people are not as well nourished as they could be in view of the food resources we have." The National Food and Nutrition Board suggested that Americans of all classes were suffering from undetected latent malnutrition (Biltekoff 2013, 53). Americans refused to eat the way scientists thought they should. Given wartime labor needs and supply issues, this was a national security problem (Biltekoff 2013, 46–79; LeBlanc 2019, 89–125).

By military directive the Office of the Quartermaster General set up a new Food Acceptance Division to figure out why soldiers were throwing away their rations. "For the first time in history," noted one Division report, US soldiers "lived for long periods of time solely on commercially produced and processed foods" (Dove 1946, 188). Scientists working at the Food Acceptance Division set out to predict which processed products soldiers would eat and which ones they would refuse. The Food Acceptance Division, alongside Mead's Food Habits unit at the National Research Council, became a cradle for the study of taste and pleasure. Scientists at the Division studied the neurophysiology of taste and smell as well as the psychology of food preferences. They measured and classified different odor and taste thresholds. The Division developed a nine-point hedonic scale for taste tests, which could be used to predict food choice and consumption (Meiselman and Schutz 2003, 200–203). After the war Food Acceptance Division scientists brought their consumer research methods to the processed food industry.

One of the first scientists to contract with the US Quartermaster Food Acceptance Division was physiological psychologist Paul Thomas Young, who became a founder of the modern science of pleasure ("Paul Thomas Young" 1965, 1085). Young was convinced that homeostasis was wrong. Hunger was not about needs or bodily regulation. Instead, Young saw hunger as a feeling of anticipation and enjoyment, an expectation of pleasure. Hedonic hunger was fueled not by the stomach nor by contents of the blood but by the sensory, "proprioceptive" pull of tastes like sweetness (Young 1949, 108). Lab rats led the way to Young's world of pleasure and vulnerability. Young ran rats through series of food preference tests:

he set out two foods, usually liquid solutions of sugar and casein (milk protein), in the two ends of a Y-shaped box, so that rats had to choose between one path and the other. He observed what efforts rats would make to get access to sweet stuff rather than the good-for-them source of protein. He measured how fast the rats ran and how much pain they overcame to get to sugar. He observed how much sugar they consumed at different concentrations.

Young's rats ate for sweetness, not for health. Despite attempts to "train" them to prefer other foods, the rats always came back to sugar. Even protein-deficient rats ran faster to sugar than to casein. They ate sugar even when they were satiated. "Psychologists can abandon the view that dietary need is essential for adequate motivation with food," he concluded (Young 1948a, 310). His rats were clearly not eating because they were hungry or needed more energy. They were eating because sugar tastes good. Young called this the "palatability" factor. "One can argue," Young (1948a, 296) wrote, "that rats take what they need to maintain homeostasis. One can also argue that rats take what they like (find palatable) regardless of need."

These rats' hunger served not need but pleasure. Hedonic hunger, as Young imagined it, was provoked by the qualities inherent in foods. "Palatability" was an affect, a feeling of pleasure or displeasure, "the immediate affective reaction (liking or disliking) of an organism which occurs when a food stimulus comes in contact with the head receptors" (Young 1948a, 310). Chemoreceptors in the mouth, nose, and gut lit up in response to a palatable stimulus. In the hedonic theory of hunger, eating is "a chemoreflexive act" (Young 1941, 152). Perhaps, as another researcher suggested, "sweeteners may also act to prime the appetite" ("Session 2B" n.d.). In other words, *the taste of sugar makes us hungry*. Hedonic hunger did not involve scarcity, motivation, or learning. Rats did not learn better when they were hungry for sweet-tasting foods. They might be more "motivated," running faster and over-coming challenges to get to sugar, but they did not learn to get through a maze any quicker for sugar than for protein (Young 1947, 66). Nor could the rats be trained to prefer a less palatable food, when given the choice over time. Hedonic theories disconnected hunger from work and learning. This was all about pleasure (Dror 2016, 247).

Hedonic pleasure was not the same as the "reward" that Edward Thorndike and the behaviorist psychologists offered to their animal subjects. Young's lab rats were not motivated by lack or deprivation: in most experiments they had eaten a full standard diet before being exposed to the sugar and casein. They ran because they anticipated "enjoyment": "when we use the word enjoyment we are thinking of the palatability of a specific food, the affective response of an animal" (Young 1948b, 284). In his experiments rats consumed far more sugar and salt than their bodies required. They consumed more when the liquids tasted stronger; their greatest intake was at a liquid sugar concentration of 18 percent. The amounts they ingested varied with taste, not with bodily needs (Young 1948a, 301).

Hunger for pleasure might even drive animals to self-injury. Young's rats were willing to submit to strong and painful electric shocks to reach the sugar at the end of their box. Young's colleagues found that magnesium-deficient rats refused to eat magnesium when offered. They speculated that magnesium deficiency actually might feel good: "It is well-known that a feeling of well-being is not always associated with the best possible physical status nor the ultimate welfare of an individual. Examples that may be cited are those of alcoholism, narcotism, and the euphoria that may occur in high altitude anoxia" (Young 1952, 251). Pleasure could lead to dangerous things. Perhaps, Young (1948a, 293) proposed, people who craved sweets, leading to overweight and disease, had inherited more sensitive taste receptors than other people's. Perhaps some people inherited especially strong sensitivity to sweetness. Young pointed to known genetic determinants for taste and olfaction. Some parents and their children could smell a certain substance at low concentrations, while others failed to notice it at all. Perhaps "innate differences in sensory structures, especially in the senses of taste, smell, and touch, may explain why some individuals select food wisely and others do so less wisely" (Young 1948a, 293). Hunger depended on an internal tendency to become aroused, on how strongly one feels a sensation.

Perhaps some people experienced stronger reactions to pleasure than others. Unlike theories of homeostasis, which took all animal bodies as self-knowing and self-balancing, hedonic theories differentiated those who were particularly vulnerable to pleasure, sensation, and overconsumption. Sugar industry–funded researchers found that while both wild and domesticated rats preferred liquids that tasted sweet, they consumed vastly different amounts. Wild rats consumed 12 percent more calories of a sugar solution than a standard liquid; domesticated rats drank 87 percent more (Kare 1969, 49–56). G. C. Kennedy (1952, 579) found that rats with fat bodies responded more strongly to a food's palatability, eating smaller amounts of unflavored foods and far greater amounts of palatable foods than nonobese control rats. Some chemosensors appeared more porous and vulnerable than others.

Processed food producers paid keen attention to this emerging science of taste, pleasure, and preference. The Food Acceptance lab's methods spread through corporate America, as alumni went on to work in the consumer research divisions of the Coca-Cola Company, the Pillsbury Corporation, the Lipton Corporation, and Hunt-Wesson Foods (Meiselman and Schutz 2003, 203). Division scientists ran experiments in the 1960s where panels of taste testers were asked to compare the hedonic value and relative acceptability of "different flavors of a single product type." The study's authors then took their pleasure-magnitude scale to Hunt-Wesson and later worked as consultants to multiple large food-processing companies (Moskowitz and Sidel 1971). Lead author Harold R. Moskowitz (1971, 388) studied perceptions of differences in the taste of sweetness and the feeling of sugar's "pleasantness, or affective dimension." Moskowitz became a renowned expert in teasing out subjects' preferences for subtle variations in flavor composition and famously innovated new niche varieties of common processed foods from pasta sauce to sodas (Moss 2013, 50–51).

. . .

A sugar pot reaches up and flips a light switch in the brain: the Sugar Information ad (see Figure 8) drew that imagery straight from the emerging field of neural physiology. In the early 1950s neural physiologists located a "hunger switch" in the brain's hypothalamus. By poking brains in specific areas, scientists made animals eat uncontrollably or starve themselves. At first, scientists believed that they had discovered a mechanism for homeostasis. The hunger switch, they thought, would flip on or off in response to bodily needs. But they soon found that things turned out otherwise.

Targeting a single brain site led to dramatic results. For decades, physiologists had noted that patients with damage to the base of their brains began to eat uncontrollably. Animals with damage to the same area grew far fatter than their peers (Hetherington and Ranson 1940). Yale physiologists John Brobeck and Bal K. Anand used a thin needle with an attached electrode to lesion highly targeted areas at the base of rats' brains. They found that injury to a specific site in the middle of the rat's hypothalamus caused it to eat continuously, so much that its body grew extremely obese. Some of those operated rats slept continuously, and others became irritable and aggressive. "Five of them were really vicious," biting their handlers at every opportunity (Anand and Brobeck 1951, 128). When one of Brobeck's rats died, he wrote: "I did an autopsy and found the gastrointestinal tract from the pylorus all the way up to the incisor teeth tightly packed with chewed up chow pellets" (Brobeck 1993, 226). The rat ate to death.

A second kind of operation, which damaged a different area at the sides of the hypothalamus, turned rats into passive ascetics who refused to eat altogether. Rats with lesions on the sides of their hypothalamus stopped eating and starved to death. Anand and Brobeck (1951, 138) believed that they had found the on and off switches for the "urge to eat": one part of the hypothalamus turned hunger on, and the other inhibited, or turned it off. They called these sites the brain's "feeding center." The hunger activated by this brain switch, though, did not resemble the hunger that behavioral psychologists produced by depriving rats of food. None of the usual motivation tests (maze learning, lever pressing, running speed, overcoming painful electric shocks, lifting weights) worked on the lesioned rats. Behavioral psychologists assumed that they could measure the intensity of hunger by how animals reacted to those tests. Food-deprived rats with normal brains increased their performance; the hungrier rats were, the harder they worked to get food.

But operated rats, with a damaged hypothalamus, showed no interest in working or overcoming challenges. They did not expend any extra effort to get food and had no interest in food that didn't taste delicious. When food appeared, especially highly palatable food, they just kept eating and did not stop. The operated rats challenged psychologists' belief that they could understand hunger by watching rats work for food. Work played no role in this new experimental setup. Brain switches, not behavior, ruled this new kind of hungry rat (Miller, Bailey, and Stevenson 1950). Something more than food deprivation appeared to make these rats hungry. These rats did not eat because they needed to. They ate in response to neural signals, to chemosensory pleasure, to context and cues. They ate for deliciousness. This kind of hunger had no clear limit or end. At its extreme this insatiable hunger even led to death.

Sugar ads drew their appestat claims from work that began in Anand and Brobeck's lab. The ads boasted that their claims had support from "research scientists at one of our leading universities." Although the ads named no names, they likely were referring to Jean Mayer, professor in the Harvard School of Public Health Department of Nutrition, and his "glucostatic" theory. Mayer did his PhD work at Yale University, around the time when Anand and Brobeck's stereotaxic experiments on brain lesions stimulated rats to overeat or starve themselves to death. Mayer learned to perform these operations and began to search for the mechanism that turns the feeding center on and off. He believed that he had found the "physiologic basis for the hunger state and the hunger behavior," in blood sugar (Mayer 1955, 17). Mayer was a scientist in the mold of Walter Cannon, committed to nutrition as a program of social regulation and reform. After fighting with the Free French forces during World War II, Mayer completed a PhD on vitamin A and became nutrition officer for the newly formed United Nations Food and Agriculture Organization (FAO). "I decided," he wrote, "that my duty was to help build a peaceful and prosperous international order as a complement to my five years of war against Fascism" (Mayer 1977, 179). During his brief tenure at the FAO, Mayer served on committees setting universal standards for protein and calorie requirements. He later traveled with UN delegations to Asia and Africa, including a fact-finding mission to Biafra, which led Mayer to campaign against the use of famine as a weapon of war.

In line with his political commitments, Mayer oriented his research program around homeostasis. He assumed that animal bodies were capable of regulating themselves. The brain, blood, organs, and muscles coordinated to keep inputs level with output. Mayer sought to uncover the chemical and neural pathways for self-regulation. He brought his static sensibility to the emerging science of neurophysiology. Hunger, for Mayer (1953, 16), was a regulatory mechanism: "Feelings involving desire for food or satiety . . . represent a conscious expression of one of the most precise regulatory devices in biology." Mayer, early in his career, used pedometers, stop-motion photos, and respiratory devices to track food inputs and energy outputs. Mayer found that food and activity levels did generally balance out, except that sedentary subjects tended to eat more than they needed (Mayer

1977, 182). This was Mayer's first indication that homeostasis did not function well for all subjects.

In his work on rats, Mayer noted that their brains were particularly sensitive to variations in blood sugar. Levels of glucose in the blood fluctuated more quickly than any other factor or nutrient, like fat or protein. He found that rats injected with glucose (or, relatedly, with amphetamines) would quickly lower their food intake. Mayer proposed that the brain contained glucoreceptors that were sensitive to blood sugar levels. In the mid 1950s he found that the substance gold thioglucose damaged cells in the hypothalamus and also caused obesity in rats—thus establishing a connection between glucose, a specific site in the brain, and obesity (Mayer 1977, 186). He believed that he had found the lever that turned the feeding switch on and off. "In this glucostatic view, hunger would be integrated among the mechanisms through which the central nervous system ensures its homeostasis" (Mayer 1953, 14).

But—this is the part that the sugar ads left out—most animals in Mayer's study failed to achieve long-term equilibrium between their energy intake and output. Some of his rats grew fat. The "day-to-day regulation" of fluctuating blood sugar was "not sufficient to insure constancy of body weight" (Mayer 1955, 18). The rat observations resonated with data showing obesity rates rising in the 1950s United States. Mayer spent the 1960s trying to figure out why homeostasis failed. The answer, he believed, was emotion: emotions cause "metabolic and endocrine changes, which in turn increase or decrease hunger." Emotions worked against homeostasis: they turned hunger on and off but could not "regulate" it (Mayer 1966b, 5).

In contradiction to the sugar ads citing his research, Mayer (1966a, 725) told clinicians treating obesity that "there is little to say for the extensive consumption of sucrose." "The best advice I can give about sugar in any form," he counseled, "[is] eat less" (Mayer 1972). As he took on a public and political role in nutrition policy in the 1960s, Mayer criticized food companies' misguiding messages and manipulation of consumers' emotions. In 1969, President Richard Nixon appointed Mayer chairman of an ambitious White House Conference on Food, Nutrition and Health. Mayer and his congressional allies skillfully maneuvered the conference to achieve lasting impacts on American food policy: easier access to food stamps for the very poor, the end of surplus commodity distribution, national nutrition guidelines, food labeling, and more aggressive controls on false advertising (LeBlanc 2019, 179–198).

Mayer's political work addressed a population increasingly understood as vulnerable to manipulation by food industry interests. The vulnerable person was poor, uneducated, and easily swayed by sensory information from taste to packaging and advertisement. A profile of obese Americans emerged, casting them as damaged in their capacity for managing emotion and judgment. Their vulnerability to pleasure and sensation appeared equivalent to brain damage in animals

(Frohlich 2024, 91–97). Some public health professionals directly accused food processing companies and advertisers of exploiting vulnerable populations for profit. In 1969, Dr. Tore J. Mita, a nutritionist at the Public Health Service Indian Hospital in Pine Ridge, South Dakota, condemned companies for marketing useless products to the poor: "I deplore the fact that millions of economically and educationally disadvantaged consumers are unwittingly spending their scarce money for worthless food products." Nutritionists could not afford to wait hopefully for public education to change consumer habits, in the face of "the million dollar budgets allocated by a segment of the food industry for the far-reaching communications media to glamorize and encourage people to consume innumerable 'nonfoods'" (Mita 1969, 1157). Mita (1969, 1158) demanded that the "burden of responsibility" for a healthy diet be shifted from the shoulders of consumers to the food processors themselves, who should be required to produce, market, and sell only nutritious foods.

. . .

Sugar Inc.'s appestat advertisement might not evoke laboratory rats and brain lesions for most subscribers to *McCall's* or *Reader's Digest*. However, most viewers of the sugar ads likely would have shared some of the "pharmacological optimism," which infused 1950s American culture (Campbell 2007, 84). Tranquilizers, from chlorpromazine to Miltown, circulated widely and promised to smooth out consumers' mental rough edges. Pharmaceuticals appeared poised to solve and regulate nonconformities of all kinds. Who knows, perhaps a little spoonful of sugar just might do the same for food-related nonconformities. The notion of a substance "curbing" or "turning down" problematic desires and feelings would have been very familiar to magazine readers of this era.

The "appestat" shared many underlying ideas with mid-twentieth-century neuropharmacology. Neuropharmacology combined older psychoanalytic assumptions and more recent brain science. Desires, cravings, and behaviors could be traced to specific sites in the brain. Feelings were understood as chemical functions. Chemical substances (drugs or sugar) served as technologies for investigating the brain and altering behavior. Some people (and animals) were seen as more vulnerable than others to the pull of pleasure and "the external forces of suggestion, substance, and impulse." Those forces drew them to perform acts beyond and despite their own free will and self-control into a spiral of psychopathology. They were unable to stop, despite the negative consequences. Nancy Campbell (2007, 20) has named these factors as the defining qualities of the twentieth-century American drug addict. The same qualities were applied to overeaters.

Hunger and drug addiction research in the 1940s and 1950s co-created a template of the vulnerable, hypersensitive, damaged, and irrational brain. Excessive hunger for food and for drugs could be understood as parallel (even equivalent) biochemical-psychological "disorder[s] of desire" (Campbell 2007, 25). Many of the same research scientists and sites were implicated in both hunger and addiction science. Access to the brain, in this era before imaging technologies, relied on direct stimulation of specific brain sites or on administration of chemicals. Two tools and two disciplines converged around drugs and food: behavioral observation and neurophysiology. Scientists poked at brains or administered substances—drugs, hormones, sugar—and observed the resulting changes in animal behavior. Behaviors and brains were reconfigured as metabolic.

This encounter of brain and behavior, drugs and food, converged in the 1940s at the Yerkes Laboratories of Primate Biology in Florida. Yerkes Lab researchers mobilized hunger as an experimental and epistemological tool for understanding brain and body function. In 1940, S.D.S. Spragg published an experimental protocol for producing morphine addiction in four Yerkes Lab chimpanzees. Spragg's work suggested that chemical addiction could happen in nonhuman animals and was not unique to the human psyche. Addicted animals appeared to challenge psychoanalytic theories of addiction as a character defect rooted in early childhood experiences or as a social-cultural construct. Spragg described addiction in purely physiological and behavioral terms. Addiction gained "a firm organic basis" (Spragg 1940, 125). He designed his experimental setup as a paired test of hunger and drug addiction. Chimpanzees were presented with two boxes, each with a color-matched key. The black box contained a banana and the white box a syringe. Food-deprived chimps unlocked the black box and ate the banana. Morphine-deprived chimps, whether or not they were food-deprived, went to the white box and removed the syringe. Chimps often handed the syringe to the researcher, sometimes physically pulling their human handlers toward the injection room. Chimpanzees in withdrawal chose the syringe over the banana, even when they were hungry. Spragg (1940, 14) interpreted both chains of action, unlocking and opening either the white or the black box, as behavioral indications of "desire."

Hunger drive tests, in which food-deprived animals solve puzzle boxes to access food "rewards," lay the groundwork for midcentury drug addiction research. Spragg suggested that drug addiction involved an "appetitive component" (Dewsbury 2003, 253). Addiction, like overeating, represented a departure from homeostasis. "Drug addiction, whether in the human or the chimpanzee subject," Spragg (1940, 125) wrote "can be considered as a state of equilibrium, the departure from which creates a condition that generates powerful motivations to restore that equilibrium—motivations that pervade the behavior of the organism and predominate over other, normally primary, desires." Hunger for bananas, hunger for morphine, desire and behavior, converged in the Yerkes Lab chimpanzee cages. In 1944, Yerkes Lab director Karl Lashley invited his former PhD student, Donald Hebb, to take up a research position there. Hebb spent the next three years meandering from studies of chimpanzee phobias to dolphin social intelligence. He expended most of his intellectual energy on a theoretical attempt to bridge the fields of behavioral psychology and neurophysiology. This effort, published in 1949 as *The Organization of Behavior: A Neuropsychological Study*, attempted to explain what was going on in the brains of hungry, addicted, and other animals.

Hunger, wrote Hebb (1949, 200–202), was "equivalent to addiction": "Hunger established in the presence of lowered blood nutrients, and having the effect (through eating) of raising them, would be physiologically the equivalent of an addiction—biologically valuable, but still an addiction." Hebb imagined what was happening in the brains of humans and animals like Spragg's chimpanzees. Their brain cells, stimulated repeatedly by the same chemical agent (like morphine), began to interact in a fixed set of patterns. Metabolic changes, stimulated by food or morphine, set off that preformed pattern. The brain cells responded to sensations and internal chemical changes and formed regular repetitive reactions. Brain cells' patterning and direction were more complex than on-off switches, stimulus and response, arousal and reaction (Hebb 1949, 72). Brain activity was not a simple reaction to animals' bodily needs. No steady regulator guaranteed equilibrium and homeostasis (Hebb 1949, 179). What an animal did depended on the activation of already formed cell assemblies, both recurrent and anticipatory (Hebb 1949, 135). Instead of one-way switches, Hebb's brains were continuous feedback loops.

Hunger, like addiction, could not be understood as simple homeostasis. No automatic meter existed in the blood or stomach, adjusting metabolic levels to meet bodily needs (Hebb 1949, 204).. Hebb (1949, 190) cited Paul Thomas Young's argument that hunger was more than homeostasis. Some brain activity, "something like thinking," had to intervene between external sense perception and internal bodily movements (Hebb 1949, xvi). Hunger and addiction disorganized brain activity, which translated into unstable and disturbed behavior. "Even in experienced subjects the need of food has disintegrating effects," Hebb (1949, 192, 205) wrote. "The relation of hunger to emotional disturbance is notorious. . . . There is an inescapable relation between drug addictions, food habits, and chronic emotional disturbance." Deprived animals were disturbed, restless, uncomfortable, in pain. Only when hunger or addiction was sated could brains stabilize and function.

Hebb drew inspiration from Spragg's chimpanzee experiments to conceive hunger and addiction as brain-based events. Hunger and addiction were functions not of homeostasis but of neural circuitry. Neural assemblies formed associations between sensory events—the taste of food or the sensation of a syringe's needle—and feelings of euphoria or satisfaction. By repeating the same association over and over, feelings and behaviors became locked in. Spragg's chimpanzees showed some signs of relief and satisfaction even from a drugless saline injection. That simple sensation connected to past relief triggered neural cells to follow a fixed pattern. Hebb suggested that the same effect appears in the act of tasting, chewing, and swallowing: the sense experience of food brings relief long before the body's needs are met. Hunger and addiction, for Hebb, both functioned as disrupters of cell assembly. Brain processes could easily be thrown off.

. . .

If hunger and addiction were parts of the same scientific-neurological complex, American drug policy and food policy in the 1950s stood (and today still stand) at opposite extremes. In the realm of food, producers and marketers are free to promote their wares unfettered. In the realm of drugs, the public response is total and violent. Cold-turkey abstinence is often the only option for addicts, whether by rehabilitation or incarceration. At the Rockefeller Institute for Medical Research, Vincent Dole imported hunger research into the study of addiction, with large-scale policy implications. Dole and his collaborator, Marie Nyswander, challenged the legal and punitive dichotomy between food hunger and drug hunger.[3] Their research did not use animal subjects; it focused entirely on humans, mainly addicts in search of recovery. Dole and Nyswander's work culminated in a historic push to move drug policy away from abstinence and toward maintenance, functioning, and harm reduction.

Dole began his medical research career in the 1940s steeped in questions of drive, motivation, and deregulated homeostasis. He studied the role of human fat tissues and protein deficiency in weight gain and loss, and confirmed the value of low-salt diets in treating hypertension (Dole et al. 1954; Dole 1959; McCarty 1984). "I'd been interested in the appetite control systems," Dole (1989, 332) recalled," and I had a feeling that there was absolutely open territory in the whole question of behavior, and to what extent metabolism had to do with drive." His move from obesity to drug addiction in the early 1960s occurred serendipitously: a colleague about to begin a sabbatical year asked Dole to fill in as chairman of the Health Research Council's Committee on Narcotics. But the move fit perfectly with his research concerns at the time.

Dole questioned why researchers and policy makers treated narcotics differently than food, when both kinds of substance increasingly appeared to stimulate the same physiological processes. At the outset of his drug research, Dole (1989, 334) recalled, "the question I asked myself was, 'What's so bad about narcotics?'" Stimulating pleasure was not on its own a reason to condemn consumption. After all, he reasoned, a glass of wine or a nice meal also produced euphoric effects, to no one's concern. The only logic behind the differential treatment of the two types of substances, which both produced metabolic effects, had to be ideological (Dole 1989, 339). With Nyswander, an experienced rehabilitation clinician, Dole set up a clinical program in 1964 to put heroin and morphine addicts on a stable daily dose, to replace cravings and disorder with stability and equilibrium. This approach paralleled his experience with obesity treatment, in which clinicians adjusted levels of protein in patients' diets and observed the effect on their weight. Quickly it became clear that adjusting protein levels and morphine doses did not cause analogous effects. Narcotics acted too rapidly for the body to establish equilibrium.

But Dole and Nyswander found that patients taking the opioid agonist drug methadone were able to reach a stable state, free of the extremes of euphoria, craving, and withdrawal. Methadone patients lost their appetite for heroin and had no withdrawal symptoms; many regained stable work and family lives. Very quickly, Dole and Nyswander's methadone maintenance protocol ballooned in size. Methadone treatment spread from one clinic to a network of New York City clinics treating tens of thousands, to a national program promoted and funded by the Nixon administration (Dole 1989, 340–341). He attempted to convince a skeptical law-enforcement community, and the general public, that narcotic addiction was a disease and not a moral failing. Treating opioid addicts with methadone, Dole (1989, 341) argued, was like treating diabetics with insulin.

In his later writings, Dole drew a line straight from his research on obesity and abnormal food consumption to drug addiction. He understood both behaviors as "symptoms of metabolic defect" (Dole 1989, 338). Although we like to think that we choose what we eat, Dole (like Hebb) believed that "all ingestive behavior is in some way responsive to the biochemical state of the body." Eating and drug-taking stemmed from biochemical effects. Hunger, for narcotic drugs or food, produced metabolic changes in the body and brain. This chemical dynamic directed what people choose to do. In this, Dole drew from the lineage of Spragg, Hebb, and Young. "Behavior, even the apparently free-willed decisions of man," Dole (1965, 211) wrote, "is powerfully determined by chemical events in the organism. The addict, slave to a chemical, illustrates this dramatically."

Methadone produced an effect in Dole and Nyswander's heroin addicts, like the effect that Sugar Information Inc. promised would result from a teaspoonful of sugar. "Somewhere in the body a simple chemical change induced by the narcotic [or alimentary] chemical—a depletion of transmitter substances in neurones, for instance, or the release of hormones—changes mood and motivation" (Dole 1965, 211). A spoonful of sugar, like 40 grams of methadone, could eliminate craving, desire, and deregulation. Hunger and addiction control designed a new form of self-maintenance: biochemical maintenance of the neurophysiological self. The metabolic brain needed constant maintenance. It was vulnerable to destabilizing influences, sensations, or substances. Far from self-regulation and homeostasis, hunger appeared as a physiological disorder. Hunger captures vulnerable brains, rendering those brains' carriers unable to control their own eating. Cravings may not be under control of the conscious will, and containing them required hypervigilance. Vulnerability, here, refers to hypersensitivity and heightened pleasure. Vulnerability is reinforced by environmental seductions, palatability, sweetness. All these feelings were promised to disappear with a spoonful of the right corrective substance.

· · ·

Scientific research on food cravings led to a serious problem: If hunger works like an addiction, hooking people on foods that their bodies may not even need, what does this mean for markets? How can a free market work if consumers are incapable of making rational choices? The ideal of the market depended on individual freedom of choice. What could that freedom really mean if consumers were misdirected by sensory manipulation, glucose dependency, and "trained" or fabricated hungers? What if the marketplace created hungers that destroyed consumers' health? *What if the market itself made us sick and hungry?* Drawing on techniques developed at the Food Acceptance Division, food processors test for the right combinations of sugar, salt, and fat that reach consumers' "bliss point" (point of strongest liking) and maximize consumption (Moss 2013). It is fair to say that many products on our grocery shelves, impoverished in nutritive content and overabundant in sensation, are food-deprived. Could foods themselves be sources of food insecurity?

Experts by the 1960s increasingly came to believe that misinformation, advertising, and branding could themselves be making Americans hungry and malnourished. Conveners of the 1969 White House Conference on Food, Nutrition and Health recommended that government agencies like the Federal Trade Commission (FTC) be empowered to control both food content and information (Frohlich 2024, 97). The Conference Final Report warned that "gaps in our public knowledge about nutrition, along with actual misinformation carried by some media, are contributing seriously to the problem of hunger and malnutrition in the United States" (White House 1970, 179). Experts called for strong government regulations on food producers' access to consumers' minds. Simply educating people about proper nutrition was not enough. The nature of the marketplace itself had to change.

In 1971, emboldened by the White House Conference, the FTC went after the sugar "appestat" ads. The FTC opened a case against Sugar Information Inc. and its advertising agency, Leo Burnett, for falsely claiming that sugar helps with weight loss. The commission charged that "respondents have represented and are now representing, directly and by implication, that . . . consumption of sugar and foods containing sugar, such as soft drinks, ice cream cones, or candy bars, before meals will result in reduced daily caloric intake." These advertisements "were, and are, false, misleading and deceptive" ("United States of America" 1972, 15). Sugar Information Inc. eventually settled the case and its two decades-long "appestat" ad campaign came to an end.

In that same year, Gerald Thain, assistant director of the FTC Food and Drug Advertising Department, publicly blamed advertisers for hunger and malnutrition: "Recently, it has become clear that, although we are a part of the most affluent society in the world existing at any time, we are not a well fed nation." False advertisements, he warned, undermined the "basic right" of all Americans to "proper food and proper nourishment" (Thain 1971, 3). False advertising prevented consumers from accessing a nutritive and healthy diet and made American hunger worse. Thain praised the White House Conference on Food, Nutrition and Health for enabling the FTC to pursue food companies who publish misinformation.

As a result of the White House Conference, the FTC opened complaints against multiple food producers for making false and unscientific statements about their ingredients. In a move that seems impossible today, the FTC did more than force companies to cease publication of misleading ads. Companies were required to publish "corrective advertisements" in the same media outlets where the original ads appeared, to inform consumers that they had been misled. Thain admitted that "the proposed corrective advertising remedies has had [*sic*] enormous repercussions. One article in the trade press recently described corrective advertising as a 'doomsday' weapon." But, Thain (1971, 7–8) argued, it was the only way to undo the harms to consumers and to the market, caused by lies and manipulation. Choices and desires stimulated falsely had to be contained and undone.

Echoing the White House Conference report, Thain listed three interconnected forms of malnutrition: deprivation, unbalanced diets, and diet-related diseases. The ills of poverty, misguided spending, and overconsumption were all expressions of the same problem: a market out of whack. This was a collective, national problem in need of a collective solution. To emphasize that Americans share a universal stake in the problems of hunger and malnutrition, Thain appealed to an imagined tradition: "Today many concerned Americans, viewing what they consider to be the deterioration of the quality of life, yearn for the life pattern of an earlier, simpler era . . . [when] we were a nation which expected and presumed pure, healthy foods flowing forth from the rich land." Since that imagined time (the memory of which itself effaces the violence inherent in obtaining land), the complexity and expansion of food markets had complicated consumer choices. People learned about food indirectly and via mass media channels. Malnutrition had become an American problem, in part, because of corporate manipulation (Thain 1971, 2–3).

In testimony opposing the new, more activist FTC policies, General Mills Corporation chairman C. W. Cook echoed the same wistful origin story but with a different ending. Cook presented the big food producers' objections at an FTC hearing in October 1971. In his testimony he recalled his mother buying milk and butter for her family from the local farmer. Those days, however, were in the past. "Tremendous changes in the technology of food processing and distribution . . . have made us a far better fed people than we would have been, despite the fact that we still have a way to go before we achieve optimum national nutrition." Advances in food production, Cook warranted, could not have happened without advertising to inform consumers how to find products. Advertising brought new and beneficial goods to consumers. "We in business . . . feel that the public interest is also served when the consumer is offered a maximum of freedom of choice in the marketplace under a system of fair competition" (Cook 1971, 3–4).

The FTC debates articulated a basic question: How does consumer choice respond to hunger? What does freedom of choice mean in the context of sensory manipulation, media messaging, palatability, and preference curves? Thain and

Cook recognized that something had shifted in postwar America. Sugar producers themselves noted that by 1960 two-thirds of sugar consumed in the United States came in the form of processed goods, in "a complete reversal of conditions which prevailed before World War II" (Hickson and Sugar Association Inc. 1960, 33). Nourishment was mediated in new ways, which both produced and alleviated hunger. Market-generated hungers generated financial opportunity and consumer choice, and also ill health and malnutrition.

. . .

In the wake of the Sugar Information Inc. settlement with the Federal Trade Commission, the sugar industry turned to more subtly effective information campaigns. The newly formed International Sugar Research Foundation subsidized scientific research favorable to the industry. Foundation-sponsored research directed public attention away from sugar's most dangerous effects on heart disease, diabetes, and obesity, and instead focused on the single issue of tooth cavities. The solution to a high-sugar diet, they proposed, was to brush your teeth. Sugar's critics were branded as "food faddists." As Christine Kearns and her colleagues found in their analysis of advertisements and publications from the 1970s and 1980s, the Sugar Association followed the tobacco industry playbook for "information laundering" (Kearns, Glantz, and Apollonio 2019, 15).

In 1973 popular magazines printed a full-page spread of a white woman extending her arm toward the reader, her hand holding a glistening caramel-topped ice cream sundae. The heading above her promised to give "the plain truth about your sweet tooth." The ad copy read: "Do you recall the messages we brought you in the past about sugar? How something with sugar in it before meals could help curb your appetite? We hope you didn't get the idea that our little diet tip was any magic formula for losing weight." Dieting is "complicated," it continued, and "research hasn't established that consuming sugar before meals will contribute to weight reduction or even keep you from gaining weight" (Sugar Information Inc. 1973). This was the corrective advertisement mandated by the new FTC guidelines, as part of its settlement with Sugar Information Inc. The advertisement's stated purpose was to reeducate the consumer and undo the harms of misguided appeals. And yet the lustrous image of an ice cream sundae beckoned. . .

Sugar might not switch off the appestat, the ad concedes. But it feels good. Having printed a retraction statement as required by its settlement, Sugar Information Inc. pivoted to a new theme. The FTC settlement order specified that future ads were allowed to include "accurate representations of refined sugar's role in and contribution to a balanced diet . . . [and] accurate representations of any non-nutritional characteristic of refined sugar" ("United States of America" 1972). This characteristic, in the 1973 ad, was pleasure. Sugar, the ad continued, "is a food you enjoy." With this corrective ad, Sugar Information Inc. left behind the electrical switches and homeostatic regulation of the 1950s and openly embraced hedonism.

FIGURE 9. "The Plain Truth about Your Sweet Tooth." *Source*: Sugar Information 1973.

The ad promises that sugar will make you feel good. "It helps you bounce back." Drawing from psychological language, Sugar Information offered consumers pleasure. Sugar "gives you a sense of satisfaction and well-being. A nice little psychological lift" (Sugar Information Inc. 1973). In the end, hedonism and marketing, as we all know, won.

6

# Weapon of White Supremacy

Hunger, in the postwar American South, was an instrument of ethnic cleansing. In December 1962 field secretaries of the Student Nonviolent Coordinating Committee (SNCC) warned that local Mississippi authorities were starving out sharecroppers who tried to register to vote. "A new economic squeeze is being put on Negro citizens here. . . . Hunger and violence are apparently being used to curtail voter-registration efforts" (SNCC 1963). SNCC began a Voter Education Project in the Mississippi Delta in 1961. In response, county welfare offices began to restrict access to welfare and food aid. SNCC and its affiliates in the Council of Confederated Organizations (COFO) estimated in 1963 that twenty-two thousand people in the Delta had been left "destitute . . . as a result of being denied work or state welfare aid because of increasing economic pressure against Negro voting efforts" (Stilt 1963, 1).

Hunger was a weapon of white supremacy. "White elites used hunger as a weapon," writes Monica M. White (2017, 21), "starving anyone who sought the right to participate in the political process into compliance." Following a site visit to Huntsville-Madison County, Alabama, in 1968, Professor Theodore James Pinnock concluded: "It is obvious that the unwritten plan of the white power structure in the rural counties of AL is to make things so economically difficult for the Negro and poor Caucasian that they have no alternative but to leave" (in De Jong 2016, 49). Bobby Smith II (2019, 2) has described how "local, state, and national actors in Mississippi used 'food power'—the use of food as a weapon or an element of power—to maintain white supremacy and undermine the civil rights movement." Southern elites chose to starve out African Americans who pursued political and economic autonomy.

Food and agriculture were central to the strategies of both white supremacists and civil rights activists in the 1960s South (De Jong 2016, 26; Smith 2023, 9).

Southern landowners altered their crops and tools to reduce their dependency on Black labor. Cotton acreage declined massively in Alabama and Mississippi, in favor of livestock and other crops. As a result, SNCC field secretary Robert Moses (2001, 7) observed that "economic necessity no longer acted as a constraint on the virulence of white racism" on the plantations along the Mississippi Delta. White landowners received price supports to reduce production and keep fields fallow. On the cotton fields remaining, the mechanical cotton picker shifted social and economic leverage toward landowners and away from workers. New Deal farm policies prevented Black workers and landowners from accessing federal support. Farm laborers, like domestic workers, were not covered by Social Security. Displaced white farmworkers found work in industry; Black farmworkers were shut out. Those who did not migrate North became underemployed seasonal laborers. White southern political leaders imposed policies designed to push Black residents out of the South (De Jong 2016, 34–36).

Moses, a leader of SNCC's voter drive in the Delta, wrote in December 1962 to Martha Prescod at the University of Michigan SNCC chapter:

> Just this afternoon, I was sitting resting, having finished a bowl of stew, and a silent hand reached over from behind, mumbling some words of apology and permission, and stumbled up with a neckbone from the plate under the bowl, which I had discarded, which had consequently some meat on it. The hand was back again, five seconds later, groping for the potatoes I had left in the bowl. I never saw the face, I didn't look. The hand was dark, dry and wind cracked, from cotton chopping and cotton picking. Lafayette and I got up and walked out. What the hell are you going to do when a man has to pick up a leftover potatoe [*sic*] from a bowl of stew? . . . We met last Sunday to initiate a drive for food and clothing for Negroes in the Delta. (Moses 1962)

Again in US history, starvation served as an instrument of violence to displace nonwhite people whose presence and labor were extraneous to the accumulation of white wealth. White supremacists reorganized land, labor, and welfare to block Black residents' access to sources of food. These gestures were most obvious in the American South but also played out in the organization of housing and labor in the urban North.

As Laurie B. Green has pointed out, media reports and politicians from the 1960s to this day refer to hunger in the United States as if it were a natural outcome of personal misfortune. What many Black Americans suffered in this period is more accurately described as programmatic starvation (Green 2017). Doctors with the Medical Committee for Human Rights (MCHR), who volunteered in support of civil rights actions, bore witness. "Most people [here] are malnourished," Dr. Herbert Krohn told a Freedom Summer volunteer in Alabama. "I saw a child with a classical case of malnutrition such as you would read about in concentration camps" (quoted in Hartford 1965). "To starve" is a transitive verb. To defend themselves against programmatic starvation, African Americans in the 1960s rural South and urban North undertook "survival experiments," informed by their own experience and by medical knowledge. Survival experiments were forms of organization, technology, and communication that imagined and built alternative, nourishing futures. Black people recognized that food and hunger were wielded against them as a weapon and reconfigured their food networks to build "emancipatory food power" (Smith 2023, 2).

Cooperative farms in the Mississippi Delta and free breakfast programs in the urban North experimented with new ways of producing and distributing food. Community organizations built networks of mutual aid. Drawing upon strategies of "collective agency and community resilience," these groups practiced cooperative survival economies (White 2018, 5–11). Participants in the 1968 Poor People's Campaign and the National Welfare Rights Organization testified to Congress and pushed for changes to welfare policy. Collective actions, protests and boycotts, challenged low wages at work and high prices at the grocery store. These survival programs sought nutritive, economic, and political autonomy from a system of labor, food production, and distribution, which was designed to dispossess people.

• • •

The biography of Mrs. L. C. Dorsey, Mississippi sharecropper, civil rights activist, and public health leader, illuminates how Black people in the American South organized in response to their programmatic starvation. Dorsey drew from her life experience to articulate a political theory of hunger and power. She grew up in the 1940s on a plantation in the Mississippi Delta. She described how families hustled to survive, planting vegetables, catching rabbits, picking berries and pecans from common lands on the levy to sell for cash. Those who were unable to take care of themselves were "included in the network of support on the plantation. Everybody always planted some extra vegetables, saved the extra rabbits that they caught, for those families" (Dorsey 1992). Mutual aid, planting, and foraging compensated for a lack of money. Despite long hours of work in the cotton fields, Dorsey's family—like the others on plantations—never cleared a profit from the plantation landowner. "You get all these advances, and at the end of the year you settle up, and you're supposed to have money, and we never had any" (Dorsey 1992). At the yearly reckoning, the landowner always claimed that cash advances, purchases at the plantation store, and "overhead" expenses ate up the value of the sharecropper's cotton. As she later recalled:

> I figured out, I had excellent teachers in these little one-room school houses who taught us incredible stuff, like how to keep books, basic bookkeeping, in math classes and stuff. I decided, and I'm not sure how I arrived at this conclusion, and I'm sure Miss Higgins, who was my teacher, influenced that by impressing us with the importance of knowing how to do these things, so that we would be more responsible in managing our money and stuff. So somehow I made the quantum leap from learning all that stuff, and decided that the reason black folks never cleared any money from this operation was because we didn't keep any records. (Dorsey 1992)

Reckoning value on the plantation served as a mechanism for labor control. As Caitlin Rosenthal (2018, 3) has written in her business history of slavery and scientific management, "control has always been at the heart of modern accounting practice." Slaveowners in the nineteenth century, as Rosenthal shows, were among the most sophisticated bookkeepers anywhere. Later, in the Jim Crow years, plantation owners used accounting practices and, relatedly, debt peonage, as leverage over their workers. Loading some workers with debt and forgiving others' debts, owners were able to encourage some workers to stay and force others to seek work elsewhere (Rosenthal 2018, 180).

Mathematics and bookkeeping were technologies of labor management. As an eighth-grader, Dorsey understood this and decided to keep her own score.

> I got a Blue Horse notebook. . . . The paper was sewn in and then it was covered with a piece of stuff. Not like the frivolous stuff you have now that falls apart. But we set it up, and I set it up the way I had learned in school with expense columns and income columns, and every day I would come home and listen to the market on the radio, where they broadcast how much cotton was selling for. Helena, Arkansas, had that every day between eleven and twelve. I forget the name of the radio station. And every thing we got, I listed in that expense column. (Dorsey 1992)

When the time for reckoning came, Dorsey proudly gave her father the notebook and explained its entries (he could not read or write). She expected a payment of over two thousand dollars and was "positively ill" with disappointment when her father returned with a few hundred. This was the first year her parents had cleared any money at all, and they were more than satisfied, but the amount did not square with her careful accounting. Later she came to suspect that her father had not showed the notebook to anyone, because he understood the challenge that it posed to the landowner's authority.

Dorsey identified math as a technology of labor control in the American South: "I mean, I had latched on to what was wrong with the whole plantation system." Sums in the ledger determined a family's access to food. Plantation owners disbursed credit, sold survival goods, and set the rate of repayment at harvest. Dorsey came to realize, when her father returned with far less money than she had reckoned, that math alone was not enough to reverse the structural oppression, which it supported. "At that point, I decided that there was no fairness in the system," she recalled, "and that somehow people had to escape the system. Because it was not ever going to be a situation where you could do anything to make it work for you. I mean, that was the end of me assuming responsibility for an unfair and unjust world" (Dorsey 1992).

Dorsey married and began a family; three years later, her young family was asked to leave the small plantation where they lived. Their landowner had purchased a mechanical cotton picker and no longer needed them. "I experienced deprivation in a different form than I had ever had at home, because there was hunger." She learned to work the local rules for surplus commodities distribution and barely kept her children fed. She applied her bookkeeping skills to balancing rent payments, electricity bills, and weekly food purchases. She chopped cotton when she was able. Dorsey described her experience of hunger:

> I had one horrible, nightmarish night [in 1965] where we cooked the last food at noon. It was enough food at noon for everybody to get enough to eat, and we went to bed that night hungry. . . . you can't appreciate how horrible that is unless you've lived through it. It's one thing to be hungry yourself. It is an entirely different thing to know that your children are hungry, and to put them to bed knowing they're hungry, and listen to them cry themselves to sleep. It is even more devastating, and it hurts even to talk about it now, to have the older children, who are only ten or so, be just as hungry but try not to let you hear them cry. That is something that helps you understand why women become prostitutes, why people rob and break in stores, and why they take what they want to deal with this. (Dorsey 1992)

Dorsey understood her family's hunger as a consequence of marital relations, agricultural transformation, legal power, and anti-Black racism. Her husband drank, failed to bring his paycheck home, and did not gather food supplements as her father had done. Neighborly mutual aid networks served as a last resort. Her family had no access to land for growing survival crops. In her gendered role as mother, Dorsey was responsible for keeping her children fed and was deeply responsive to their suffering.

Dorsey understood her family's hunger in relation to law, power, and racism. Hunger led her to "understand why women become prostitutes, why people rob." Hunger resulted from law, and to escape hunger meant to break beyond law. This was why "[people] take what they want to deal with this." Her experience with hunger was part and motive for her activism for civil and economic rights. Antihunger action required a challenge to legal power over Black people. Civil rights work gave Dorsey tools to analyze and intervene in her community's history. In the Freedom Summer of 1964, SNCC and COFO organized volunteers to converge upon the South and mount a large-scale voter registration drive. Freedom summer volunteers set up schools, to counter the historical underinvestment in Black education. These schools were meant to be antihierarchical, imbued with the "awareness that students brought with them valuable knowledge and experiences" (Dittmer 2009, 53). The Freedom Schools taught math, reading, health, and Black history in relation to the civil rights movement.

Later, Dorsey was selected to enter employee training for the Head Start childcare program, funded by the 1964 Economic Opportunity Act, which offered her further access to politically-grounded education. Civil rights education opened new and other worlds. "We were learning, and it was a whole new world," Dorsey (1992) said. "I read all the stuff they brought as voraciously as I had read the Freedom School material, because it opened up another whole world, that being in the plantation, and the limitations of the educational experiences that the plantation had offered, had denied us. And I realized that there was a hunger there that

I hadn't recognized that was akin to this whole business of keeping records in that Blueback notebook when I was thirteen." Dorsey's synthesis of hunger for change, hunger for learning, and bodily hunger echoes across African American cultural history. Hunger, literacy, and empowerment are powerfully interconnected in the African American literary tradition (Warnes 2004).

Frederick Douglass's autobiography evokes the pain of bodily and intellectual starvation, seeking wheat bread and the "bread of knowledge." Richard Wright (2005 [1944], 16), in his autobiographical novel *American Hunger*, wrote of feeling hunger as a "deep biological bitterness." Wright (2005 [1944], 282, 382) described a hunger that extended beyond food: a "hunger for insight," "a hunger for life." In 1964 and 1965, Dorsey volunteered with COFO, recruited by Fannie Lou Hamer, and began to mobilize sharecroppers to register to vote. She felt an echo of the earlier "magic" of math. "I felt an excitement that somehow what we were doing, and the magic of the vote, was going to eradicate all of the inequities that we were experiencing. . . . The only other time I had that kind of high, for lack of a better term, was that year that I was keeping books to show Mr. Carl that we knew what he was doing, and we were going to break up this nonsense of taking all our money" (Dorsey 1992).

In response to Black residents' mobilization, white landowners tightened control over access to communal food resources. In other words, they sought to starve Black workers out. Local authorities in Dorsey's town closed off access to the levy, where pecan trees grew on public federal land. Landowners refused to allow sharecroppers to plant gardens of turnips and other survival crops. Enclosing common food resources in this way had two effects: it criminalized poverty survival tactics like gleaning pecans; and it controlled poor Black people's labor and access to land (Williams and Freshour 2022, 43). As described in chapter 3, plantation owners used food advances to maintain tight labor control. Sharecroppers relied entirely on loans from landowners to bridge the months between the November harvesting season and March, when landowners took the cotton to market and distributed the shares; loans were contingent on remaining in the employ and good graces of the plantation owner. If a worker attempted to escape this cycle of debt, they would be met by violence and criminalization. Food advances were tools of power. Welfare agencies collaborated with this structure of political and labor control by making access to benefits contingent on obedience.

County welfare officials responded to civil rights mobilization by enacting a requirement that an employer or "responsible person" sign a complicated form before any applicant could receive food. However, "due to the voter registration drive . . . , the 'responsible people' are not particularly inclined to favors for the Negro" ("Ruleville Miss." 1962). Several counties like Leflore County, the site where Emmett Till was murdered, chose to replace their federal commodity surplus program with food stamps. Unlike surplus commodities, stamps required money deposits that were too expensive for most laborers. The number of residents receiving aid plummeted.[1] Dorsey (1992) explained that "Black people were totally dependent on white people for everything that had to do with their survival." If one plantation owner decided to eject a Black family from the plantation, they were blacklisted and would not find work or food anywhere else. Federal surplus commodities, the only other source of food, might delay starvation, but they also served as mechanisms for white authorities to further tighten control. Collective mobilization and voting held a status analogous to education and bookkeeping in Dorsey's fight against exploitation. In her struggle they were tools of liberation from subjection and starvation. The fight over the value of labor, the fight to vote, and the fight against hunger were one and the same.

Like many other activists in the region, Dorsey saw that white landowners responded to the civil rights movement by starving Black residents out. Plantation owners warned her not to bother bringing sharecroppers back home once she led them to the voter registration desk. Sharecroppers who tried to register risked losing their homes, work, and subsistence. "When people started mumbling about civil rights and human rights and political rights . . . ," Dorsey (1992) noted, "there was a conscious move by white landowners to clamp down. One of the things that they did was actually put in place those things that would result in people being starved to death." In 1967 she was recruited to bring her local organizing skills to the newly opened Tufts-Delta Health Center. The Delta Health Center, funded by Lyndon Johnson's Office of Economic Opportunity, was established by physicians and social workers connected to the Medical Committee for Human Rights and is widely recognized as one of the first community health centers in the United States. The Delta Health Center was organized around principles of community accountability. Dorsey (1992) was hired to teach residents "how to go to the Welfare Department with records and demand your rights, how to go to elected officials and get things done in your community."

Delta Health Center founder Jack Geiger turned the Center's pharmacy into a food pantry. Center leaders called neighborhood meetings, where they asked residents about their needs and goals. They found that "food is always the number one priority. When we first came to the Delta the people said, over and over again, health services are wonderful, . . . we're happy to have it here—but for the love of God, could you spare some food?" (Geiger 1969, 2438). At the Center, Dorsey founded and managed the North Bolivar County Farm Cooperative, a cooperative of area residents who pooled their labor to grow food for their families and to sell at local markets (Hatch 1992). Neither state officials nor the federal Office of Economic Opportunity were enthusiastic about these experiments in subsistence undertaken by a health center. Geiger told the story of when the Office of Economic Opportunity "sent someone down to scream at me when I was giving away food and charging it to the pharmacy. I said, 'What's wrong with that?' He said, 'The pharmacy is for drugs and the treatment of disease.' And I said, 'The last time I looked in my medical textbook, the most effective therapy for malnutrition is food.' And he went away" (Geiger and Cohen 2017). Geiger's "therapy for malnutrition" was a political intervention. The diagnosis of malnutrition created possibilities for community-based mutual aid, cooperative production, and education. By framing poverty relief as medicine, rather than welfare, the Delta Health Center shifted the locus of power away from local welfare boards, run by White Citizens' Council members, to federal agencies.

Years later, having earned a PhD in social work, Dorsey became the Delta Health Center's director. She continued to serve her community for many years. Her lifelong survival experiments mobilized math and accounting, political organizing, historical education, health services, and cooperative agriculture. All of these skills were necessary to resist labor control and ethnic cleansing by starvation.

. . .

A group of displaced sharecroppers, mobilized by SNCC and the Mississippi Freedom Democratic Party, met on January 29, 1966, at the Mount Beulah Center in Edwards, Mississippi, "to talk about their problem: being hungry and poor." Many of the people at the Mount Beulah meeting were homeless and without a means of subsistence. Many were fleeing violence. The hundreds of attendees included a group of sharecroppers who had been evicted from the Andrews plantation near Dorsey's home, when they had tried to strike for better working hours and higher wages. In the backlash to that strike Dorsey (1992) "saw the horror that could happen to you when you didn't belong to a white man. That was what we saw with the Andrews' people. Everybody got kicked off that plantation, and every plantation was alerted not to hire them." They all lived in "a system that really controlled you through the threat of starvation."

SNCC field secretary Charlie Cobb was present at Mount Beulah and described the desperate circumstances behind this mobilization. In response to civil rights advances, plantation owners and local authorities stripped Black citizens of the means to survive in Mississippi. Cotton-picking machines, which had begun to appear in the mid-twentieth century, appeared everywhere and displaced tens of thousands of workers. White Citizens Councils, white supremacist organizations formed in response to the Supreme Court ruling on school desegregation, controlled local welfare boards. Employers sealed off access to jobs. County officials cut access to welfare. Black residents were left with two choices: "leaving the state in search of opportunity elsewhere, or starving" (Cobb 1966, 1).

Cobb (1966, 2) recorded testimony from one resident to the effect that local welfare officials "gonna keep us hungry as we been all our days. We still ain't gonna have no food. I'm thinkin bout gettin them [nonpoor] folks off that [county welfare] board and putting some of these folks on who know what it means if you go in the kitchen to cook an you ain't got but half a package of beans an 8 kids to feed—you got to put enough water in that pot to have some likker, so when the beans run out, the likker go roun into gravey an you have somethin to sop."

Participants testified to their experience of living hungry, with extending gravies and prolonged, worried sleep. Another resident testified: "We heard Mr. Johnson speak about poverty. He's gonna restrict poverty. Everybody's gonna get well treated. When it [welfare] be issued out through that Sunflower [County] KKK, you just ain't gonna get it. While they're figuring an all like that, you have these peoples on the plantation who are starving" (Cobb 1966, 2). "If the food that's somewhere down for us poor peoples in Mississippi doesn't be given to us," several people warned, "I guess somebody'll have to go try and take it. An that's not gonna be long" (Cobb 1992, 6).

A group of fifty people, led by COFO volunteer and Mississippi Freedom Democratic Party delegate Unita Blackwell, decided to occupy the nearby abandoned Greenville Air Force Base. Instead of waiting to receive welfare from local or federal authorities, they wanted to establish conditions for their own survival. "We are here because we are hungry and cold," they announced. "We demand food. We are here because we are hungry. Our children can't be taught in school because they are hungry. . . . We demand jobs. . . . We demand income. . . . We want to decide what foods we eat" (MFDP 1966, 1). They claimed the buildings for homes and training centers, and the land for farming. Within weeks, US military police came to clear them from the base and their experiment in survival came to an end. But the national publicity that they generated opened a new chapter in the political history of hunger in the United States.

Senator Robert Kennedy and the Senate Subcommittee on Employment, Manpower and Poverty heard about the Greenville Air Base incident and traveled to Jackson, Mississippi, in April 1967 to gather testimonies. Kennedy's visit, covered widely in national media, is commonly characterized as the moment when Americans "discovered" hunger in their own country (Green 2017). Of course, the only people doing the "discovering" were the senators and television viewers. People on the ground did not need to discover anything. The senators heard from Unita Blackwell, MFDP leader Fannie Lou Hamer, and Marian Wright, who was then a National Association for the Advancement of Colored People (NAACP) lawyer representing welfare clients in the Delta. Blackwell made clear that hunger and starvation were weapons of white supremacy. She described poverty relief as a direct result of her community's mobilization and resistance: "Senators, I want you all to know that in Mississippi if it had not been for civil rights it wouldn't have been no poverty program, because this is what people started out to get enough initiative to stand up to try to say could they do something for themselves, and that's what started the whole thing" (*Hearings before the Special Subcommittee* 1967, 594).

Blackwell, Hamer, and Wright explained to Kennedy and the other senators how local welfare boards denied civil rights activists their legitimate benefits. They told the senators of pervasive hunger and how "poverty programs are being discouraged in the way of saying, you can't participate in civil rights" (*Hearings before the Special Subcommittee* 1967, 548). They demanded that federal authorities take authority for food and welfare programs away from states and counties that used hunger as a tool of violence. "[Local control], along with the purchase price requirement, meant that many of the poor would not benefit from the food stamp program. In fact, it could almost be said that in some part of the South these features of the program created, rather than solved, the social problem of hunger" (DeVault and Pitts 1984, 548). Kennedy asked Blackwell: "What happens when people don't get the commodities [denied to them by local administrators of federal welfare programs]?" She answered: "They starve" (*Hearings before the Special Subcommittee* 1967).

As poor people and civil rights workers made clear, the white power structure across the cotton-growing region undertook a near-genocidal campaign of deprivation. In an echo of the withholding of food rations from Native peoples at the turn of the twentieth century, plantation owners and county welfare boards colluded to starve Black residents out of the South. Fannie Lou Hamer told a journalist: "Down in Mississippi they are killing Negroes of all ages, on the installment plan, through starvation. If you are a Negro and vote, if you persist in dreams of black power to win some measure of freedom in white-controlled communities, you go hungry" ("Going Hungry" 1968, 9). In the wake of the 1967 Senate hearings that gathered testimony in Jackson, conditions in the Mississippi Delta became a reference point for speaking about hunger in the United States. Poverty, malnutrition, and hunger elsewhere in the United States were compared to conditions in the Delta, which in turn were compared to conditions in Africa or Latin America. This led to debates about the specificity of hunger, malnutrition, and starvation. If hunger in Mississippi was the result of a coordinated campaign of starvation, what did hunger represent in the urban North? Doctors and activists began to profile a space extending all the way across "the wealthiest nation in the history of the world," in which "millions of men, women and children are starving" (Citizens' Board 1968, 7, 9).

"Frequently throughout the Mississippi Delta," wrote physician Raymond F. Wheeler, "we heard charges of an unwritten but generally accepted policy on the part of those who control the state to eliminate the Negro Mississippian either by driving him out of the state or starving him to death. At first, the charge seems to me beyond belief" (Wheeler 1967, 26). Wheeler led a group of Ivy League physicians, mobilized by the Southern Regional Council, on a tour of Mississippi's Humphreys and Leflore counties immediately following the 1967 Senate subcommittee hearings in Jackson. Doctors visited the homes of families enrolled in a federally funded early childhood education program. Wheeler noted the "common practice" of white plantation landlords forbidding their tenants from planting a subsistence garden, even when ample space for one existed. He and his colleagues spoke with families who were declared ineligible for surplus commodities or food stamps, "even though they have literally nothing" (Wheeler 1967, 5). One mother with whom Wheeler spoke "summed up the question of diet in a single, poignant sentence: 'These children go to bed hungry and get up hungry and don't ever know nothing else in between'" (Wheeler 1967, 13–14).

Doctors with Wheeler on the Southern Regional Council's tour of Mississippi "saw children whose nutritional and medical condition we can only describe as shocking—even to a group of physicians whose work involves daily confrontation with disease and suffering." They reported:

> In child after child we saw: evidence of vitamin and mineral deficiencies; serious, untreated skin infections and ulcerations; eye and ear diseases, also unattended bone diseases secondary to poor food intake; the prevalence of bacterial and parasitic disease, as well as severe anemia, with resulting loss of energy and ability to live a normally active life; diseases of the heart and the lungs—requiring surgery—which have gone undiagnosed and untreated; epileptic and other neurological disorders; severe kidney ailments, that in other children would warrant immediate hospitalization; and finally, in boys and girls in every county we visited, obvious evidence of severe malnutrition, with injury to the body's tissues—its muscles, bones, and skin, as well as an associated psychological state of fatigue, listlessness, and exhaustion. (Brenner et al. 1967, 4–5)

If charges of deliberate, programmatic starvation at first had seemed "beyond belief" to Wheeler and his companions, by the end of their tour he was convinced. Wheeler came to see Mississippi as "a kind of prison" for "semi-starving people" (Wheeler 1967, 27).

The Senate subcommittee hearings and the Southern Regional Council report inspired further and broader reporting. In July 1967 the Field Foundation recruited Wheeler to join an ambitious national survey, the Citizens' Board of Inquiry into Hunger and Malnutrition in the United States. Board members included doctors and public health experts, law professors, a Brookings Institution economist, religious and charitable leaders, union representatives, the presidents of Morehouse and Clark colleges, Dolores Huerta of the United Farm Workers Union, and Vine Deloria Jr. of the National Congress of American Indians. The Citizens' Board assembled data and carried out hearings and field trips in Kentucky, San Antonio, Alabama, Mississippi, on a Navajo Reservation, in South Dakota Indian country, Florida migrant labor camps, and poor neighborhoods of Boston, New York, and Washington, DC. The reporters of the Citizens' Board (1968, 9) wrote that "we find ourselves somewhat startled by our own findings, for we too had been lulled into the comforting belief that at least the extremes of privation had been eliminated."

The Citizens' Board mapped a geography of displacement and violence—a zone of American settler colonization—through the spread of hunger. Board members "found concrete evidence of hunger and malnutrition in every part of the United States where we have held hearings or conducted field trips" (Citizens' Board 1968,

9). Many of these sites were situated at the borderlands of US settler-colonialism, near the Mexican frontier, on Native American reservations, on plantations, and in mining communities. In northern cities the Citizens' Board visited immigrant neighborhoods and areas settled by displaced plantation workers. Notably, the Citizens' Board tied starvation in the rural South to hunger and malnutrition in the urban North. They emphasized that "these conditions are not confined to Mississippi." Their report identified a "great group of people" in the northeastern United States "living just at or below a minimum level of subsistence." The report documented severe malnutrition in Baltimore, Boston, Cleveland, and New York. Doctors in the Bronx recounted cases of anemia and other forms of malnutrition prevalent in children, and widespread hunger in the days before welfare checks came in. Psychiatrist Robert Coles, who worked with impoverished children in Georgia and Boston, argued in the report that the starvation of Black Americans impacted both the North and the South: "When a sick, chronically malnourished child leaves a plantation or mountain hollow for Chicago or Detroit, rural poverty becomes urban poverty" (Citizens' Board 1968, 32). Wheeler compared what he saw in Boston's poor neighborhoods to his previous experiences in the South and concluded that "the problems [in Boston] are only different in degree from what we have seen elsewhere" (quoted in Citizens' Board 1968, 18).

Historian Greta de Jong has theorized that the hundreds of thousands of Black Americans exiled from the South in the 1960s "were the first to experience the transition from free labor to displaced persons that awaited millions of other workers in this new era of economic restructuring" (de Jong 2016, 17). These displaced people's condition of abandonment and deprivation, justified by ideologies of free market, limited government, and individual liberty, would be replicated across the United States in the late twentieth century. The Citizens' Board (1968, 4) report showed some awareness of this process, even as it cast hungry people as "useless mouths": "wherever we have gone we have seen the multitudinous cast-offs of an economic system which, bewilderingly, can build up ever greater national achievements without affecting the immense and economically useless pockets of the impoverished." The violence of ethnic cleansing through starvation could not and would not be contained geographically to the South.

. . .

Readers of the *New York Times* on May 21, 1968, opened the newspaper to a three-column advertisement captioned, "This Baby Is Dying of Hunger." The ad urged readers to tune into a CBS special report that evening, which would reveal an "incredible, shocking truth" (Martin 1972, 186). CBS's broadcast on "Hunger in America" brought the Citizens' Board's narratives into the living rooms of millions of American households.[2] Guided by the resonant voice of reporter Charles Kuralt, viewers of "Hunger in America" followed the itinerary of the Citizens' Board investigators, with some important deviations. Viewer reactions were strong: in the week after the show aired, CBS received more than five thousand letters, and constituents "deluged" the Senate Subcommittee on Employment, Manpower and Poverty (*Hunger and Malnutrition in US* 1968, 53) with phone calls and letters of concern.[3]

Viewers of the televised special report met local doctors and their patients in the borderlands of San Antonio, tenant farms in wealthy Loudoun County, Virginia, a Navajo reservation near Tuba, Arizona, and sharecroppers' shacks in Hale County. But CBS completely excised Northern cities from its program. Despite the Citizens' Board's insistence that Northern urban poverty was connected to Southern starvation, CBS producers skipped over the Bronx, Boston, Detroit, and Cleveland. For a Northern urban audience, the broadcast created a geography of the hungry other. "Hunger in America" begins with Mexican Americans in San Antonio, where, we are told, "unemployment is high" and "100,000 people are hungry all the time" (Carr and Davies 1968, 3:30). A priest named Father Ruiz leads the camera into the homes of his parishioners and explains what it means for them to be hungry. When hunger becomes visible, "when you begin to see hunger in the faces of people," by then they have already lost sensation and "they no longer feel hunger" (7:00). Viewers learn that poor residents of San Antonio survive on surplus commodities, which lack fruit and vegetables. Commodities keep them alive, but it is a poor life. "The poor are alive because they eat. They are malnourished because of what they eat. Fat people can be hungry people" (14:20). Vera Burke, director of social services at a local charity hospital, complains that patients cannot afford to follow the diets prescribed to cure their nutritional illnesses, especially adequate protein intake. She leads the camera through three wards for malnourished infants. When the babies leave the hospital, she says, they go home "where there is no milk" (16:50).

Medical authorities are the main protagonists in this documentary; they validate the veracity of hunger. In Loudon County, Dr. Steven Graninger explains that seven thousand families have severe nutrition problems; in his eyes the problem is that tenant farmers have too many children and not enough food. Graninger blames these white farmers' condition on a cycle of "constant misery": "these people with no past to be proud of and no hope for the future, seek immediate forms of enjoyment" (37:35). In Tuba, Dr. Jean Van Duesen accompanies the camera into the homes of Navajo families, patients who "continually face the medical problems caused by lack of food." Like Burke, Van Duesen denounces the starchiness of federal surplus commodities, "what I would call a white diet, . . . actually a very poor diet." Van Duesen shows viewers an infant at the public hospital, whom she has diagnosed with kwashiorkor, protein-calorie malnutrition. "The is a disease that was first seen in South America and Africa. It's not supposed to exist in the United States but it does." Van Duesen recounts that she sees infants with marasmus, "total, total protein-calorie malnutrition" (46:50). A third of these cases died in the hospital.

Finally, Dr. Raymond Wheeler leads the camera into Miss Carlyle's home in Hale County, Mississippi. Wheeler prefaces the visit by explaining that "slow starvation has become part of the Southern way of life." The *CBS Reports* segment leaves it to Miss Carlyle, not Wheeler, to explain the social context for her family's starvation: "White people don't care how you live. . . . I imagine I feel like it's because children going to school, doing a little voting, something they never have did." When pressed to justify her statement that "white people don't care," Miss Carlyle refuses to take the bait: "I know they don't care. I don't have to think they don't care. I know they don't care" (48:03). Unlike in his written report, Wheeler does not validate Miss Carlyle's statement on air. The "Hunger in America" segment pulled a theme from the Citizens' Board report and repeated it at every location: hungry people, especially children, were irreversibly damaged. Malnourished babies at the Tuba Public Hospital "may have permanent damage to the brain and inability to read and write" (33:50). In their first year undernourished children in the South "fall behind . . . and they never catch up" (42:55). The poor diet of tenant farmers' children in Virginia "affects brain tissue, . . . the ability to think and to learn. The worst damage is done during infancy. The brain damage is not reversible. It can't be changed, one year from now or five years from now" (20:56).

Mikal Raz (2013) has shown how poverty discourse in the 1960s figured poor people, especially poor Black people, as deficient. Poor people were thought to lack sensitivity, culture, and maternal care. The "deprivation hypothesis" focused attention on "what is missing rather than what is there, on deprivation rather than on differences or strengths and coping mechanisms," and left a long legacy in social services and education (Raz 2013, 24). The "Hunger in America" broadcast thus transmitted and amplified this view of the poor as damaged and lacking. Government officials reacted strongly. US Secretary of Agriculture Oroville Freeman gave an angry press conference days after the broadcast to denounce its "shoddy journalism, . . . distorted, oversimplified and misleading picture of domestic hunger" (Martin 1972, 189). A congressman from San Antonio tasked the Federal Communications Commission with investigating whether CBS producers lied when they portrayed babies in his city dying of hunger. The FCC expressed concern about the evidence for CBS's reporting but refused to censor the network over the content of its claims. Mississippi congressman Jamie Whitten, chair of the powerful House Agricultural Appropriations Subcommittee, was said to have persuaded FBI agents to launch an investigation into the broadcast's producers and contributors. Jean Mayer (1971), one of CBS's scientific advisers, wrote that "almost anyone who was seen in the picture was interrogated, some repeatedly." In its most explicit and pointed message, the "Hunger in America" broadcast indicted the US Department of Agriculture and its management of the food stamp and surplus commodity programs. "In this country," Charles Kuralt concluded, "the most basic human need must become a human right" (Carr and Davies 1968, 49:47).

· · ·

Starvation in the United States, for Robert Wheeler and for many medical experts, was "beyond belief." Investigators for the Southern Regional Council "found it hard to believe we were examining American children of the Twentieth Century" (Brenner et al. 1967, 5). Medical practitioners and hunger researchers struggled to articulate and respond to these reports, which originated outside of their professional circles and societies. Some reacted with shock and a transformed sense of professional responsibility. "While we have been studying 'hyperglycemia in tuco-tucos' and 'mouse liver nucleic acids,'" despaired one nutrition researcher, "we have not investigated the problem of pre-school malnutrition in our own back yards" (Latham 1968, 2). Other experts reacted defensively; if they had not noted or studied the problem previously, it must not exist. To diagnose hunger in the United States was to diagnose neglect, violence, and inequity. This, to many, was beyond belief.

As soon as American hunger and starvation appeared in the public consciousness, experts questioned the nature of this diagnosis. Perhaps there was hunger—but it couldn't be a real, medically validated hunger. Some experts argued that hunger itself was an empty category that could not be diagnosed or measured and therefore should be eliminated from the medical vocabulary. Hunger's scientific validity was challenged, at precisely the peak of its social and political power. How did experts not see or believe what was happening in their own backyard? John F. Mueller (1969, 1413), president of the American Society for Clinical Nutrition, lamented that "most of us were so concerned with the enormity of the problems in developing countries of the World, that we forgot our own problems." Was this a question of "forgetfulness?"

Mueller blamed a sense of complacency in the aftermath of the "vitamin era" and successful treatment of specific deficiency diseases like beriberi and pellagra. During most of the twentieth century, nutritionists battled successfully against deficiency disease. They identified the vitamin or mineral associated with a particular set of symptoms and developed pharmaceutical or industrial palliatives. Thiamin and riboflavin entered into the standard bag of flour; iodine was added to table salt; vitamin D got mixed into milk bottles. Simple deficiencies were resolved with a single supplement, and nutritionists rightfully felt a sense of mastery and triumph at having cured them. With the important exception of the two world wars, concerns about hunger and starvation faded into the background of these exciting developments. Two conditions challenged the vitamania of twentieth-century nutritionists: obesity and hunger (Moran 2018, 112, 137). Both were generalized metabolic conditions that resisted attempts to contain them with a pill or supplement. Mueller (1969, 1413) offered another, more uncomfortable explanation for nutritionists' neglect of the hunger around them: experts felt "some degree of indifference fostered by an unwillingness to become 'involved.'" In other words, they refused or avoided naming what they saw. Some scientists, particularly in nutrition, preferred to maintain discussion on a technical, apolitical level. To name hunger and starvation was to acknowledge the violence of American society (Biltekoff 2024, 14).

Many experts looked at these cases of malnourished children and thought of Africa and Latin America. Doctors and researchers who had worked with the Rockefeller Foundation and USAID to alleviate hunger in the global South, were shocked to discover the presence of severe malnutrition in the United States. One nutritionist wrote, in reaction to the CBS broadcast, that as "a physician who has dealt with a great deal of kwashiorkor and nutritional marasmus in Africa, it was eye-opening to sit in a comfortable U.S. home and to see cases of these serious nutritional diseases displayed in Texas and Arizona" (Latham 1968, 3). Citizens' Board member Alfred Haynes, a Johns Hopkins University professor of public health, expressed a similar sense of dissonance: "We associate [kwashiorkor] with Africa, Asia and other parts of the world, but one of our medical colleagues found cases in a field trip to the Indian reservations" (*Hunger and Malnutrition in US* 1968, 17). The National Nutrition Survey found in Texas and Louisiana "signs and indices of malnutrition of essentially the same incidences and severity as found in low-income Central American families" ("Malnutrition and Hunger" 1970, 273). Could medical terms that experts used to describe poor, hungry, underdeveloped peoples in the global South—malnutrition, undernutrition, starvation—apply equally within the borders of the United States? Hunger debates skirted the question of American empire and settler-colonialism.

Medical experts on the Citizens' Board struggled to reconcile the condition of poor Americans with their experiences as development experts in the informal American aid empire. Haynes found "children, while living in the United States, [who] seem to conform more to the pattern of developing countries. They are not what we would call sick but they have not been able to achieve their potential" (*Hunger and Malnutrition in US* 1968, 16). But Haynes and the Citizens' Board distinguished between their observations and "the extreme famine state with which some of us have had first hand familiarity abroad." More concerning, they argued, were "the far vaster numbers of Americans who never get enough to eat, who never get adequate nutrition, who waste away or suffer the corpulence and gross overweight of a diet comprised almost entirely of starches" (*Hunger and Malnutrition in US* 1968, 31).

Some nutritionists resisted *Hunger USA* as a challenge to their own authority and expertise. The Citizens' Board (1968) report centered and highlighted poor people's testimonies. To some experts, this was an error and an affront: a poor person's story about feeling hunger had no scientific validity, as their hunger represented no more than a subjective feeling. "Hunger is a physiological or emotional state . . . very often [directed at] something having no direct relation to nutrition." A well-fed person might get hungry for a "steak or a popsickle [*sic*]" (Youmans 1970, 1123). Obese people tend to feel hungry all the time. Truly malnourished, even starving, subjects may not feel any hunger at all. John B. Youmans, professor at the Vanderbilt University Medical School, spent his career surveying the nutritional status of large populations from Tennessee to Pakistan by massive data collection, dietary observations, physical exams, and laboratory analyses. Youmans (1970, 1123) accused reporters of using the term "hunger" "primarily for its emotional and political impact without reference to its actual physiologic meaning." To this, Dr. Alfred Klinger retorted that physicians must heed the voices of the poor: "We [must] recognize that medicine is as much a social science as a biological one" (Klinger, Mendelsohn, and Alberts 1970, 682).

Dr. Herbert Pollack led the charge against *Hunger USA*. Pollack, a diabetes and nutrition expert at George Washington University and consultant to the US State Department, spoke out against the Citizens' Board report. He may have been motivated by his ties to the conservative Institute for Defense Analyses, which sent typed copies of his critique to federal policy makers (Pollack 1968, 32). Or he may have felt personally affronted by the CBS broadcast. Pollack owned a cattle farm near Leesberg, Virginia, where he served as governor of the Middleburg Hunt and member of the Loudoun County Medical Society (Smith 1990). He and his associates may well have taken offense at the way that CBS depicted Loudoun County as a site of deprivation and malnutrition. Where the Citizens' Board or CBS reporters saw "hunger," Pollack argued, they had no idea what they were looking at. They lacked scientific grounding. In his view, *Hunger USA* was based on little more than "a series of anecdotal testimonial presentations" (Pollack 1969, 480). Reporters may have observed symptoms of what looked like malnutrition, but Pollack did not believe their claims about the nature of the problem.

In his critique Pollack employed a technique that had already been sharpened by the tobacco industry in its defense against public health activists (which is still employed today by climate change deniers and the sugar industry). Naomi Oreskes and Eric Conway (2010, 13) call it the "tobacco strategy": invoking multiple possible causes and explanations, to foster a sense of uncertainty and paralyze policy action. What looks to an average observer like deprivation, Pollack argued, might well be something else. Inadequate access to food, or "primary malnutrition," was only one possible explanation (he thought it the least likely explanation) for these apparent symptoms. Pollack (1969, 486), for one, "[had] yet to hear of such a case [of infantile malnutrition] that was the result of poverty." He ran through *Hunger USA* and at almost every stop found alternative causes for what the reporters saw.

Low birth weights in San Antonio might be inherited rather than nutritional; Mexican babies, Pollack suggested, should not be measured to the same standards as Anglo babies. Swollen bellies might be caused by umbilical hernia, not protein-calorie malnutrition. Elderly people might be too lonely and isolated to seek the food that they need, rather than too poor. Blackfoot Indians surveyed by the Public Health Service might not have accurately reported how little they ate. A prevalence of anemia in Harlan County, Kentucky, might be caused by parasites, bone marrow disease, excessive bleeding, or by drinking too much milk. Intestinal parasites or digestive diseases might prevent the body from absorbing nutrients, even when someone is eating plenty of food. Infectious diseases might "increase metabolic demands" by drawing excess energy away from the body, causing fevers or other symptoms. Many symptoms that appeared to be linked with malnutrition might be something else entirely (Pollack 1969, 480). Extra food, Pollack (1969, 488) warned, might even make some of those conditions worse. If there really was a serious malnutrition problem in the United States, Pollack (1969, 486) suggested, public health authorities would have noticed a change in overall rates of sickness and death. They had not.[4]

Above all, Pollack suggested that the real problems lay with poor people themselves, with their ignorance and incompetence. Inadequate welfare was not to blame. The proper diagnosis for this condition was not primary malnutrition, or lack of access to food, but secondary malnutrition caused by "lack of knowledge of nutritional value of foods and poor management of household budgets" (Pollack 1969, 480). "It becomes apparent that what the [Citizens' Board] observers are really declaiming is the failure of people to participate in the food stamp and commodity programs," rather than the insufficiencies of federal programs themselves (Pollack 1969, 481). Pollack (1969, 481) bemoaned "the lack of understanding or an inadequate education" in rural areas. Poor people's food choices, not inadequate wages and welfare, led to dietary deficiency. Southern Democrats and their allies repeatedly blamed malnutrition on the purported ignorance of Black women (Moran 2018, 115).

Pollack's arguments were echoed by Secretary of Agriculture Oroville Freeman in his defense against charges that federal food aid criminally neglected the poor. In testimony to Congress, Freeman cited Harvard Public Health professor Frederick Stare to the effect that "there are no hard facts" on how many people are hungry or malnourished in the United States. Like Pollack, Freeman criticized reports relying on anecdotal testimonies and ran through a list of alternate explanations for apparent symptoms of malnutrition. Above all, Freeman argued that government agents cannot be responsible for guaranteeing proper food choices in a poor and ignorant population: "it is not possible for them to spoon-feed every person in the country" (*Hunger and Malnutrition* 1968, 243–244).

Everyone saw the same images of poor children on their television screens. Doctors and nutritionists fought, in policy briefs and in the pages of medical journals, over what it was that they all saw. In a debate that still continues today, experts questioned the medical grounds for a diagnosis of hunger. Were these children severely malnourished, merely undernourished, simply hungry, ignorant, or just plain poor? Was this condition an objective illness or a subjective feeling, a medical question or a political one, and who ought to determine the answers? Doctors with the Southern Regional Council, after traveling through Mississippi, were categorical. They diagnosed not malnutrition but starvation. The Council doctors rejected the malnutrition diagnosis, for a very different reason: "We do not want to quibble over words, but 'malnutrition' is not quite what we found; the boys and girls we saw were hungry—weak, in pain, sick; their lives are being shortened; they are, in fact, visibly and predictably losing their health, their energy, their spirits. They are suffering from hunger and disease and directly or indirectly they are dying from them—which is exactly what 'starvation' means" (Brenner et al. 1967, 6). Testimonies gathered by Wheeler and his colleagues insisted that we remember the violent relations underlying these conditions. To starve was, and is, a transitive verb.

. . .

Poor people did not want to wait for experts to agree whether they were hungry, malnourished, deprived, deficient, undernourished, or starved. In October 1970 two dozen activists with the National Welfare Rights Organization (NWRO), Radical Action for the People and the Welfare Coalition, disrupted a workshop at the Missouri Association for Social Welfare conference on "The Dimensions of Hunger." Dr. Arnold Schaefer was scheduled to present the results of the National Nutrition Survey, which had launched in response to the publicity around the *Hunger USA* report. Welfare activists shouted Schaefer down, crying, "Let the people talk." They called for welfare workers to disrupt their agencies' complicity in suppressing clients' access to support. The protesters demanded "that experts stop studying hunger and do something about it." As Ms. Huella Scales said, "We can't eat studies" (Canfield 1970).

Poor people's activism spread across the United States in the late 1960s. As Annelise Orleck (2011, 2) has documented, "the poorest of the poor, despite daunting obstacles, transformed themselves into effective political actors who insisted on being heard." The 1964 Economic Opportunity Act opened spaces and resources for community organization. Across the country, poor people built and maintained urban housing cooperatives, farming cooperatives, community health clinics, welfare rights organizations, renters' rights groups, and community development corporations (Orleck 2011, 20). The Chicago Freedom Campaign and Union against Slums mobilized urban residents to fight against discriminatory city policies (Laurent 2018, 124–127). United Farm Workers fought for living wages and safe working conditions in the agricultural fields of the western United States. The NRWO united poor activists across the country who campaigned at local welfare boards demanding their legal right to welfare benefits, food, and housing (Piven and Cloward 1977, 272–353).

In cities as in rural areas, welfare activists challenged the structures of welfare administration, wage control, and the free market for food and rent, which produced scarcity and deprivation and upheld white supremacy. Restrictive welfare provisions were aimed at women of color across the United States. Activists in the urban North and West understood the parallels of their own situation with that of Southern workers. One of the most radical acts undertaken by NWRO was to mobilize poor women to demand welfare benefits, to which they were already legally entitled (Piven and Cloward 1977, 284). They challenged moralistic, punitive, and paternalistic "man in the house" rules, which monitored single women to ensure that no potential male breadwinners stayed overnight (Piven and Cloward 1977, 295). By 1969, NWRO grew to twenty-two thousand activists, mainly centered in the Midwestern and Northern cities; 85 percent of its membership was Black (Piven and Cloward 1977, 317).

In May 1968, in the aftermath of Martin Luther King Jr.'s assassination, the Poor People's Campaign occupied a tent encampment called Resurrection City on the Capitol Mall. At the center of Resurrection City, organizers erected a massive ten-by thirty-two-foot open mural titled "Hunger's Wall." Slogans for "Chicano Power," "Sisters of Watts for Human Dignity," "Uhuru or Revolution," "Cosmic Brotherhood," and "Love, not War" cover the wood panels. Above all of it stands an image of a Black man speaking out. "BROTHERS AND SISTERS," the text behind him reads, "HUNGER *IS REAL* AND YOU BETTER BELIEVE IT!" (NMAAHC 2021).

Activists with the Poor People's Campaign testified by invitation of senators on the Committee on Labor and Welfare, some of whom had visited Mississippi the year before. Mrs. Leona Hale of the Fort Berthold Reservation (in Newtown, North Dakota) testified: "We had a good life when the games [for hunting] were there. Now they are gone. I live on this [surplus] commodity and I have diabetes and I can't live on this canned chopped meat in exchange for what they took away from me. My people are starving at home" (*Hunger and Malnutrition in US* 1968, 115). Myrtle Brown of Marks, Mississippi, asked why white children were able to eat in school and not Black children. "Nothing from nothing is nothing," she said. "I have to go to Washington to see I get some rights. I am not only pleading for myself but I am speaking for the whole nation of poor people" (*Hunger and Malnutrition in US* 1968, 117). Benjamin Ortiz, high school student from Camden, New Jersey, linked hunger to settler-colonialism and white supremacy: "That is why I am starving, because you think, 'Everything in this country is mine'" (*Hunger and Malnutrition in UW* 1968, 127).

In 1969 the Black Panther Party (BPP) required that each of its chapters across the country set up a breakfast program for children every school morning. Party leaders understood hunger as the root of a "vicious cycle" ensnaring Black people across the country: "They TELL US, you're hungry because you're poor. . . . You're poor because you haven't got the best jobs. . . . You can't get the best jobs because you're uneducated, and you're uneducated because you didn't learn

FIGURE 10. Plywood panel mural created and displayed in the Resurrection City encampment on the National Mall in Washington, DC, during the summer of 1968 (detail). Painted text at the top of the panel reads: "Hunger's Wall: Tell It Like It Is." Source: Collection of the National Museum of African American History and Culture, Gift of Vincent DeForest.

while you were in school, and you didn't learn while you were in school because you weren't interested." While acknowledging the link between access to food and school performance, the Panthers refused experts' conclusion that poor people were irremediably damaged. "The root cause of this problem is not mental incapabilities or cultural deprivation, but HUNGER" (Potorti 2017, 94). The Panthers targeted neighborhood businesses and employers who "thrive off of the Black Community like leeches" and perpetuate hunger in their communities. "Hunger is one of the means of oppression and it must be halted" (Black Panther Community News Service 1969, 3).

The Black Panther Party's survival experiments were engaged with science, medicine, and history. They were political and technical. Black Panther Party member David Lemieux later recalled the reasons why the Party began to serve free breakfast to children in 1969. "Studies came out saying that children that didn't have a good breakfast in the morning were less attentive at school, and less inclined to do well, and suffered from fatigue. I mean, there's all sorts of scientific reasons to have a good breakfast in the morning. And we just simply took that information and a program was developed serving breakfast to children" (quoted in Nelson 2016). Survival programs like the Black Panthers' combined local knowledge, federal antipoverty resources, and scientific and medical expertise. Medical knowledge, disseminated via television reports, popular press, and medical volunteers, informed political and economic actions in the South and urban North. Freedom Schools developed political theory and historical grounding, through students' and teachers' collaborative work. Impoverished people navigated and redirected welfare and public health programs, notably President Lyndon Johnson's War on Poverty and antihunger measures, toward broader political ends of life and liberation.

Survival programs countered racist assumptions that hunger, joblessness, and outmigration were the natural consequences of economic modernization. Cooperative farms and businesses, mutual aid networks, self-help education,

and training built alternatives to structures that exploited Black people (De Jong 2016, 29). Many of these programs failed not because they were unsustainable, but because they were actively suppressed by those in power (Smith 2019). Survival programs "show a contradiction in the system": hunger is neither a natural state nor an inevitable side effect of economic change. "If the Black Panther Party can do all of this with no money," asked BPP member Jamal Joseph, "how is the richest government in the world allowing people to live in poverty and hunger and on the street?" (Mukherjee 2017). Hunger was—and is—a programmatic policy, not a fact of nature.

7

# Carceral Hunger

*Struggling to be free, to stay sane. If not this, then what? . . . Must I turn my*
*cheek and be happy to plainly exist? Miserable, but existing. Eating, drinking,*
*consuming crap—but existing. Fuck that! I will do what i can.*
—HERIBERTO SHARKY GARCIA, "IF THE FUTURE IS NOW: REVOLUTIONARY
ABOLITIONIST ART AND PRAXIS FROM THE UNDERSIDE OF
WHITE-AMERICAN CIVIL SOCIETY," 2018

Some two million people in the United States are made hungry, on purpose, every day. They are incarcerated in American detention centers, jails, and prisons (Sawyer and Wagner 2023). Some are made hungry by the withholding of food; many, many more are served food that is disgusting, spoiled, tasteless, and ultraprocessed. Prison officials use hunger as an instrument to control inmates' behavior. In addition, the nature of prison food itself causes hunger. Prisons fulfill regulatory requirements for calories and nutrients (when state requirements exist) in the cheapest, least nourishing forms possible: processed meats, "mechanically separated chicken," soy filler, piles of white bread, yellow cake, vitamin powders. "With the exception of a few good meals, the chow was lethal," rap artist Albert "Prodigy" Johnson wrote of his time in a New York penitentiary, "you get hungry between meals. . . . Plus when they feed you, you only get served in portions. You're lucky if you know people, you can get an extra piece of chicken or something. But you be hungry" (Johnson and Iandoli 2016, 3, 7).

Carceral hunger brings together many themes explored in this book: behavior modification, punishment, and reward; starvation wages and labor control; consumer choice, processed foods, and craving; and the liberatory politics of refusing hunger. Private food service providers like Aramark furnish worthless and disgusting meals, incentivizing extra purchases at privately run commissaries. Incarcerated people work for pennies an hour (if they are paid at all) to afford cheap food and other basic goods at inflated prices from these commissaries. Prison authorities use food service and commissary access as technologies of behavior control and punishment. But inside prisons food can be a tool for sociability, creativity, and resistance for incarcerated people. Prison hunger strikers mobilize collectively to refuse carceral hunger.

Anthony Ryan Hatch (2019, 76) has suggested that "raw starvation is not a major problem in U.S. prisons, but well-designed hunger is." What kinds of hunger are *well-designed*? How is hunger produced in the absence of raw starvation? Carceral hunger stems from a total lack of control and predictability, when someone cannot know whether their needs will be met from day to day and can do nothing about it. Carceral hunger results from working for starvation wages, which never provide close to enough money to buy healthy food. Carceral hunger is caused by industrial, cheaply made ultraprocessed foods (described below as *nutritus*), and food vendors who inflate prices for junk food because they know that their clients have no other choice but to buy from them. Carceral hunger removes people's control over their time, wages, access, sociability, and bodily autonomy. Carceral hunger is racist and racially targeted. It devalues and depresses. In sum, carceral hunger describes a combination of food insecurity, food oppression, and food apartheid, which impacts whole communities both within and far beyond prison walls.

"I was hungry," one formerly incarcerated person told the Maryland Food and Prison Abolition Project. "Some days I couldn't sleep. You'd be irritable. You're hungry, you know. It affected me pretty bad . . . I had to get a [prison] job so I could eat" (MFPAP 2021, 207). According to one survey, 94 percent of incarcerated people in the United States (in a survey size of 250) "did not have enough food to feel full" (Soble, Stroud, and Weinstein 2020, 9). A prisoner in Ohio told the Incarcerated Workers' Organizing Committee: "I'm hungry every day" (IWOC/Action Cooperative 2018, 13). A whopping 80 percent of people surveyed by the IWOC complained that they had been denied meals or given too little food in the past year (4). A respondent from a Kansas prison wrote: "The portions on the trays are very small and I'm always hungry even after I eat" (14). An incarcerated person in Missouri described how strict time limits at the canteen prevented them from eating a full meal. A person in California described prison officers "taking my food from me" (14).

A 2023 meta-analysis of prison ethnographies in Canada and the United States found that "those in custody complained about being constantly hungry" (Woods-Brown, Hunt, and Sweeting 2023, 11). "Constant feelings of hunger are, for many imprisoned individuals, the defining aspect of their time spent incarcerated" (MFPAP 2021, 30). "Carceral logics," write Ashanté Reese and Joshua Sbicca (2022, 8), "permeate the experience of eating in general for poor, Black, and Brown people. . . . The state regularly polices poverty instead of addressing how racial capitalism perpetuates the lack of access to basic needs like healthy food." Brian Williams and Carrie Freshour (2022, 38) name "the production of hunger" as one of the defining features of carcerality. Circuits of hunger and carcerality extend prison logics beyond prison walls—sometimes directly, as when prisons (still) use convict labor on agricultural plantations (Reese and Carr 2020). Welfare rules and regulations create another circuit of carcerality. Workfare requirements criminalize those who do not have a regular job. Welfare benefits exclude most of those who are not employed, making it impossible to survive (Dickinson 2019, 9). The most marginalized welfare recipients—Black women, formerly incarcerated people, and single mothers—are not free to live fully. Welfare rules create hunger by design (Tani 2016, 273, 280). Carceral hunger is produced, programmatically, every day, across the United States.

Plantation prisons starved their captives. Prison laborers worked fields where enslaved people had labored, under conditions of extreme violence (Reese and Carr 2020). State-owned plantation prisons kept their captives under conditions of forced labor, terror, and deprivation through most of the twentieth century and arguably still today (Oshinsky 1997, 223–248). As Williams and Freshour (2022, 43) point out, plantation prisons were filled with Black people caught up in the criminalization of their own survival. Common sources of food were cut off by strict trespassing and vagrancy laws. These prison farms made use of a well-established instrument for labor control on the plantation—namely, starvation. Cummins Farm, a plantation prison in Arkansas, became the site of a judicial reckoning over carceral starvation. The State of Arkansas purchased farmland in 1902 on a site that once belonged to the Cummins slave plantation and has been running a penal farm there ever since. In 2022, Cummins Farm received an Arkansas "Century Farm" prize in recognition of its long existence. State Corrections secretary Solomon Graves celebrated this "opportunity to spotlight the Department of Corrections' Agriculture operations. Many people aren't aware that the Division of Correction manages over 20,000 acres of farmland, saving taxpayers between $5 and $6 million a year through inmate consumption and providing inmates with farm-fresh food and valuable agriculture job skills" (Bass 2022). Today, prison laborers at Cummins Farm and other plantation prisons are still not paid any wages for their work (McDowell and Mason 2024). In 2001 six Cummins Farm correctional officers were found guilty of torturing inmates (Nelson 2002).

Beginning in 1965, Cummins Farm prisoners filed multiple legal cases against the Arkansas Department of Corrections for cruel and unusual punishment. The findings were (are) devastating. District Judge J. Smith Henley described Cummins Farm as "banishment from civilized society to a dark and evil world completely alien to the free world" (*Holt v. Sarver* 1970). Prisoners worked the fields all year, ten hours a day, six days a week, under surveillance of "trusty" convicts who had been armed with guns and charged by the prison wardens with maintaining discipline. No wages were paid; the only way to earn money was to sell blood to the prison-run blood bank (*Holt v. Sarver* 1969). If a prison laborer fell behind in the field and failed to meet his quota, the assistant warden whipped him on the buttocks with a five-foot-long leather strap (*Talley v. Stephens* 1965). Some prisoners were forced to stand for hours on an unstable "teeter board." Some prisoners were tortured with electric shocks from the wires of a battery-operated crank telephone (*Jackson v. Bishop* 1967).

FIGURE 11. "Superintendent M. L. Royster set the pace of the workday at the prison farm which could often stretch 12 hours or more," Virginia State Prison Farm, June 24, 1961. *Source*: "From the Archives" 2023.

When Judge Henley barred Arkansas from employing these forms of corporal punishment, prison authorities shifted to the use of isolation cells. As many as eleven men were kept in an eight-by-ten-foot cell with a drinking fountain and an uncovered toilet that flushed from the outside. Prisoners kept in twenty-four-hour isolation received squares of "grue," pushed under the grating of the cell door (*Holt v. Sarver* 1969). Grue consisted of "meat, potatoes, vegetables, eggs, oleo, syrup, and seasoning baked all together in a pan and served [twice a day] in four inch squares" (*Holt v. Sarver* 1969). At first Judge Henley did not object to grue, even as he ordered the prison to cease torturing prisoners and to improve intolerable living conditions (*Holt v. Sarver* 1969). Higher courts overruled Henley and determined that the grue diet was a form of forced starvation—a cruel and unusual punishment. An Appeals Court decided that the Eighth Amendment guarantees a right to "the basic necessities of human existence . . . including light, heat, ventilation, sanitation, clothing and a proper diet" (*Finney v. Arkansas Board of Corrections* 1974). Cummins Farm could no longer legally starve prisoners as punishment.

Arkansas was not an exceptional case in this regard. The Virginia Penal System, for most of the twentieth century, similarly held most of the state's incarcerated men on prison farms, alongside several field camps for road gangs and other worksites. Prisoners at State Farm Penitentiary in the 1960s worked corn fields with mules for twelve or more hours each day ("From the Archives" 2023). Those who fell behind or refused work at the penal farms were punished with rations of bread and water. One cold day in 1968, several men incarcerated at Virginia Bland Correctional Farm refused to work. All those who refused, and some who were believed to have incited the stoppage, were punished. Charles Lee Melton, whom the guards accused of agitation, was sent to solitary confinement and fed a diet of only bread and water "because the administration disapproved of his 'attitude'" (*Landman v. Royster* 1971). Melton was confined to solitary at two different work camps from December to March 1968 and from July to September 1970. He received four slices of bread and water two times a day, two days out of three. While in solitary confinement in 1970, Melton's weight fell from 160 to 140 pounds (*Landman v. Royster* 1971).

Also in 1968, inmates at the Virginia State Penitentiary struck from prison industry jobs (paying fifteen cents an hour), and in response prison officials imposed months of solitary confinement and a diet of bread and water (Hillyer 2019, 1–2). A District judge found in 1971 that Virginia practiced "disregard of constitutional guaranties of so grave a nature as to violate the most common notions of due process and humane treatment." Judge Robert Merhige enjoined the State of Virginia to end bread and water punishment. Merhige condemned bread and water on three grounds—scientific, psychological, and penological. In the decision he wrote:

> Bread and water provides a daily intake of only 700 calories, whereas sedentary men on the average need 2000 calories or more to maintain continued health. . . . The purpose and intended effect of such a diet is to discipline a recalcitrant [*sic*] by debilitating him physically. Without food, his strength and mental alertness begin to decline immediately. It is a telling reminder too that prison authorities enjoy complete control over all sources of pleasure, comfort, and basic needs. Moreover, the pains of hunger constitute a dull, prolonged sort of corporal punishment. That marked physical effects ensue is evident from the numerous instances of substantial weight loss during solitary confinement. (*Landman v. Royster* 1971)

Bread and water meals weakened both body and mind, and arbitrarily wielded control over the life and death of incarcerated people. "As a technique designed to break a man's spirit not just by denial of physical comforts but of necessities, to the end that his powers of resistance diminish," wrote Judge Merhige, "the bread and water diet is inconsistent with current minimum standards of respect for human dignity" (*Landman v. Royster* 1971). Virginia, like Arkansas, was enjoined to stop forcing people in prisons to work by starving them.

In 1978 the Supreme Court took up the Arkansas case—now named *Hutto v. Finney*, after T. Don Hutto, supervisor of the Arkansas Department of Corrections, and incarcerated petitioner Robert Finney. Justice John Paul Stevens upheld the Appeals Court decision on the grue diet. What constituted a "basic necessity" and a "proper diet"? Stevens, like Merhige, turned to the science of nutrition: the National Academy of Sciences had set a daily caloric minimum for active adult men at 2,700 calories and sedentary men at 2,000. Stevens determined that Cummins Farm grue provided fewer than 1,000 calories per day. In addition, Stevens noted that "practically all inmates [in punitive isolation] are losing weight" on the grue diet. "'Grue' might be tolerable for a few days and intolerably cruel for weeks or months" (*Hutto et al. v. Finney et al.* 1978). The cruel and unusual impact of a starvation diet, for Stevens, depended on its measure. Still today, *Hutto v. Finney* remains the Supreme Court standard for judging the constitutionality of prison diets: by duration of punishment and measures of weight loss, daily calories, and nutrients (Cuellar 2022, 500; McKeithen 2022).

Hutto, the Arkansas Department of Corrections director who gave his name to the definitive court case on programmatic starvation in prisons, began his penal career on a state prison farm in Texas. He was appointed superintendent in Arkansas in 1971 and became deputy director of the Virginia Department of Corrections in 1976. He went on to cofound of one of the first and largest private prison companies in the United States. The Corrections Corporation of America (CCA)—later rebranded CoreCivic after a journalist exposed terrible conditions in CCA prisons—gained contracts with state correctional agencies and with federal immigration authorities. Today some 8 percent of state and federal prisoners are incarcerated by private prison companies including CoreCivic (Bauer 2018a). The company named a facility in Texas in Hutto's honor. First built as a prison, it was converted to an immigrant family detention center that, as of 2018, held mothers who had been separated from their children (Baur 2018b). The Hutto Detention Center was the site of a 2015 mass hunger strike by detained immigrant women.

In Arkansas, Virginia, and elsewhere through the 1960s and 1970s, "litigation became a form of resistance to the deprivations of prison life" (Hillyer 2019, 2). This avenue of protest and redress did not remain open long. In the 1980s prison authorities, legislators, and courts imposed increasingly difficult restrictions on prisoners' access to court review (Hillyer 2019, 5). Grue did not disappear into the past. Rebranded as Nutraloaf, grue continues to circulate as punishment in prisons and jails across at least eighteen states (Soble, Stroud, and Weinstein 2020, 12). Nutraloaf describes a paste of food ingredients—leftovers, mechanically separated chicken, beans, oil, powdered milk, vegetables, chunks of bread, sometimes apples or raisins—blended together and baked into a loaf, cut into squares, and generally served cold in a paper bag. The loaf is used as a punitive measure and seems to be employed mostly for behavior control. A Vermont corrections commissioner described Nutraloaf as "a way of providing nutrition in a mechanism that dissuades inmates from throwing feces, urine, trays and silverware. . . . It tends to have the desired outcome. Once the offender relents, we stop with the nutraloaf" (Ring 2008).[1] The loaf is usually dense and highly caloric, and contains essential nutrients. Nutraloaf is designed to taste "blank, as though someone physically removed all hints of flavor" (Ruby 2010). George Eng, who was subjected to Nutraloaf while in solitary confinement in New York, recalled it as grainy and hard. "The reality is that you're starving," he told the *New York Times*, but I would taste it and just throw it away" (McKinley 2018).

Nutraloaf exploits the limitations of *Hutto v. Finney* (Cuellar 2022, 526). If a punitive diet contains sufficient calories and nutrients, if there is no measurable weight loss, it does not count under *Hutto* as cruel and unusual punishment. Samuel LeMaire filed a complaint against the Oregon State Prison in the early 1990s, after he was confined to the prison's Disciplinary Special Unit and fed Nutraloaf as punishment for aggression and misbehavior. Circuit Judge Stephen S. Trott denied LeMaire's complaint. Trott's decision repeatedly notes that LeMaire was a heavy man, who "unlike the Hutto inmates who lost weight, has actually gained some sixty pounds in confinement. . . . Nutraloaf provides an excess of nutritional requirements. . . . LeMaire is not being starved. He is being fed, and he is being fed adequately" (*LeMaire v. Maass* 1993).[2] Since LeMaire received essential nutrients and did not lose weight, the court reasoned, he was not made hungry.

The shift from grue to Nutraloaf indexes a shift in carceral modes from forced labor to behavior control, from starvation to *nutritus*. Prisons are required to maintain inmates' weight and provide a minimum number of calories and nutrients. But the courts do not care much how they do it. A judge in Wisconsin allowed Nutraloaf on the grounds that "food served in prison must be nutritious, but it does not have to be delicious or even particularly appetizing" (*Prude v. Clarke* 2011). Although raw starvation is widely condemned today as a form of torture, feeding people painfully impoverished foods has become normal and normative.

. . .

*Prison food makes people hungry.* Prison food is edible detritus, *nutritus*. "I feel . . . bloated," an incarcerated person told the Maryland Food and Prison Abolition Project. "I feel like I'm full and after a while I just felt like I haven't ate anything" (MFPAP 2021, 95). Zachary Starnes, who spent four years in the Oklahoma State Reformatory, told journalist Brianna Baily (2020) that while in prison he was wracked by hunger: "Those meals, when you eat them a couple hours later, you're starving . . . a few hours later, those carbs are going to turn into sugar and you're not going to be full anymore." Baily notes that Oklahoma spends an average of 75 cents to 85 cents per meal for people in its prisons. Kenneth, formerly incarcerated in West Maryland, echoed Starnes's experience:

"Basically, after you eat any one of your trays, at least two hours after that you'll be hungry again" (MFPAP 2021, 31).

Prison food, as reported by incarcerated people, is "spoiled" and "undercooked," "all processed, not enough protein/whole grains, fresh fruits/veggies, most calories from white sugar/white pasta/white bread. Bad shit!" (IWOC/Action Cooperative 2018, 13–15). About 80 percent of people surveyed by the Impact Justice organization labeled the food as "unappetizing in taste and smell." Respondents described prison food as a "nasty, mushy, goulash-type mixture" or "rubbery, chewy, slop on a plate." Most commonly, they described prison food as "unhealthy," "processed," "junk food," "non-nutritious," and "malnourishing" (Soble, Stroud, and Weinstein 2020, 23, 29).

Prison food is cheap. The California Department of Corrections spends about one dollar for every meal served—half of what it costs to serve one school lunch and about a third of the cost of a meal from Veterans Affairs (Soble, Stroud, and Weinstein 2020, 76). Most states spend fewer than three dollars per day for each inmate's food, and the state of Wisconsin reports that it spends a single dollar per day (Soble, Stroud, and Weinstein 2020, 87). Food expenses constitute 4 percent of Texas's overall prison budget (Soble, Stroud, and Weinstein 2020, 7). There is constant pressure to cut costs by substituting ultraprocessed foods that can be quickly reheated and that require no preparation. Nancy Porter, food service director of corrections for the State of North Carolina and president of the American Correctional Food Service Association, described the challenge of building a meal containing sufficient calories and nutrients. "We are using public money to fund correctional food service, and the public wants us to feed inmates for the least amount of money possible. . . . . We have to watch the markets and see what happens. When turkey was cheap, we started blending turkey with beef products, making a cost-effective mix. We are always looking for something else we can use to develop menus that can increase protein, which costs the most" (Stein 2000, 208). This is why prisons serve mechanically separated chicken (puréed carcasses with bone fragments removed) and soy filler, alongside mounds of bread, pasta, cookies, and cake (*Smego v. Aramark Food Servs. Corp* 2013).

Cake, it seems, is ubiquitous in prison. Darlene, formerly imprisoned in the Northeast, told Amy Smoyer: "They'd give you cake, cake. . . . You get it almost every morning for breakfast, a piece of cake with your oatmeal, a piece of cake with your freno, a piece of cake with your eggs, a piece of cake with everything. . . . I just can't understand the logic behind the menu" (Smoyer and Lopes 2017, 247). Miguel, who served time on the West Coast, told Impact Justice that "sometimes they serve a giant slab of coffee cake as the breakfast entree. It must be like a thousand calories" (Soble, Stroud, and Weinstein 2020, 30). At first I was taken aback when I learned about all the cake. I didn't know how to understand the omnipresence of a sweet dessert, which I associate with pleasure and indulgence. "Let them eat cake," said Marie Antoinette. Is cake not a symbol of wealth and luxury? How can incarcerated people suffer so deeply and so widely from hunger when they are eating cake all the time?

Serving cake with every meal seems coherent only from the perspective of what Will McKeithen (2022, 59) has called "carceral nutrition." It goes back to *Hutto v. Finney*. Prisons must supply sufficient calories and nutrients. Some states mandate that corrections departments supply precise levels of calories, protein, and vitamins; others require that meals be approved by a registered dietitian. The American Correctional Association (ACA) publishes nutritional guidelines for ACA-accredited prisons. Cake, like bread, pasta, biscuits, and so on, fills a specific function: to pack the most calories into the cheapest possible form. (Cheap, because US agricultural subsidies sink the cost of processed food ingredients like wheat, soy, and corn syrup.) Cake is a filler food. Theo told Impact Justice: "It's as if someone handed you two Snickers bars and called it dinner" (Soble, Stroud, and Weinstein 2020, 50). Conversely, fresh fruits are excluded from prison meals to prevent home brewing of fermented alcohol (Hardy 2016). Alongside caloric foods like cake, prisons serve sugar-sweetened vitamin powders to convey required nutrients. These powders have so much food coloring that they stain everything they touch, which, along with their strong chemical taste, does not encourage consumption (Soble, Stroud, and Weinstein 2020, 24; MFPAP 2021, 53).

Theo's callout to Snickers brings us back to sugar, craving, and control (see chapter 5). Cake is making imprisoned people in prison hungry and malnourished. Sugar, the food that promised to relieve hunger and maintain life, is doing the opposite. (Same for its cheaper substitute, high-fructose corn syrup.) In the carceral context sugar recalls plantation convict leasing, when starving men performed forced labor cutting cane (Reese 2021). Sugar and its isomorphs continue to cause harm to people in prison. One incarcerated person told the Maryland Project: "[Correctional staff] will allow you to have all this bread, and they give us a lot of noodles, which is starch. That just turns into sugar. So, I can see why the [people] here are increasing diabetics" (MFPAP 2021, 97).

Cake might also be understood as a tool for behavior control. Corrections officials told Impact Justice that they considered heavy foods with sugar and fat useful to "encourage lethargic and docile behavior" (Soble, Stroud, and Weinstein 2020, 105). The Maryland Project calls cake and other heavy processed foods a "'tranquilizing' biotechnology deployed to deplete energy and thus hinder the potential for resistance" (MFPAP 2021, 103). The timing of access to food in prison is also tightly controlled and often unpredictable. Many prisons limit meal time to fifteen or twenty minutes, including time spent waiting in line to be served. Out of fear or disgust, imprisoned people often eat so quickly that they do not taste their food (Soble, Stroud, and Weinstein 2020, 52; MFPAP 2021, 42–43). Officials can shift meal times to odd and unpredictable hours, serving lunch at 3 p.m., dinner at 4 p.m., and breakfast twelve hours later (as in an example in Maryland

[MFPAP 2021, 31]). One Michigan Department of Corrections officer put it starkly: "Food is a control mechanism" (Perkins 2018).

In 2020, Raymond B. Skelton filed a class action suit against the New Jersey Department of Corrections (NJDOC) for serving food so devoid of nutrition that it violated the Eighth Amendment rule against cruel and unusual punishment. Skelton's complaint put forth the obvious: high-calorie starches and sugary vitamin powders do not meet any standard of healthy nutrition. "NJDOC serves a diet to prisoners, including diabetics, of grits, overcooked carrots, white bread, greasy processed meats, cookies, cakes, white rice, sugary drinks, margarine, and constant potatoes—all foods to be avoided by diabetics. . . . Even if the menu as designed is what is actually served, it does not stand the most basic nutritional scrutiny." NJDOC, Skelton charged, had "removed virtually every fruit and vegetable critical to human health and replaced it with pasta, white flour, and starches" (*Skelton v. NJDOC* 2020). This case was dismissed on a technicality, but others challenging the *Hutto v. Finney* nutrition standards will certainly follow.

Corrections departments employ a common legal defense against such lawsuits: in thirty-eight states, corrections offices contract with registered dietitians to certify their menus' nutritional content. Dietitians have become arbiters of what meets the courts' standards at the lowest possible cost. Their conflict of interest is evident—they are employed by the agencies whose standards they are asked to review—which might explain why dietitians regularly approve meal plans so far askew from known nutritional standards. Prison dietitians are asked to certify whether the menus meet state and federal standards, not whether they provide adequate nutrition (Hardy 2016). A detainee at the Kane County Detention Center in Illinois, for instance, complained about insufficient and unsanitary food (served by the Aramark Corporation), which caused him gastritis and severe vomiting. His legal case failed because the Detention Center's menus were reviewed periodically by a certified dietitian (*Becerra v. Kramer* 2017). Arguably, at least some prison dietitians are legitimizing nutritional torture.

Even in a tightly controlled prison environment, some dietitians and corrections officials place responsibility on incarcerated individuals for their own health and weight. Women at the South Dakota Women's Penitentiary complained about unhealthy meals and weight gain. In response, the prison developed a "wellness program" offering a lower-fat meal option and classes to "educate inmates on the importance of proper weight, nutrition and daily exercise" (Stein 2000, 509). Similarly, an Oregon women's prison instituted a Healthy Food Access Project, which reduced the daily calories served to all women in the prison who had diabetes (Firth et al. 2015). Dietitians at the California Correctional Health Care Services provide individual nutrition counseling, where they "emphasize education to empower the patient to make good decisions regarding their diet and take control of their health issues" (Hardy 2016).

Prison commissaries also create an illusion of consumer choice and responsibility. Prison jobs pay starvation wages, often a few cents per hour (on average, $3.45 per day). Most of this labor goes toward keeping the prison itself going, especially the food service. People who refuse to work are often disciplined. Prison wages are necessary to purchase basic hygiene items and supplemental food from the commissary, which is often operated by a private company (Sawyer and Wagner 2023, 801). Food items for sale do offer materials for control and creativity in one's own eating, but they do not offer much nutrition and they are extremely expensive. Impact Justice found that three in five respondents could not afford commissary purchases; many went to great and dangerous lengths to get access to money for food consumption (Soble, Stroud, and Weinstein 2020, 11). Without these supplements, "[people] just wake up and go to bed hungry'" (MFPAP 2021, 30).

. . .

What kind of hunger is produced in prisons by cake and vitamin powders? This hunger does not generally come with weight loss or starvation.[3] It is a different kind of hunger, caused by impoverished products and insecurity. As described, carceral hunger removes people's control over their time, wages, sociability, and bodily autonomy. Not knowing, day to day, whether your needs will be met or when. Not having enough money to be sure that you will not be hungry that night. Carceral hunger helps to understand a kind of hunger that is produced by having irregular, unpredictable access to cheap filler foods. In other words, carceral hunger is a form of food insecurity.

The concept of household food insecurity emerged out of a period around the 1980s when poverty became increasingly criminalized. Instead of seeking structural solutions to racism, poverty, lack of housing, and hunger, policy makers focused on controlling individual pathologies and behaviors—from welfare fraud to petty crime (Hinton 2016, 105). Stories depicting fraudulent "welfare queens" spread through the media and political speeches (Kohler-Hausmann 2017, 187). States cracked down on a perceived wave of welfare fraud, even as they withdrew benefits for people not receiving regular wages. Poor people on welfare were arrested for crimes of survival, trying to make some extra money to top off insufficient welfare payments (Kohler-Hausmann 2017, 203). Punitive policies, carried out by welfare officials and the police, targeted urban Black and Brown mothers and youth.

The Reagan White House declared that hunger did not identifiably exist in the United States and that representations of hunger were fraudulent. "We've had considerable information that people go to soup kitchens because the food is free," Reagan counselor Edwin Meese commented in 1983, "and that that's easier than paying for it." Meese denied that there was any evidence of real hunger in the country (Hoffman 1983). Meanwhile the number of food banks and demand for charity food exploded in this period (Fisher 2017). Welfare was reconfigured as support for low-wage earners and denied to the unemployed; support was withdrawn from single parents. In the process, more and more people came to rely on food pantries (Dickinson 2019, 3; Kohler-Hausmann 2017, 123). Activists and scholars sought to measure real hunger in the United States, to debunk the narrative that welfare and food bank recipients were all cheaters.

Nutrition researcher Kathy Radimer profiled a kind of hunger that she named "household food insecurity." Radimer spoke with women who sought help from food banks in upstate New York in the late 1980s. Her interviewees were not starving like people pictured in UNICEF and Food for Africa campaigns in the media at that time. But they were suffering. A woman she named Gay told her, "I'm not *hungry* hungry." Gay said, "going *hungry* hungry is when there is absolutely nothing in the house. But also going hungry is when you have to eat the same thing all week long and you have no variation from it and you know sooner or later you're going to run out of that, too" (Radimer 1990, 206). Gay, and other women Radimer spoke with, described something other than starvation. "The gist was that the food eaten was enough that the women knew neither they nor their children were going to die of starvation, but also they knew it wasn't as much as they should eat, as they needed to be healthy, as they wanted to eat, as they were used to eating, etc." (Radimer 1990, 192).

Radimer drew from Gay's and others' experiences to coin a new definition of hunger as food insecurity. Food insecurity, she proposed, is "the inability to acquire or consume an adequate quality or sufficient quantity of food in socially acceptable ways, or the uncertainty that one will be able to do so" (Radimer, Olson, and Campbell 1990, 1546). Food insecurity included some elements of deprivation, such as skipping meals and cutting portion sizes. But it also meant eating in ways that made women feel degraded and unhealthy. It meant eating nutritus. And it meant constant worry about having enough. Food anxiety—worrying that the food you have will run out before you are able to buy more—is a defining characteristic of food insecurity (Radimer 1990, 211). So much more could and should be said about Radimer's extraordinary work on food insecurity and its impact on national and global food policies. For my purposes here, Radimer's concept of food insecurity names the distinction that I describe above, between raw starvation and nutritus. Never feeling truly full. Not knowing if your needs will be met, or when. Being surrounded by what Imani Perry has called "deprived productions": "The stuff that goes to the confined, and that is produced for the confined, is stamped with the imprimatur of 'less than'" (Perry 2018, 160).

Food insecurity points to historical connections between carceral hunger, anti-welfare, and tough-on-crime politics—from the War on Poverty to the War on Crime (Hinton 2016; Kohler-Hausmann 2015, 87). Erika Camplin (2016, 10) has remarked that the Prison Industrial Complex took off at the same time, around the 1970s through the 1980s, as production of impoverished, ultraprocessed food, and withdrawal of the welfare state. Poor people and people of color were captured in overlapping regimes of enclosure and insecurity. At the same time, people arrested for crimes of survival were demonized as not deserving: as one judge wrote about prison food, "to the extent that conditions are restrictive, indeed, even harsh, they are part of the penalty criminal defendants must pay for their offenses against society" (*Johnson v. Williams* 1991).

Food insecurity is a defining experience for people impacted by incarceration. Welfare reforms in the 1990s instituted a double punishment for crimes of poverty: people convicted of dealing drugs could be barred from receiving food stamps for life. West Virginia, in 2016, blocked more than twenty-one hundred people with drug felony convictions from receiving SNAP benefits (Born 2018). Formerly incarcerated people in the United States are food insecure at almost twice the national average rate (Testa and Jackson 2019). A 2013 survey found that 91 percent of people recently released from prison were food-insecure, and nearly four in ten had not eaten all day because they could not buy food (London and Jones 2021). When we note that 113 million people in the United States have an immediate family member who spent at least one night in prison or jail, the community effects of punitive food insecurity come to light (Sawyer and Wagner 2023). Criminalizing poverty and impoverishing criminals means that whole communities are made food-insecure.

. . .

"We have decided to put our fate in our own hands. . . . Power concedes nothing without demand" (Crawford and DuGuya 2011). Tens of thousands of imprisoned people have staged hunger strikes over the past few decades. Hunger strikes are perhaps the most powerful form of collective resistance to incarceration. If hunger is the defining experience of imprisonment, the hunger strike is "ultimate practice of freedom involving food in a prison" (Ugelvik 2011, 56). Hunger in prison is a tool for psychological and physical control, which the hunger strike turns back upon itself. Prison hunger strikers reverse and "interiorize the power of the state" (Feldman 1991, 237). Incarcerated people oppose carceral hunger with forms of collective counter-conduct that "utilize the tools of government against government" (Banu 2014, 65). Hunger strikers "turned their hunger on its head" (Camacho 2023, 181). They publicly reproduce—and thereby refuse—a relation that they already experience every day. Prison hunger strikers are always already hungry.

Over the past fifteen years, hunger strikes have taken place in prisons across the United States: California, Kentucky, Michigan, and Washington. Incarcerated people in Alabama staged at least twenty-seven hunger strike actions between 2013 and 2017 (Sheets 2017). The largest prison strike in 2013, at its peak, included more than thirty thousand people in California prisons, some of whom struck for a life-endangering sixty days (Reiter 2014, 581). In that same year, 106 of 164 prisoners at the Guantanamo Bay military prison camp went on hunger strike; many were forcibly fed (Associated Press 2013).

FIGURE 12. "We Support the Prisoners' Hunger Strike," poster at hunger strike solidarity protest at Corcoran State Prison, July 13, 2013. Source: Photo by Steve Rhodes (CC-BY-NC-ND 2.0).

When prisoners hold a hunger strike, they publicly name their own hunger. Hunger becomes a collective identity and a basis for collective action. Prison hunger strikes echo past and present coalitions of the hungry—from the 1930s Hunger Marches to the Poor People's Campaigns. Like these campaigns, prison hunger strikes are often led by self-consciously interracial coalitions who come together around shared experiences of hunger (Crawford and DuGuya 2011; Reiter 2014, 590). Hunger strikes fit in a long and enduring collective movement of the hungry. Hunger strikers refuse to ingest refuse, nutritus. They claim an existence beyond living like trash. Kentucky prisoners in 2010 struck against high commissary prices and prison food contaminated with worms, rocks, cardboard, and insects (the state prison system had contracted with Aramark to provide meals for $2.63 per day) (Reuter 2010). In 2014 twelve hundred immigrant detainees at the Northwest Detention Center in Tacoma, Washington, staged a hunger strike to demand "Better food—Better treatment—Better pay—Lower commissary—Fairness" (Montange 2017, 509; Hernandez 2017, 103–33). A thousand prisoners at Michigan's Kinross Facility refused to eat meals one day in 2016 to protest poor food service by private contractors Aramark and Trinity, ranging from maggot infestation to employee drug running and corruption (Egan 2016). Heriberto Sharky Garcia, incarcerated at California's Folsom State Prison, smuggled a video of himself refusing food during a 2018 hunger strike (Pilkington 2018). Garcia (2018) stated his refusal to take in nutritus: "Must I turn my cheek and be happy to plainly exist? Miserable, but existing. Eating, drinking, consuming crap—but existing. Fuck that! I will do what i can."

Hunger striking is one strategy that people in prison use to deal with being fed crap. Mutual aid is a less visible form of resistance to carceral hunger. People in prisons practice forms of community food security, sharing resources and cooking together. J., incarcerated in Maryland, explained that "we try to help people that doesn't have anything . . . we just take some of our stuff and we donate it to them to make sure they have their hygiene and food that they need" (MFPAP 2021, 40). Another person at the same prison told the Maryland Project how he and others make welcome bags for new arrivals: "'Are you okay? Are you hungry?' There are guys that are in prison that will look out for you" (MFPAP 2021, 40). If a group accumulates enough supplies from the commissary, they can make a "hook up," a collective meal composed of ingredients like ramen noodles, pouches of tuna, hot sauce, peanut butter, perhaps an onion or pepper from the kitchen. Anthony Ryan Hatch (2019, 79) pays respect to the "maker culture" displayed in such collective experiments in pleasure and survival, "in which their ability to produce palatable food out of refuse should amaze and astound."

Like hunger strikes demanding better food, mutual aid posits hunger as a collective affliction requiring collective action. Mutual aid points toward collective possibilities for sustaining life in prison. Hunger strikes, when carried out over a long time, challenge the very structure of carceral hunger and incarceration. Long hunger strikes reclaim control over the state's ability to generate slow death. James Crawford and Mutop DuGuya, imprisoned in solitary confinement in California's Pelican Bay Prison, announced the first in a long series of hunger strikes in 2011. Pelican Bay hunger strikers recognized that the function of solitary confinement was to kill them slowly: "Some of us have already suffered a slow, agonizing death in which the state has shown no compassion toward these dying prisoners. Rather than compassion they turn up their ruthlessness. No one wants to die. Yet under this current system of what amounts to intense torture, what choice do we have? If one is to die, it will be on our own terms" (Crawford and DuGuya 2011).

Hunger strikers make visible and reverse the state's power to kill them slowly. Long hunger strikes publicly reveal the ultimate goal of imprisonment, which is to eliminate people. Kelly Lyle Hernandez (2017, 1) has named this fact and its historical origins: "Mass incarceration is mass elimination. . . . Incarceration operates as a means of purging, removing, caging, containing, erasing, disappearing, and eliminating targeted populations from land, life, and society in the United States." Men incarcerated in Pelican Bay recognized that all those in solitary were targets for elimination. "This hunger strike will be carried on by all races, New Afrikans (Blacks), Mexicans (i.e. of all walks), whites and others who realize [that] we are silently being murdered by CDCR/CCPOAA Union as well as the US judicial system" (Crawford and DuGuya 2011). Crawford and DuGuya refused to exist in a "state of organized debility," whose end point is slow death (Kalina 2019, 60, 69). In this they poignantly echoed hunger marchers and strikers from an earlier era, like the Missouri cotton field strikers of 1941 who said that "it is better we die than live as we have been living" (UCAPAWA, CIO, and James 1942, 5).

Hunger strikers visibly make their own bodies, their biologies, political. As anthropologist Alan Feldman (1991, 230) wrote, hunger strikers engage with "the political manipulation of their bodies [as] a managed project." Feldman described how Irish Republican hunger strikers in the 1980s projected their own lives and bodies onto a broader historical trajectory. They imagined that their own biological time would align with historical, political time, and that their own physical decline would shift the course of Irish history (Feldman 1991, 233). The decline of one biological existence, the death of one hunger striker, could put into motion a new historical epoch. The hunger strike opens a field of historical possibility and transformation. Heriberto Sharky Garcia (2018) envisioned the creation of "the New Human, a new 'species' of being modeled on the needs and immediacies of the colonized masses." In the meantime, Garcia wrote, he was "struggling to be free, to stay sane. If not this, then what?"

8

## Ozempic

Who gets to escape captive markets and deprived productions? In 2023 a global craze erupted for the hunger-reducing drug Ozempic (semaglutide, also sold as Wegovy). "Vitamin O" invaded the news and social media. Some consumers publicly trumpeted their weight loss success; others hid their use of the drug to avoid social stigma and judgment. Though Ozempic had been approved to treat diabetes, many diabetics struggled to fill their prescriptions as off-label users ate up the available supply (FDA 2023). Many eager weight-loss consumers turned to illicit internet purchases of semaglutide compounds. Users without insurance coverage paid $900 for a month's supply of Ozempic, or $1,350 monthly for the higher dose of semaglutide in Wegovy (Synott 2023).

As one might expect, access and usage followed class divides. Rich neighborhoods were consuming Ozempic at twice the rate of low-income areas that were more impacted by metabolic diseases (Goldstein 2023). Sales grew so high that by late summer 2023, the market value of Danish pharmaceutical company Novo Nordisk, producer of Ozempic and Wegovy, was larger than the rest of Denmark's entire national economy (Nelson 2023). Ozempic promises consumers a pharmaceutical escape from hunger. This chapter considers the science of hunger suppression, desire, longing, and capitalism. I trace how Ozempic could come to be understood by one of Novo Nordisk's own research affiliates as a project of cultural Marxist pharmacology. Food companies—in collusion with federal agriculture and trade policies, starvation wages and punitive welfare benefits—are making many people feel terribly hungry. As Julie Guthman (2015) has pointed out, human bodies are a prime target of (food) industrial growth. When "the body becomes an accumulation strategy," bodies are pressed to absorb surplus production and provide outlets for capital investment. Agro-industrial companies grow by expanding their market. Not just in competition with other producers, but also by expanding bodies' capacity to consume (Guthman 2015, 2527). Palatability, marketing, and synthetic ingredients all combine to "make ultra-processed products liable to harm endogenous satiety mechanisms and so promote energy overconsumption"—in other words, to make eaters hungry for more (Moodie et al. 2013, 671).

Food companies saturate the world with *nutritus*. Corporate strategy, industrial food design, and global deregulation combine to perpetuate hunger. Food-processing corporations have been designing food to get consumers to eat more since at least the 1950s (recall our discussion of the sugar industry in chapter 5). Starting in the 1970s, trade liberalization and deregulation opened low- and middle-income countries to processed food marketers. Phillip Baker and colleagues (2020, 2–5) have observed that as a country's income rises, ultraprocessed foods shift from a consumer good for the wealthy to a product for the poor. The ultimate frontiers of market expansion, globally, are the economically oppressed. At the same time, as market expansion for processed foods slows in the global North, another outlet for capital investment is growing exponentially: the pharmaceutical market for hunger suppressants (Guthman 2015, 2531).

What work is semaglutide doing? What is the nature of the hunger that it suppresses? "My relationship with hunger, and therefore with eating, is transformed," wrote *Washington Post* commentator Ruth Marcus in 2023 about her experience on Ozempic. "I leave food on my plate, untouched and unlamented, and do not look at the food on yours with the same longing: 'Are you gonna eat those fries?'" For another consumer the drug "shut off the intrusive constant thoughts about food" (Belluz 2023). A user named MandyM wrote in 2019 on *WebMD*: "I've lost [weight] and all interest in food or alcohol. Not caring or even thinking about food or your next meal and not worrying about how you will resist food is incredibly freeing." ("User Reviews for Ozempic" 2023). "No wonder that skinny people think heavy people have no willpower," another Ozempic consumer wrote. "Their brains actually do tell them to stop eating. I had no idea" (Tolentino 2023). A user named High Praise explained on *WebMD* that after starting Ozempic, "I'm not always starving, just feel like a normal person" ("User Reviews for Ozempic" 2023).

A user named Chris posted on *WebMD*: "Ozempic has given me the gift of low appetite" ("User Reviews for Ozempic" 2023). Chris received their lack of hunger as a gift. To no longer want, to no longer desire to consume, is for them a thing of value. Wanting, for Chris and for many other consumers posting on *WebMD*, became something so aversive that they are willing to endure great expense and physical challenges (and to consume a different kind of substance, a drug) in order to stop. Ozempic provides these users relief from thinking, longing, caring, wanting, resisting. In that opening of negative space, in that area of feeling and being that semaglutide suppresses in its users, I believe that new understandings of hunger may become clearer. This kind of hunger is a combination of longing, wanting, and thinking—a constant, fixed, involuntary attention. Hunger here implies a heightened sensitivity to changes in the nature-culture in and around us: shifts in the climate and built environment, economy, sociability, culture, and affect. Hunger responds to the world entering the body (in the form of food) and orients the body toward the world (by directing thoughts and desires). In an extractive, violent, and stochastically changing world, hunger expresses a gut feeling that things are not right.

Ozempic may release some of the burdens of hunger and longing in a violent, consumerist, and antifat world. In sociologist Scott Vrecko's (2010b, 555) words, obesity drugs offer a "means of protecting individuals from a hostile modern environment" of "hyperconsumption." The drug acts within a social and physiological milieu shaped by global market forces, social norms, expert and lay knowledges, and individual practices. Ozempic reshapes relations of longing. It leaves consumers like Marcus indifferent to the full plate of fries laying before her. For some users semaglutide makes moving through a hyperconsumptive world more bearable. And yet there is a cost to this relief. Hundreds of Ozempic reviewers on *Drugs .com* and *WebMD* recorded experiences of nausea, bloating, vomiting, diarrhea, headaches, and fatigue. Users threw up at work and while driving and had uncontrollable bowel movements that lasted all night. "If you do eat," wrote Stringa007, "you have to force yourself to eat because of the pain, dizzy spells (especially going from sitting to standing), stomach gurgles almost back to back all day, and did I mention how bad the diarrhea is? It's like giving yourself a virus that won't go away" ("User Reviews for Ozempic" 2023). For many, the side effects diminished after a few weeks of use. Some continued to feel mild nausea punctuated by "sulfuric burps." Others found themselves incapable of functioning. "I have been unable to basically leave my house for days," wrote a user named Lola ("User Reviews for Ozempic" 2023). Lola, like many users, tried to power through extreme side effects in the hope that after a few weeks or months they would subside. Those who chose to stop the drug found that its effects lasted for days or weeks.

Some users wrote that they nearly stopped eating altogether. Not only did they lose interest in food, they no longer felt any desire to eat at all. MandyM wrote: "I actually started worrying about how little I wanted to eat." GR posted: "As I began week 4, my appetite is now so reduced that I barely eat anything at all. I have to force myself to eat a meal, and even then I feel sick after a few bites." SRose wrote: "I have actually lost more weight that I intended to and can't seem to make myself eat to pick my weight back up. . . . For anyone wanting to use it for weight loss it's a hell of a way to lose it as you definitely won't have an appetite but you also find yourself feeling weak because you haven't ate anything substantial" ("User Reviews for Ozempic" 2023). Mimi wrote: "I don't have ANY appetite at all and cannot face food. . . . Yes, the 'food noise' has gone, and I no longer overeat or binge, but I feel like everything is suppressed" ("Ozempic User Reviews" 2023). User Susanne Brown told the *Global News* that "taking Ozempic is akin to 'doctor-approved anorexia.' . . . When she first started on Ozempic, it led to dangerous eating habits, where she would 'eat two pieces of cauliflower and be full.' If a patient so desires, they could stop eating entirely by taking more and more of the drug" (Mannie 2023). Some Ozempic users were literally starving. British physicians reported that they treated a woman who had bought semaglutide online, without a prescription, for symptoms of starvation (Sivaraman and Kozhippally 2020).

Reading their posts, I get the impression that these users have internalized, turned outside-in, the violence of the external world, which Ozempic had promised to alleviate. Instead of feeling compelled to respond to and to resist the cues and demands of food out in the world, these users have turned inward. They have ceased to nourish themselves. They are nauseous, bloated, and unable to ingest. They are starving themselves. These semaglutide consumers are starving themselves so that the food market cannot control them and make them always feel starving. Unlike hunger strikers and hunger marchers, who find collective identity and meaning in their actions, drug takers are profoundly alone, except perhaps on forums like *WebMD*. I sympathize. Perhaps nausea and aversion are the most consistent, logical, and preservative responses to this world.

. . .

Hunger is a scientific goldmine for two reasons. First, hunger is a key to solving what has come to be known as a crisis of obesity. Experts by the 1970s routinely characterized obesity as an epidemic (Nordsiek 1964).[1] This language of crisis is fueled by antifat discourse and by claims that "excess weight" causes metabolic, cardiovascular, and respiratory diseases. As many scholars have pointed out, such claims involve a reductive flattening of personal, biological, and cultural difference and complexity (Yates-Doerr 2015a and 2015b; McCullogh and Hardin 2013, 7). The obesity crisis nevertheless mobilizes scientists, public health experts, mass media, and public concern (Guthman 2015, 2531). More than a personal diagnosis, obesity is framed as a collective menace: "Obesity is no longer only the problem of individuals but of whole populations and nations" (Ošancova and Hejda 1975, 57; see Biltekoff 2013, 121). The specter of ballooning health-care costs places responsibility on overweight people for threatening the future fiscal health of states and communities (Dickinson 2019, 120). As the driver of a potentially costly epidemic, excess hunger becomes everybody's business.

Second, hunger suppression is a financial windfall in a world ruled by the politics of thinness. Body shaping has become a collective project of citizenship, social value, labor productivity, and personal attractiveness. It requires hard work to maintain a body that is capable of being productive in the labor force and that is politically, socially, and personally normative (Dickinson 2019, 122).[2] People who deviate from a thin, white, hetero, American norm are labeled as "undesirable populations" and are disciplined to "fix" and control their bodies (Choudhury 2022, 18; Strings 2019; Williams-Forson 2022, 89–140; Harrison 2021). Hunger-suppressing drugs promise to make people desire less and consume less, and therefore become candidates to be employed and desired (Cottom 2023). An effective drug that reduces hunger can earn billions, as Novo Nordisk has experienced with Ozempic.

Weight loss regimens are designed on the premise that the overweight subject must be motivated to become thin and healthy. The results are often violent and humiliating, when patients are blamed for their own lack of motivation to lose weight (Choudhury 2022, 16). The American Academy of Pediatricians recommends "motivational interviewing" as a first step in the treatment of childhood obesity (the final step being a prescription for diabetic or anticraving medication). In the motivational interview the pediatrician "identifies and reinforces a patient's [or parent's] own motivation for change" and "guides families to identify a behavior to change" (Hampl et al. 2023, 47). Readers of chapter 2 in this book will recognize the figure of motivation and all that it implies. Motivation, as a psychological construct, relies on a structure of pleasure and pain, punishment and reward. As we know, the original motivation experiments starved animal subjects and lured them to work with small tidbits of food. Motivation as a frame comes out of a behavioral model of human psychology that is based on deprivation.

I should not have been surprised when I discovered that the inventor of behavioral weight control was a psychologist who starved his subjects to get them to work. But I was! In 1962, Charles Ferster published a study on "The Control of Eating." Ferster was a protégé of B. F. Skinner, in whose lab Ferster trained pigeons to peck incessantly at a small disc or lever to get bits of food. Ferster learned to use rewards and punishments as reinforcers to make his subjects behave in specific ways. Most important, he kept his subjects—whether pigeons, chimps, or children—in a constant state of hunger and food deprivation; then he tracked their "performance" on lever pressing or puzzle solving (Ferster, Nurnberger, and Levitt 1996, 403). In Alexandra Rutherford's (2009, 7, 43–47) words, Ferster used hunger as a "technology of behavior."

Ferster spent two years early in his career at the Yerkes Primate Lab, where he deprived chimpanzees of food so that they would do experimental work. He maintained his chimps at 80 percent of their free-feeding weight; in other words, he subjected the animals to nearly the same regimen as the one that the Minnesota Starvation Experiment used to study the effects of extreme food deprivation in people. The chimps were made to respond to rewards (small bits of food) or punishments (in the form of time-outs) (Ferster 1958). Senior researchers at the Yerkes Laboratory were appalled by Ferster's handling of his primate subjects. One colleague recalled that "there were lots of comments made at weekly staff meetings about the psychology of half-starved animals" (Dewsbury 2003, 257). Yerkes lab director Henry Nissen complained that "you try to starve them into submission and some animals would starve themselves to death. They'd just quit working. It was like they'd lose appetite" (quoted in Dewsbury 2003, 258). Nissen believed that starvation contributed to the deaths of two chimpanzees at the lab (Dewsbury

2003, 258). Skinner later complained that "tender-hearted colleagues frustrated [Ferster's] efforts to reduce chimpanzees to a satisfactory state of deprivation" (Skinner 1981, 261).

In 1957, Ferster moved to the Indiana University Medical Center. There he applied the same experimental setup to a group of autistic children in the university hospital. Instead of imposing a starvation diet on the children, he forbade them to eat between meals. Then he exposed them to learning tasks that could earn them food or candy (Ferster and DeMyer 1962, 93–95). At Indiana University he also began to study a method of behavioral self-control for weight loss. He recruited twelve nurses from the hospital and led the women through an experimental dieting protocol based on stimulus and response, reward and punishment (Rutherford 2009, 106). Ferster seemingly did not believe in hunger as such. In his view, consistent with behavioral psychology, subjective feelings of hunger were both unmeasurable and irrelevant. "Hunger pangs, which are ordinarily taken as symptoms of hunger (from which the effect of food deprivation is inferred), are more closely related to the conditioned stimuli accompanying past reinforcements of eating than to the level of food deprivation" (Ferster, Nurnberger, and Levitt 1996, 403). In other words, hunger feelings were a result of psychological training rather than physiological need.

Ferster sought to retrain his twelve subjects' hunger feelings and eating patterns. He set out to make eating—especially pleasurable eating—feel like punishment. By pairing "pies, cakes, cokes, doughnuts, or candy" with a "known aversive event," these foods "may become conditioned aversive stimuli" (Ferster, Nurnberger, and Levitt 1996, 402). If a psychological link could be created between food and punishment, pain or displeasure, food itself would become undesirable. In practice, this meant focusing the women's attention on the "ultimate aversive consequences" of their own eating. Ferster and his colleagues trained the women to pause in the middle of a meal and verbally rehearse how eating would bring them pain, misfortune, shame, or exclusion. The researchers "probed" the women to discover "instances where overweight has affected daily life functioning, . . . pleasure, occupation, etc." (Ferster n.d. [ca. 1958]). Each woman had her own repertoire of ultimate aversive consequences (UACs).

According to archival notes on a group training session, Ferster's colleague Gene Levitt placed a piece of pie in front of each of the women in turn and asked them to recite their UACs. Miss H- said that her "Spencer corset created an unsightly roll of fat on her body which she felt was noticeable." Mrs. M- "noted that her husband is losing weight rapidly and that she would 'die of mortification' if she stopped losing weight and he caught up with her." Levitt went so far as to grade the subjects' recitations; Mrs. M- got "no better than B or perhaps B-" (Ferster n.d. [ca. 1958]). No one ate the pie, of course. Recitations of UACs were supposed to happen in the middle of meals and every time the women encountered a dessert, soda, or piece of candy. Ferster predicted that with repeated aversion training, the subjects' "feelings of hunger should disappear except just before meal-time" (Ferster, Nurnberger, Levitt 1996 [1962], 405).

Needless to say, that hasn't worked out. Ferster is truly one of the most disagreeable scientists I have encountered in the historical record. Somehow, however, behavioral self-control remains the standard first line of treatment for people judged as overweight. As soon as news emerged about Ferster's weight loss study, he began to receive letters from women pleading for his help. Mrs. G. R. Zeller (1961) wrote from California: "Recently I read an article . . . [stating] that you and your colleagues had some measure of success, that is in creating the idea of aversion to food. . . . I am at least [many pounds] overweight. It is impairing my health—my mental outlook and certainly my disposition. . . . Is there anything you can suggest to do?" Mrs. S. J. Smith (1961) wrote from Seattle on behalf of her "Fatties Club," "the members of the club and I haven't been very successful in taking pounds off or keeping off what we do remove. We were wondering if you could possibly have any other helpful ideas we could use." Ferster's self-control method found a broad popular audience in a 1972 mass-market self-help book, *Slim Chance in a Fat World* (Rutherford 2009, 108). Slim chance, indeed.

By the time that Ferster published his behavioral self-control method, the American marketplace was already saturated with weight-loss drugs. A parade of amphetamines and their derivatives—Benzedrine, phenmetrazine, phentermine, fenfluramine, ephedrine—filled pharmacies and medicine cabinets, one after the other. By the late 1960s, some 2 percent to 3 percent of the American population, or four million to five million people, were using amphetamines for weight loss (Rasmussen 2009, 238). As one weight-loss medication was banned because of toxicity, psychosis, or addiction, another took its place. Ozempic is the latest in a series of hunger-suppressant drugs, each derived from a new scientific understanding of hunger and how to stop it.

. . .

Ozempic exists because scientific research on hunger and appetite has become increasingly precise and granular. Researchers manipulate mice genes to knock out specific neuroreceptors or hormones and observe what changes result in the genetically modified mouse's eating preferences and behaviors. Real-time MRI scans track which brain regions light up when human subjects look at images of food, with or without injections of specific peptides or hormones. Nutrition labs house subjects for a day or a week, expose them to precisely calibrated kinds of food, survey their subjective hunger feelings, and track the peptides and hormones circulating in their blood. Scientists have isolated a dozen hormones and neuropeptides that influence hunger, appetite, and fullness: ghrelin, insulin, and leptin hormones for long-term energy regulation; Neuropeptide Y and CART (cocaine and amphetamine-regulated transcript) neuropeptides that stimulate hunger and fullness, respectively; and gastrointestinal hormones and peptides that sense the contents of the gut, control gastric emptying, and promote fullness. Semaglutide amplifies the work of one of those gut peptides, GLP-1.

Pharmaceutical appetite suppressants track closely with scientific developments in hunger research. Amphetamines made users more sensitive to the switches that turned appetite on and off. Addiction theories of hunger led to anticraving medications, which were designed to stop consumers from feeling pleasure. Ozempic and comparable drugs replicate the action of peripheral gut peptides. Hopes for a hunger on/off switch were revived with the discovery of the hormone leptin in 1995 (Friedman 2012). Leptin administered directly to the brain reduced food intake, and leptin deficiency caused increased eating. Five years later, the hormone ghrelin was found to produce the opposite effect (Kojima et al. 1999; Gil-Campos et al. 2006, 201). Newspapers and magazines breathlessly reproduced images of rats with and without leptin, one stick thin and the other obese. However, initial hopes quickly tapered. These hormones fail to turn off hunger effectively under conditions of increasing consumption (Schwartz et al. 2000, 662). In addition, proof that human bodies were unable to regulate themselves appeared evident everywhere. Changes in consumer patterns and body sizes across the twentieth century suggested that bodies were not set up to defend any fixed set point, whether of sugar, fat, or body weight.

The first wave of anti–food craving drugs, which came out in the 2000s, targeted the brain's pleasure receptors. As food addicts were defined as dangerously sensitive to sweetness, pleasure, and palatability, anti-craving drugs were designed to reduce pleasure. Certain neuropeptides could turn up or down pleasurable sensations. Neuroscientists identified specific neural circuits for hedonic sensation, "overlapping brain systems . . . [that] mediate drug addiction and feeding" (Dagher 2009, 30–32). Cannabinoid and opioid receptors in the brain respond to both food deprivation and intensely pleasurable tastes (Di Marzo, Ligresti, and Cristino 2009, 3). The brains of animals exposed to a high-fat, high-sugar diet had dysfunctional dopamine pleasure receptors (Hopkins and Blundell 2017, 75). Opioid and cannabinoid antagonists were found to block perceptions of pleasure. When food-deprived subjects took the anti-craving drug naltrexone, which blocks opioid receptors, sugar tasted less delicious than it had previously (Wassum et al. 2009).

Anti-craving drugs allowed people to view themselves, and act on themselves, as diseased and in need of medication (Vrecko 2010a, 43). If a drug can "cure" hunger, the corollary must be that hunger is a biological disease. "It is long past time to stop shaming people with disorders of appetite in a futile attempt to tame our own fears of loss of control," argued columnist Maia Szalavitz (2023). Addiction appears as a biological problem rather than a problem of self-control or willpower. If a drug can turn off the desire to eat quickly and fully, perhaps that desire was never under conscious control to begin with (Sanabria 2015b). Still today, most research on hunger targets the brain, manipulating pleasure receptors in the central nervous system. But it turns out that tinkering with the brain's cannabinoid, opioid, and dopamine receptors causes unwanted and sometimes severe psychiatric side effects (Vrecko 2010b, 567). Pharmacological innovation in that area has slowed as regulators forced these drugs off the market. Some scientists argued that the focus on blocking pleasure in the brain misses out on a whole realm of bodily experience.

. . .

"There is a tendency to . . . [go] straight to the brain," complained Gerard Smith in 1982. When scientists wanted to understand what made animals and people hungry, they looked to identify the neural mechanisms. "But this move is too neat," Smith cautioned. Looking for hunger and motivation in the brain "[reduced] psychology to neuropsychology." The brain alone could not reveal the full dynamic of what it meant to be hungry. "To go straight to the brain is to study the brain. But . . . motivation is not a thing in the brain but a relationship that involves the brain" (Smith 1982, 134).

In the 1970s, Smith was one of a group of researchers at Weill Cornell Medical Center who began to study appetite and eating from the opposite end of the hungry brain. They focused on the gut and asked what factors make animals stop eating. First, they sham-fed rats who had not eaten all night: food entered the rats' mouths and exited through a tube before it reached their stomachs. Those rats, whose food never touched their gut, ate and ate for hours on end, almost indefinitely (Young et al. 1974). It seemed, then, that something happened in the gut, or in the relationship between the gut and the brain, to make animals stop eating. Evidence of some factor circulating outside of the brain already existed: in the 1950s G. R. Hervey connected the blood flow of two rats, one of which had a lesioned hypothalamus that made it overeat. The second mouse, sharing the overeater's blood, stopped eating and starved (Hervey 1959). The Weill Cornell group set out to find what it was that traveled between those parabiont rats.

Thanks to the work of gut endocrinologists, the Weill Cornell researchers knew that the stomach and intestines produced their own hormones (Bloom and Polak 1978). They found that cholecystokinin (CCK), a hormone secreted when food enters the small intestine, made rats eat less. The more CCK they injected into a rat's intestine, the less it ate (Gibbs, Young, and Smith 1973, 488). When either the gut hormone or food entered their stomachs, rats performed the same "satiety sequence" of behaviors that rats usually do when they are ready to stop eating (Gibbs and Smith 1982). CCK apparently made rats feel full. Over the following decades, endocrinologists identified more than thirty gut peptides involved in appetite, leading some to call the gut the "largest endocrine organ in the body" (De Silva and Bloom 2012, 12). The gut—the stomach, intestines, and fat tissues—all seem to independently experience hunger and fullness.[3]

One gut hormone, ghrelin, increases stomach movement and makes one hungry. The other gut peptides act to delay the stomach from emptying, release digestive enzymes, stimulate glucose production in the liver, and reduce hunger. Two of the most important gut peptides, PYY and GLP-1, act through the vagus nerve to the hypothalamus (De Silva and Bloom 2012, 12). Endocrine cells in the gut have receptors that taste food, "the gut equivalent of the taste buds on the tongue that sample various components of ingested food" (Barrett 2014, 34–37). The gut releases hormones in response to specific tastes. An umami tastant alone in the gut (without any food attached) can make people feel less hungry (Cummings 2015, 717). In sum, *hunger is a gut feeling*. What does it mean to say that a gut, rather than a person, is tasting and reacting to food?

*Gut feeling* is a way of thinking about hunger that attends to sites outside of the brain, peripheral sites of sensing, knowing, and responding. Gut feelings also refer to feelings that escape conscious awareness and control. In the gut model of hunger, intestinal cells and fat cells are agents, which themselves can feel hungry or full. Eaters may not even be aware of what their guts and tissues are sensing, knowing, and feeling (Sanabria 2015b, 135). This model of hunger considers feelings that do not correspond to hedonic pleasure but rather to an unconscious sense of compulsion, of wanting something. Or the opposite of compulsion, a sense of satiety, not wanting. Emilia Sanabria (2015a) has noted that this becomes a problem—when a body can no longer be trusted to know its own limits and needs—in a context of a broken food system, in which a focus on individual eaters obscures broader cultural and corporate forces.

A new theory of affect emerged to describe this situation, when hunger and desire feel compulsive, unconscious, biological. Psychologist Kent Berridge suggested that hunger and desire should be analyzed as a collection of separate components. Berridge distinguished between *liking* something, meaning taking pleasure from it, and *wanting* something, which was more like a craving or a longing. Berridge (1996, 1) argued that these were two entirely separate processes, with distinct neural substrates. "Liking" implies a drive toward pleasure (hedonism). Regardless of bodily needs, whether one has already eaten, the pure pleasure of food can bring one back for more. "Wanting" (sometimes referred to as "implicit wanting") suggests an unconscious draw to consume something that may or may not fulfill a need or even produce pleasure. One can even want something and not like it (Berridge 2004, 195). Wanting compels one to focus attention and longing on a particular substance. Wanting is a gut feeling.

Researchers performed all sorts of experiments to separate out wanting from liking. They placed tastants (like sweetness without sugar) on rats' tongues to measure liking. They asked people how much they liked different kinds of food, then tested how hard the same subjects were willing to work to acquire those foods (which was meant to measure wanting). People who scored high on a scale of binge eating seemed to have an unusually high implicit wanting for high-fat sweet foods, even when they said that they didn't like those foods any more than others. Those people "wanted" sweet and fatty foods more then they "liked" them (Blundell and Finlayson 2011, 1217). Researchers gave other human test subjects the same food to eat repeatedly. The more the subjects ate, the less they liked it (Berridge and Robinson 2003, 509; Finlayson, King, and Blundell 2007, 989). But how much of it they ate did not seem to change how much they wanted it. Implicit wanting, researchers concluded, must be independent of homeostasis. One could keep wanting something even if one didn't *need* it, or even *like* it (Finlayson, King, and Blundell 2008, 126). The opposite of wanting, satiety (not wanting), also appears to function mostly at an unconscious level. Fullness just happens, without thought or will.

Well before Ozempic, medical interventions in the gut made patients stop wanting food. Before there were gut peptide drugs, there was bariatric surgery. In the early 1950s surgeons in Sweden and the United States noticed that patients who received bowel restriction surgery, for treatment of various diseases, tended to lose a significant amount of weight. Thus began decades of restrictive surgeries, which cut up and bypassed parts of the stomach and intestine, to get patients to lose weight. By 1970 more than thirty thousand intestinal bypass operations had been performed, although it soon became clear that the side effects of intestinal surgery were too dangerous to tolerate. The gastric bypass (diverting part of the stomach and intestine) was first practiced in 1967 and quickly became the most prevalent weight loss surgery (Celio and Pories 2016, 656–664). In the year 2018, some 250,000 bariatric surgeries took place in the United States (Lynch, Kozak, and Zalesin 2022, 1).

Following bariatric surgery, many patients no longer felt hungry. They stopped wanting food. Researchers found that bariatric surgery altered gut peptide activity (Imamura et al. 1984). It wasn't just that a smaller stomach stopped them from absorbing as much food. They no longer had a desire to eat. Mentally, they knew that they needed food, but affectively they did not feel the need (Lynch, Kozak, and Zalesin 2022, 4).[4] Even more powerfully, postsurgery patients felt satiated, overfull, every time they ate. Bariatric patients interviewed by Amanda Lynch postsurgery complained that they experienced "painful feelings or 'being sick' from taking 'one last bite'" (Lynch, Kozak, and Zalesin 2022, 5). Patients after surgery said to Lynch and her colleagues, "I don't think my body knew what hunger was" before surgery, and "I never really understood full" (Lynch, Kozak, and Zalesin 2022, 6). "Eleanor," who underwent a sleeve gastrectomy, told Lynch, "I either didn't recognize the signals before or they are much more acute now. The stomach I have now, I think it has that brain connection" (Lynch, Kozak, and Zalesin 2022, 6). Patients postsurgery said that they no longer felt guilt or regret when they were full, and that their hunger feelings were less intense and emotional (Lynch, Kozak, and Zalesin 2022, 7).

Drug researchers looked to bariatric surgery for clues to how to suppress hunger. Some asked, "Could the altered gut hormones following gastric bypass be sending 'fullness' signals resulting in sustained weight loss?" (Wren and Bloom 2007, 2125). In rat models, directly injecting gut hormones produced similar effects as bariatric surgery. If a drug could manage to deliver a combination of gut hormones that "mimic natural satiety mechanisms," it could replace surgery with the same effects (Wren and Bloom 2007, 2126). Ozempic answered that call. Enter the Gila monster. Gila monsters are the largest lizards in the United States and one of a few species of venomous lizard. They live in desert arroyos and semiarid rocky regions of the Southwest United States and northern Mexico. According to the National Zoo, Gilas have been known to eat only three or four large meals (of birds, eggs, small mammals, and amphibians) in an entire year. They carry stores of fat, move slowly, and have very low metabolism (Smithsonian National Zoo n.d.). Gila monster saliva contains the hormone exendin-4, a particularly powerful peptide that resembles human GLP-1, but is stronger and longer lasting.

A synthetic form of the Gila hormone, Exenatide, was the first GLP-1 drug to be approved for diabetics. Exenatide reduced blood sugar, slowed the stomach from emptying, and reduced hunger (University of North Carolina 2007). But early GLP-1 drugs metabolized quickly and required daily injections. Novo Nordisk figured out how to prolong the effect for a week at a time, and Ozempic was released in 2017. "Injecting ourselves with this lizard juice," worried a user named Sane on *Drugs.com*, "can't be good for us" ("User Reviews for Ozempic" 2023). Gila monster saliva (or rather, a synthetic version of it) is now teaching human bodies, especially the gut, how to stop feeling hungry all the time.

. . .

Physiological psychologist John Blundell, working with Novo Nordisk, tested semaglutide on human subjects. He found that semaglutide made users want less. They lost appetite, felt fewer food cravings, and avoided fatty, energy-dense foods (Blundell et al. 2017, 1249). Blundell and his colleagues at the University of Leeds specialized in research on wanting and satiety (not-wanting). They applied Berridge's schema of liking versus wanting experimentally and developed tools to measure the strength of implicit (unconscious) wanting (Finlayson, King, and Blundell 2007, 2008). At some point in the 2000s, Blundell and members of his research group seem to have become convinced that something extreme and dramatic had to be done about overeating. This is where it becomes really interesting for someone like me, who studies science, technology, and society. Blundell came to view this specific form of hunger, wanting and longing, as a product of late-capitalist overproduction. Furthermore, a solution, at least in Blundell's view, is to defend oneself from capitalism with pharmaceuticals. Blundell's work on Ozempic is a form of cultural Marxist pharmacology.

The fundamental problem, as Blundell and his colleagues see it, is capitalism. Desire and longing, in late-capitalist society, are sick. Overconsumption is everywhere, powered by the economic drive to expand markets. People are enticed to buy ever more clothes, gadgets, cars, appliances, and processed foods; as Blundell points out, only the latter is blamed for a global health emergency (Blundell and Finlayson 2011, 1216). The commercial marketplace pushes out ever tastier foods to attract ever more consumption. As a result, the drive to consume, perpetuated by abundance, advertising, and ease of access has damaged the general structure of desire and longing. Consumers are wanting more, far more than they need, and are never satiated. "Given this situation (abundance, palatability and promotion), together with the operation of a powerful and well- functioning reward system in the brain, it is a surprise to us that the level of obesity is not even higher than its current level" (Blundell and Finlayson 2011, 1217). Obesity is only one side effect of an all-encompassing consumer society.

Industrial food processors have our number (Sanabria 2015a; Moodie et al. 2013, 671). They know the "bliss points" for doses of sugar, fat, and salt that make foods hyperpalatable (Drewnowski and Greenwood 1983; Moss 2013). They know that liquid sugar drinks and membranous cheese puffs slip past our mouths so quickly that our taste sensors miss how much stuff just went in and leave our stomachs so quickly that the gut barely tastes them (Cassady, Considine, and Mattes 2013; Mozaffarian 2022, 1447). (The Sugar Research Foundation has known this since 1969 [55].) Food companies know that people tend to eat more ultraprocessed foods, more quickly, than minimally processed foods, even when the two types of food are similar in calories, fat, and sugar (Hall et al. 2019; Small and DiFeliceantonio 2019, 347). Processors know that they can get away with substituting cheaper synthetic alternatives—artificial flavorings, preservatives, enzymes, emulsifiers, gums, trans fats—for whole ingredients (Guthman 2015, 2529; Baker et al. 2020, 10–12). They know that human bodies can adjust to accommodate increasing food intake but tend to forcefully resist eating restriction and weight loss (Blundell and Finlayson 2004, 23; MacLean et al. 2017, 9). Companies know that environmental cues and tastes learned in childhood shape lifelong appetites (Halford et al. 2008; MacLean et al. 2017 11–12). They know that many people are stressed, overworked, with little time to care for themselves and their families, getting paid starvation wages and inadequate welfare benefits (Eyer and Sterling 1977; Chilton and Rabinowich 2012; Cheon 2021).

Food processors know that ultraprocessed meals, drinks, and snacks at bargain prices (subsidized by federal agricultural policy) offer affordability, convenience, and pleasure, and sometimes they are the only feasible alternatives in a captive marketplace. The only possible response to this situation must be to repair the whole psychological structure of desire and wanting. Current approaches that focus on behavior change and weight loss, or even taxing sugary sodas, will not help much. Telling people to lose weight and exercise more just makes them feel bad about themselves and does nothing to move the needle. The only social intervention to date that significantly reduced obesity, Blundell notes, was the economic blockade of Cuba in the 1980s and 1990s. National shortages of food and gas forced Cubans to eat less and to walk instead of driving. But that kind of violent social engineering is neither generalizable nor desirable. Besides, the world economy depends on easy access to food and fuel (Blundell 2018, 1305; see Garth 2013). Attempts to reduce the supply of unhealthy food, or to intervene on the consequences of wanting, like weight gain, are doomed to fail. Instead, the structure of desire itself must be altered. People must be helped to "manage their drive to consume" (Halford et al. 2010, 255).

It does not help simply to exhort people to eat less. This is not within any one individual's mental power. For Blundell and his colleagues the issue is "a hedonic process operating at an unconscious, compulsive level (measurable by implicit wanting)" (Blundell and Finlayson 2011, 1217). To change the way people eat, one must change what they want, lessening desire for some foods and reinforcing desire for others (Halford et al. 2010, 256). Desire, longing, and wanting must be redirected away from capitalist productions and promotions. In other words, to suppress an out-of-control hunger, one requires the tools of the Frankfurt School. Blundell cites Marxist philosophers Herbert Marcuse and Max Horkheimer to suggest that the capitalist system "controls people's behavior to the same extent as an overtly authoritarian regime." Capitalism drives people to behave in ways that do damage to themselves. Under such conditions, Blundell asks, is a scientific solution to obesity even possible? "Can biological mechanisms or psychological processes be revealed that are strong enough to resist the political and economic forces of a capitalist system, which is the basis for the world's business?" (Blundell 2018, 1305). Could scientists ever come up with a drug, a surgery, or a psychological intervention, for resisting capitalism?

Blundell wrote this reflection at roughly the same time as his research group was working for Novo Nordisk to investigate the effectiveness of semaglutide. I imagine that he must have had semaglutide in mind when he asked whether a biological mechanism exists, which was strong enough to counter the effects of capitalism. The Leeds group had for some time been calling for an antiobesity drug that would alter "our innate attraction to food and susceptibility to over-consumption" (Halford et al. 2010, 265). Ozempic, it appears, is (at least for some of its developers) a technology for surviving capitalism. I did not see that coming from a physiological psychologist working for a drug company.

. . .

Three conclusions emerge from this Ozempic story: First, industrial food producers design their products to increase consumption—in other words, to keep people hungry. This has serious consequences for health and well-being. Some people suffer deeply and experience their relationship with food as a constant battle against their own bodies. Fat shaming, diet culture, and motivational weight loss programs amplify the harm. Responsibility for managing this situation falls on the backs of individual consumers.

Public discussions of Ozempic and obesity almost never mention the companies that make the food, which makes people sick. Commentators argue over whether people are or are not to blame for what they eat, whether overeating is an addition, a disease, or a bad habit, and whether Ozempic is a proper or viable response. Some commentators lament racial and economic inequalities, the ubiquity of fast food joints, the paucity of fresh food in some neighborhoods, or the generally unhealthy food environment. But they almost always lay the burden—and shame—of managing all this on individual consumers. This situation is not new, and is not coincidental. When experts in the 1970s and 1980s warned about the ill health effects of eating too much sugar, the sugar industry responded with targeted interventions focused on the importance of daily tooth brushing to avoid cavities (Kearns, Glantz, and Apollonio 2019, 15). Corporate-funded narratives emphasize uncertainty about the causes of weight gain, even when experts agree that there is a clear correlation between the rise of metabolic disease and industrially processed foods. Food companies are systematically and scientifically manipulating our taste sensors, hormonal responses, and brain reward circuits. They are treating our sensory systems as "alienable commodities" (Spackman and Lahne 2019, 145). Their foods make us hungry by design. These corporations should be held responsible.

The second conclusion is that hunger, desire, and longing are historically determined. This is what Blundell decided when he read Herbert Marcuse while his lab was testing Ozempic's psycho-physiological effects. Consumer culture channels desires, wants, and needs in directions that reinforce domination. This is a broader way to make the point above about food companies manipulating the body's hunger responses. As Marcuse (1991 [1964], 5–6) has argued, the dominant culture creates and reinforces needs that perpetuate toil, misery, and "the struggle for existence." Hunger is manipulated and mobilized in the service of consumerism, wage suppression, overwork, and cultural norms like anti-Blackness and fat shaming, all of which cause damage. People struggling to stretch their paycheck, catching something fast to eat between shifts, or punishing themselves for perceived food transgressions have that much less energy to devote to things that will make them truly happy and well. Marcuse (1991 [1964], 5) called this situation "false needs," when people's desires are manipulated in the service of their own misery. But you don't need to subscribe to totalizing, binary judgements about true and false needs to recognize that our hungers are being played with in ways that do not serve our collective well-being. Even, in fact, in ways that perpetuate violence and harm.

The third conclusion: Ozempic tells us to pay close attention to gut feelings. If hunger and desire are historical, collective, and mediated by capitalism, then liberation goes with changing the structure of desire. Ozempic shows that such a radical restructuring is possible and that many thousands, even millions, of people are yearning for it. If only it could be done collectively, without inducing permanent nausea and astronomical medical expenses. Kent Berridge's (1996) work on wanting and liking suggests that there are subtle distinctions in the structure of desire, distinctions that many help us to recognize and respond to manipulative cues. Wanting, as Berridge describes it, is a feeling of craving or compulsion. You can want something, strongly, terribly, even when it gives you no pleasure, you don't like it, even when it is damaging. As Blundell recognized, that kind of wanting lines up with something like what Marcuse called false needs. If we take liking in its broadest sense—not just a fleeting sensation of pleasure but full enjoyment—liking offers a counterfeeling to the compulsion of wanting. What might happen if people were able to carefully, slowly, mindfully pay attention to what they truly like?

As Da'Shaun Harrison (2021, 20) has written, "thinness, as a politic, demands that one consume less, desire less, rather than make the demand that we end a World where what one desires would leave others without." Is another politic possible? Is there a different, collective mechanism, a different hunger, strong enough to resist the political and economic forces of a capitalist system? Gut feelings might lead us away from hungers that harm and toward desires that bring enjoyment. The first step toward this kind of desire is to be able to truly feel—to recognize and to analyze—our gut feelings. What is the nature of this particular hunger? Is it a numbing of pain? Which parts of this hunger feel compulsive, which parts feel pleasant, and when? Before, during, after consuming something? Listening to gut feelings requires developing the skill of interoception (Chen et al. 2021; Harshaw 2008; Berntson and Khalsa 2021). Could a careful survey of gut feelings inform a critical analysis of one's own desires?[5]

Antidieting experts encourage eaters to respect and respond to their own gut feelings. The authors of the popular antidieting book *Intuitive Eating* propose a set of principles including "Reject the Diet Mentality," "Make Peace with Food," "Respect Your Body," "Honor Your Hunger," "Feel Your Fullness", and "Discover the Satisfaction Factor." Intuitive eating encourages readers to feel and follow their own hunger cues; the authors ask readers to measure their feelings on a ten-point Hunger Scale, ranging from (1) famished to (5) satisfied to (10) painfully overfull (Tribole and Resch 2012, 68–69). Intuitive eating practitioners propose a form of "gentle nutrition," by which the body's feelings of pleasure, satisfaction, and wellness guide eaters toward foods that are good for nourishment and well-being. What if listening to gut feelings went beyond a scale of strength of feeling? What if gut feelings could also tell us something about the ways longing and desire are channeled?

What if this technique expanded beyond individual bodies, to include inquiry about the whole structure of food production, consumerism, and desire? Gut feelings are physical, social, emotional, and cultural. Gut feelings are also triggered by food shaming, fat shaming, white cultural norms, and anti-Blackness. Scholar Psyche Williams-Forson challenges the moralistic, commodified messages that direct African Americans to eat or not to eat certain foods. Williams-Forson (2022, 126) has argued that "we, as African Americans, need to be transparent about how we feel after eating certain foods: sluggish, satisfied, satiated, happy, cranky, and so on. . . . We should decide how foods feel in our bodies." What gut feelings might a universal basic income produce? What about legally mandated one-hour meal breaks and regular, predictable working hours? What hungers might be relieved by redirecting federal agricultural subsidies to support sustainable food systems? Ozempic shows that a different kind of wanting is possible. But we don't have to be satisfied with the version sold to us in the form of an injectable pen.

# Conclusion

## *They Were Hungry*

"They were hungry." In an interview with sociologist Kelly Neilsen, former University of California–Riverside (UCR) chancellor Ray Orbach recalled the low-income students who entered UCR in the early 1990s. UCR is where I teach. Many of my students are hungry. This book is a response to the question why. One reason is historical: UCR lost a quarter of its enrolled students during the 1970s and 1980s due to environmental catastrophe. Air pollution in the local area got so bad by the late 1970s that the City of Riverside called for a state of emergency. Faced with a precipitous loss of tuition funding, university leaders decided to recruit an untapped pool of potential undergraduates: local high school students. They reached out to area schools and families, counseled students how to qualify for UC admissions requirements, and welcomed new cohorts of first-generation, low-income, underrepresented youth. In this process UCR experienced a triple financial, ecological, and demographic transition, which defines the university's landscape today.

The smog has lightened since, and UCR is nationally recognized as a leader in promoting diversity, inclusive excellence, and student social mobility. At the same time, the university now depends on underrepresented students, their tuition and state funding, to finance its operations. Looking back, what struck Orbach most about the new wave of students was their drive and motivation. "We were able to bring students who not only had no one in the family who had gone to college," Orbach said, "but they hadn't even thought about it. These were first-generation students, and they were marvelous. They were hungry. They worked as hard as they could" (Hamilton and Nielsen 2021, 34). Orbach spoke metaphorically, but his words also described a material reality. Roughly half of UCR undergraduate students, according to recent student surveys, are food-insecure (University of California 2024). They were, and they continue to be, hungry. Students at UCR, across the UC system, and across the United States are taking up hunger as a collective political identity. They are staging hunger strikes, taking labor action against starvation wages, and making collective demands to end all forms of food insecurity and carceral hunger. Students are pointing the way toward a future politics of hunger.

Orbach's figurative image of UCR students as hungry and motivated took a concrete turn around 2015. The University of California began an initiative to promote research on global food systems. As part of its launch, the university financed an internal survey of food insecurity among UC students (Martinez et al. 2018). This was one of the first large-scale surveys of college food security in the United States or anywhere, and the results stunned many of us. Of the UCR students who completed the survey, 62 percent qualified as food-insecure; half of that group were deemed very food-insecure. Almost two-thirds of students surveyed were eating poorly due to lack of resources. One-third skipped meals because they could not afford to buy more food. Many of us who work and study at UCR were deeply shaken by this news. I was teaching a seminar that year on "Hunger and Famine in the Modern World," about chronic hunger and famine events around the globe. I learned from students in that very class that some of them were skipping meals due to lack of funds, and some were sleeping during the daytime to deal with unsatisfied hunger pangs.

How could this be possible? How could thousands of students be hungry at a public university in a state with the sixth-largest economy in the world? At a campus founded on an agricultural research station, in a city that once called itself the citrus capital of the world? Focus groups of food-insecure students across the nation probed the underlying dynamics and consequences. A complex of entangled issues emerged: Students have scarce time to seek out and prepare healthy and affordable food, and they lack transportation to grocery stores. Universities contract food service out to private food suppliers, and set higher wages than at local food joints, leading to high food prices on campus. Students are hit by hidden costs of off-campus housing such as utilities and other bills. Financial aid packages tend to underestimate the actual cost of attending universities like UCR. Some students do not take the loans in their financial aid packages, because they don't want to fall into debt; then they find themselves unable to earn enough to live and study at the same time. Others take on heavy loans and live in a state of anxiety about paying them off. On top of that, many students face eligibility restrictions for federal welfare, SNAP (food stamp) benefits, and Pell grants. Many students are caring for and financially supporting family members, children, or elders. Food-insecure students encounter shame, stigma, and accusations of poor financial decision making (Henry 2017; Meza et al. 2019; Fortin, Harvey, and White 2021).

Students expressed fatigue, anxiety, anger, and frustration with themselves and their institutions. They spoke of their struggle to focus on lectures and schoolwork, to find sources of affordable food and time to eat between tightly packed work and school schedules. They described a feeling of alienation from their studies and their social world, unable to go out to restaurants or bring their own lunch to a study group session. Black, Latinx, and Native American students, former foster youth, LGBTQ+ students, and students caring for family members all respond to UCR surveys with much higher rates of food insecurity than other groups of students (University of California 2024). Students identified as food-insecure had lower grades, on average, than food-secure peers (Phillips, McDaniel, and Croft 2018). Meanwhile, a union-financed study, also released in 2016, found that more than two-thirds of staff members employed by the University of California (of those who responded to the study) qualified as food-insecure (Drier, Bomba, and Romero 2016).

Over the past few years, food security reports and surveys have proliferated. Tens of thousands of students have answered two or six or ten questions designed by the US Department of Agriculture (USDA) to track individual food security. Reports describe an acute crisis nationwide: the HOPE Lab found that two-thirds of community college students in the United States suffer from food insecurity (Goldrick-Rab, Richardson, and Hernandez 2017, 1). Social surveyors identified levels of food insecurity between 10 percent and 75 percent among different groups of college students; almost all surveys found that food insecurity among students far outmeasured food insecurity among US households (Nikolaus et al. 2020; Nazmi et al. 2019). At UCR and beyond, student hunger has become a matter of concern.

Some commentators, faculty and staff, expressed skepticism that students really were experiencing an actual food-security crisis. Skeptics noted that USDA household food-security surveys consistently identify between 12 percent and 15 percent food-insecure households in the United States. How could students experience food insecurity at rates three or five times higher than local families? Perhaps, one skeptical faculty member suggested to me, the food-security measuring instrument does not work properly with students. Perhaps the survey identified as "food-insecure" habits and events common to the college student experience. Which student hasn't skipped a meal on occasion? Some commentators suggested that students just need to buck up; some recalled their own lean college days, living on beans or ramen noodles. But activists and scholars pushed back. No student today can afford college just by cutting corners and eating ramen. Over the past forty years, state governments have divested from higher education, just as underrepresented, low-income students began to enter college in large numbers. Universities in the United States now enroll more low-income students than middle-income students, and tuition dollars, not public taxes, fund most university operations (Fortin, Harvey, and White 2021, 243). Students are on the hook for increasing fees even as the cost of living and housing soars. A public education today does not resemble the student experience of the 1970s or the 1990s.

Well before the University of California released its student food-insecurity survey, student activists fought to address the crisis of entitlements in their midst. Activists for undocumented student rights built the first food pantry on UCR's campus in 2013 as a collective response to student hunger. Mafalda Gueta, president of the UCR Chicano Student Center's PODER program, explained that "undocumented students constantly have to fill that [financial] gap, so some of them work two jobs or try to find scholarships that don't require residency or citizenship. A lot of students go hungry because they choose to pay their rent instead of eating" (Magat 2015). Undocumented students are excluded from federal programs like Pell grants and SNAP (food stamp) benefits. As students nationwide campaigned for legal status, financial aid, and educational access, UCR students with Undocumented Student Programs and Chicano Student Programs sought to care for each other's material needs. They relied on university seed funding, grocery and cash donations, and volunteer student labor to start a mobile food pantry on campus. Student pantry coordinators quickly realized that many documented students also suffered from food insecurity. A student parent association stepped in to help with food distribution, as part of its own mutual aid program. Student volunteers at the mobile pantry handed out grocery bags to fill with apples, lettuce, and canned goods. Gueta noted that food insecurity had grown to a campuswide student issue (Magat 2015).

After the UC food-insecurity survey came out, student activists pushed to raise awareness. Political science major and student government leader Melina Reyes went on a five-day hunger strike in 2016, supported by fellow students, to press the issue of food insecurity on campus (Avila 2016). Activists showed up at university leaders' town halls and public events, demanding an adequate response to this issue. They organized rallies at the Belltower, a central meeting point on the quad. Student organizations set up public showings of documentaries on food insecurity, solicited student-run solutions, and organized meal plan donations. A student in my class wrote a series of articles in the UCR student newspaper highlighting the food-insecurity survey and student responses to it (Ismail 2017a, 2017b, and 2017c). Student government leaders campaigned on the issues of food and housing insecurity, and succeeded in galvanizing state legislators to provide funding for emergency food and housing. The student food-insecurity survey became a rallying point. Student organizer Crystal Brachetti explained that "essentially, we are just trying to show administration that we're aware that there are 62 percent of us that are hungry and we're not OK with it" (Ismail 2017a).

Students and staff mobilized to serve students suffering from hunger. Students established and fought to preserve a university-sponsored community garden. Two students who conceived and built the first UCR food pantry, Ana Coria and Daniel Lopez Salas, later became university staff members coordinating (respectively) Undocumented Student Programs and the official, expanded campus food pantry. A student founder of the community garden, Fortino Morales, went on to direct universitywide sustainability efforts. Staff and students now grow and harvest fresh food from the garden to supply the pantry. In 2016 my students and I visited the student food pantry, which at that time was located in a small closet behind a student meeting room. Pantry director Grecia Marquez-Nieblas described the pressing needs on campus and invited all of us to get involved. I began to attend working group meetings of staff, students, and faculty around basic needs. Being a historian, I brought what skills I had to the table and set out to write this book. I hoped that I could contribute material to situate individual experiences with hunger in deeper, collective histories.

The writing of this book is indelibly marked by the historic UC graduate student and postdoc strike of fall 2022. I remember standing in a conversation with graduate student organizers and hearing a student call to fight against "starvation wages." That exchange was the origin point of the chapter on starvation wages and hunger marches of the Great Depression. That conversation and others like it reoriented my research to pursue more closely the connections between hunger, learning, and labor exploitation. More generally, the strike of fall 2022 compelled me to be keenly aware of the conditions of my own work and my responsibility to those who have fought such battles over time. (Here I am writing a book about hunger, in the middle of a labor action against starvation wages!) I do not remember that student's name, but I thank them for their insight and for making clear the historical connections between the student labor action of 2022 and the world-historical struggle against hunger and starvation wages.

One of the high points of the 2022 strike happened in early December, as classes were officially coming to a close (though many already had been cancelled). University dining halls across the UC system were "liberated." Organizers surrounded the cash tills and declared the dining hall free and open for all. They invited students who had no more credit at the dining hall, those who could not afford a meal plan, and food-insecure community members to gather at the hall and eat what they needed. By imagining mutual aid as a weapon against the war on subsistence, and specifically by targeting an institution that is designed to promote social welfare and mobility, organizers brought back to life the historical tradition of the hunger marchers. "Today," declared organizers at UCR, "we are reclaiming the resources that are ours; resources we shouldn't have to pay to access in the first place. Food insecurity is violence" (AbolishUCR Collective 2022). This research comes out of a lived encounter, shared with colleagues, students, and staff at UCR,

FIGURE 13. "Food Insecurity Is Violence." Source: AbolishUCR Collective 2022.

who advocate for recognition and repair of hunger and food insecurity on campus. My research is responsible to them and to others who may feel shame or alienation due to hunger and food insecurity. Hunger is not your fault.

. . .

Hunger is not a natural, biological, or genetic destiny.[1] It is not just a matter of choices and habits. It is not a switch that you can turn off, or an addiction. Hunger is a technology. This book shows how hunger is produced, on purpose and to specific ends. Hunger is a tool, an instrument. Hunger focuses and narrows the horizon of desires and needs. Hunger drowns out other thoughts, feelings, plans, and concerns. Hunger cannot be ignored.

Hunger serves to advance a logic of elimination, a logic of debt and labor, a logic of behavior control, and a logic of commodification. By "logic" I mean a set of knowledges and ideologies, power relations, and forms of subjectivity. Knowledge, power, and subjectivity together constitute a discursive and material formation, an apparatus for shaping worlds (Escobar 2011, 46). A logic of elimination targets specific groups of people for dispossession and disappearance. A logic of debt and labor forces people to work in order to survive. A logic of behavior control employs regimes of motivation to punish or reward specific actions. A logic of commodification manipulates desire and longing toward commercial aims.

Throughout this book we have seen a logic of elimination play out through starvation, land seizures, and forced displacement, economic and cultural assimilation, and imprisonment. At several junctures in US history, state agents and their collaborators set out to eliminate people. Indian agents and army units systematically destroyed Native sources of food and replaced them with rations conditional on obedience (the "starving process.") In Mississippi in 1967, Raymond Wheeler and the Southern Regional Council identified a "policy on the part of those who control the state to eliminate the Negro Mississippian . . . by starving him to death" (Brenner et al. 1967, 26). Stringent welfare rules close off access to common resources and criminalize survival (thus, by implication, foreclosing one's continued existence). In American prisons hunger is a key component in broader regimes of containment and elimination. Targets of elimination, violence, and displacement were (and are) blamed for their own suffering. Poor and starving people were said to be lazy or criminal. Eugenicists and racists proposed that "inferior" peoples were doomed to disappear. This logic negates the existence and thriving of whole cultures and peoples. The subjective side of elimination is a sense of loss of self, and shame for one's own feeling of diminishment.

People caught up in logics of elimination fought back, and continue to do so. Work by the Native Food Sovereignty Alliance, the NDN Collective Land Back campaign (Pieratos, Manning, and Tilsen 2021), water protectors at Standing Rock (Estes 2019), tribal entities such as the Karuk Department of Natural Resources

(Norgaard 2019), and land trusts like the Tongva Land Conservancy reveal and reverse the logic of elimination. Black food justice organizations such as the National Black Food Justice Alliance (Reese and Cooper 2021), Community Services Unlimited (Haasberg 2020; Garth 2020), North Bolivar County Good Food Revolution (Smith 2023), Black Farmers Market initiative, and the Detroit Black Community Food Security Network (White 2018) work toward emancipatory food power. The California Reparations Task Force, Restitution Study Group, the Equal Justice Initiative, and other reparations movements fight for repair of intergenerational state and corporate violence against Black people in America. Incarcerated people and their allies in organizations like Impact/Justice (Soble, Stroud, and Weinstein 2020), Maryland Food and Prison Abolition Project (MFPAP 2021), and the Youth Justice Coalition hold rallies and hunger strikes to protest continued confinement and deprivation.

When workers must follow orders if they want to survive, this is an example of the logic of debt and labor. Employers activate this logic when they leverage starvation wages, debt, scrip, and food advances to maintain control over workers. Hunger channels workers to serve specific ends, as when welfare agencies required work in exchange for relief. Scrip and furnish (food advances) exemplify the power of debt: plantation and coal mine owners purposefully kept their workers hungry as a tool of coercion. Food aid works in a parallel way at an international level, as when US president Lyndon Johnson pressured India to industrialize its agriculture in exchange for famine relief. Student debt functions according to this same logic, forcing students to channel their studies and ambitions toward jobs that will support their debt burden.

The logic of debt and labor, starvation wages, and punitive welfare policies is undergirded by ideology: hunger as a whip, driving people to work. Antiwelfare politicians argue that hunger is a necessary stimulus to labor and productivity. Conversely, they blame poor people for their own situation; if one is hungry, one must not be working hard enough. Starvation wages marked a worker as abject, subaltern, undeserving. Similarly, credit card debt, underwater mortgages, or unpaid car loans appear as personal failures, not as systemic forms of economic pressure. History shows us powerful stories of collective resistance to debt and labor coercion. The Hunger Marchers of 1930 and 1931 built a national coalition across race, ethnicity, gender, and rural/urban divides all around a common identity: of being made hungry. They turned hunger into a powerful common cause. Mutual aid networks such as the neighborhood aid described by L. C. Dorsey, the Freedom Farms Cooperative established by Fannie Lou Hamer, and the Black Panther Party breakfast programs made survival into a collective project. Since 2011, the Debt Collective has worked to disrupt the coercive power of personal debt. The Collective functions as a debtors union; it purchases packages of outstanding medical, student, and credit card debts (which are resold on financial markets), and forgives them. In the process the Debt Collective (2020) reveals that the logic of debt and labor is collective and structural, not simply a question of individual blame and responsibility.

The logic of behavior control employs punishments and rewards to nudge, motivate, and coerce. Psychologists set up this structure of behavior control in animal laboratories, and from there it spread to schools, prisons, workplaces, drug treatment centers, and weight-loss programs. This logic reflects a utilitarian ideology that sums up human experience as pleasure and pain. Aversive feelings discourage certain preferences and behaviors; pleasurable feelings make one want to do more. As these feelings repeat, one automatically avoids certain behaviors, while other behaviors become habits. Edward Thorndike taught schoolteachers to impose such regimes of repetition, punishment, and reward on their students. Charles Ferster's behavioral weight-loss program had dieters recite their worst fears and shames ("ultimate aversive consequences") while staring at a piece of pie. Prisons enact the most violent and coercive expression of behavior control, imposing hunger (in the form of an inedible, indigestible diet) as punishment. In all of these examples the punishment is always stronger than the reward.

This logic assumes a pliable, influenceable subject—like the "starved personality"—whose feelings and actions may be undone, broken down, and recast. This subject's attention is focused on relieving hunger, pain, and aversion, and seeking relief and pleasure. They are hypersensitive, responsive, and suggestible. They follow external cues and directions. They must work to direct their "willpower" repeatedly toward specific ends. Hunger is a tool to create such a pliable subject. This is often in the service of a racial project, as when would-be saviors infantilize nonwhite people with scripts about how they need to change their diet, exercise more, and practice willpower (Moran 2018, 133; Williams-Forson 2022, 16). It is difficult to undo such pervasive ideologies of motivation, habits, and self-control. Antidieting activists challenge punitive weight-control programs. Unconditional parenting and antigrading approaches to teaching relieve behaviorist pressures on children. Removing moral rules around welfare, making welfare support unconditional, is another step in this direction. All of these approaches refuse the logic of behavior control, punishment, and reward.

Chapter 8 outlined a critique of commodified structures of desire and longing. Food companies manipulate taste preferences and the neurobiology of hunger, in order to make us hungry to consume. Government subsidies for wheat, corn, and soy encourage industrialized agriculture, massive livestock operations, and highly processed foods. But suppressing hunger is also commodified in the form of weight loss drugs and diet plans. Commercial interests like Weight Watchers and Novo Nordisk benefit from diet culture and fat shaming. Liking food, pleasurable eating, family food histories, rich Black and Indigenous food cultures are shamed. In the absence of real, intentional pleasure, all that remains is a battle between cravings, willpower, and drugs. A logic of commodification is expressed through feelings of wanting, longing, and craving.

Resistance to logics of commodification is possible, even at the most everyday level. Chefs and scholar-activists like Catriona Rueda Esquibel and Luz Calvo call upon us to decolonize our diets. By this, they mean to actively resist the lure of commercially processed foods, which keep people sick and weak. Ancestral knowledge, recipes, seeds, plants, and growing techniques offer protection, nourishment, and cultural healing. For scholar Psyche Williams-Forson (2022, 126–128), decolonizing diet requires a space free of racist food shaming, for Black people to "decide how we want to live our culinary lives." Black food and eating call for "praise and celebration" rather than "shame and embarrassment." Cooking, Esquibel and Calvo (2013, 3) say, can be a "revolutionary act."

Hunger and eating, alongside personal indebtedness, are surely among the most moralized areas of American culture. Blame and shame run thick. This book shows that hunger and debt are historically intertwined. Cultural tropes around debt and eating sound very similar: critics accuse their targets of making bad choices, being weak in the face of temptation, unable to control themselves. My goal is to loosen the shame that knots around individuals, their wishes and choices. At the same time, I have no interest in replacing social blame (around debt, or body weight) with purely biological explanations about how hunger is a disease or an addiction. Instead I point to connections and movements that address hunger, debt, and their logics as regimes to be resisted collectively.

ACKNOWLEDGMENTS

This book was nourished by powerful communities of scholars and activists. You would not be reading this without the brilliant, compassionate, incisive draft readings by Audra Wolfe (The Outside Reader), Rachel Moran, Nancy Campbell, Hannah Landecker, Cathy Gere, Jade Sasser, and Emmanuel Saadia. Each one of them read an entire draft and pushed me to learn more and to say exactly what I mean. Emma Spary, Anya Zilberstein, Patrick McCray, and Suman Seth carefully combed through an early version of chapter 2; their excitement, confusion, and questions were formative as I built out the book project.

Faculty and staff who are building a new Department of Society, Environment, and Health Equity with me at the University of California–Riverside (Chikako Takeshita, Juliann Allison, Ellen Reese, Jade Sasser, Bronwyn Leebaw, Cathy Gudis, Cassia Roth, Michelle Raheja, Tanya Nieri, Kim Yi Dionne, Jennifer Syvertsen, Chioun Lee, Josie Ayala, and Brenda Robinson) have taught me fierceness, patience, hilarity, strategy, and playing the long game with discipline and accountability to students and our communities. Thanks to Juliet McMullin, Sage Whitson, Vorris Nunley, and Dylan Rodriguez for your leadership and your company. Colleagues in the Department of History have taught me to support compromise, and history graduate students have modeled collaborative leadership (thanks to Kate Mower, Margaret Hanson, Kat Boniface, Hailee Menchaca, and Audrey Maier). The Health Inequities Faculty Commons, led by Kim Yi Dionne, Jennifer Syvertsen, and Tanya Nieri, hosted legendary desert writing retreats where many of these chapters advanced.

Thanks to Jennifer Hughes and Erica Edwards for founding the UCR Mid Career Research Initiative, to Goldberry Long for writing workshops, and to Freya Schwiy, Covadonga Lamar Prieto, Susan Zieger, Mariam Lam, Alejandra Dubcovsky, Molly McGarry, and Sarita See for your company. The UCR STS Coffee Hour opened a space for new encounters across disciplines; thanks to Chikako Takeshita, Sherryl Vint, David Lo, and Norm Ellstrand for many excellent afternoon conversations and collaborations. Every one of these collaborations owes its existence to the UCR Center for Ideas and Society and its executive director, Katharine Henshaw. One of the best service experiences I've ever had was alongside Devon Sakamoto, Karen McComb, Daniel Lopez Salas, Grecia Marquez Nieblas, and many students in the UCR Basic Needs Working Group.

Many thanks to the History of the Recent Social Sciences society (HISRESS), Philippe Fontaine, Jeff Pooley, Mark Solovey, Jamie Cohen-Cole, Craig Calhoun, Katerina Liskova, and Suzanne Schmidt. The UCHRI 2023 Food Futures group (led by Charlotte Biltekoff, Julie Guthman, Jade Sasser, and Elizabeth Hoover) taught me about dreaming as scholarship. Cal STS and its conveners (Joe Dumit, James Greisemer, Colin Milburn, Carlos Andres Barragan, and Tim Choi) teach me about performance, dancing, and hiking as research. Colleagues in History of Science Society (HSS) teach me about institutional change and how to have fun along the way; these colleagues include, among others, Rosanna Dent, Lois Roisson, Ayah Nurridin, Emily Merchant, Samantha Muka, Sarah Pickman, Kristine Palmieri, Alexandra Hui, Sarah Qidwai, Michael McGovern, Don Opitz, and J. P. Gutierrez. I am lucky to find myself repeatedly on panels organized by Julia Alejandra Morales Fontanilla, Emily Yates-Doerr, and Laura Meek. Thanks to the Hunger in the Americas panel at HSS: Eve Buckley, Joel Vargas Dominguez, Stefan Pohl Valero, Helen Anne Curry, Timothy Lorek, and Adriana Salay Leme (who I am so fortunate to have met through this research). M. Murphy and Joanna Radin are inspirations.

I was lucky to co-conspire with Michael Pettit, Jaci Young, and Kira Luissier about the history of psychology and to co-organize a lovely series on theory with Robert Brain and Edward Jones-Imhotep, both through the Center for the History of Science, Technology and Medicine. Scholars involved with the Nutrire Collective (Alyshia Gálvez, Natalí Valdez, Emily Yates-Doerr, Jessica Hardin, Megan Carney, Abril Saldaña Tejada, Hanna Garth, Leonore Manderson, Megan Warin, Sarah Chard, Emily Mendenhall, Maggie Dickenson, Emily Vasquez, Heather Howard, Ariana Ochoa Camacho, and the late Adele Hite) teach me what an intellectual community of care and activism can be and do. Nathalie Morris, Robin Coste Lewis, Debbie Weinstein, and Laura Stark are my anchors and inspiration. They teach me about vulnerability and refuge as a scholarly and personal ethic.

Thanks to my parents, Charlene and Dan Simmons, and to my alloparents, Yossi Saadia, Jan Basu, Jim and Judy Meyers, and Mark Dillon.

The research for this book received vital support from archivists, including Lizette Royer Barton at the Cummings Center for the History of Psychology and Joel Christie in the Federal Trade Commission Office of the Secretary, who took a whole hour of his time to explain the history of FTC corrective advertising cases in the 1970s. Staff at the Industry Documents Library provide an invaluable public service. UC Press editor Kate Marshall enthusiastically welcomed me to the Food Studies series at UC Press, and Chad Attenborough offered patience and expertise in making this book happen.

The epigraph from Wahunsenacawh is from Samuel Gardner Drake, *Biography and History of the Indians of North America, from Its First Discovery*. The epigraph from Fannie Lou Hamer is reprinted courtesy of *The Progressive*. The epigraph from Kari Norgaard, Ron Reid, and Carolina Van Horne is reprinted courtesy of MIT Press. And the epigraph from Impani Perry is reprinted courtesy of Duke University Press.

This project was supported in part by the University of California Office of the President MRPI funding MRP-19–600791, and an Andrew W. Mellon Term Professorship at the Center for Ideas and Society, University of California–Riverside. My existence is supported by Emmanuel Saadia and Lazare Simmons-Saadia. You are the best. I love you.

## INTRODUCTION

1. In 1793, Chikamauga warriors attacked Wears Fort, cut corn from the field, stole his horses, killed hogs and cows, and broke his grain mill. In retaliation, Wear and a group of volunteer militiamen invaded the village of Tallassee, killed fifteen people, and took four women hostage for the return of his stolen property. (What did he expect when he built a house in the middle of a highway?) (Sharp 2014a).

2. For documenting Wear family history, I thank my mother, Charlene Wear Simmons; my aunt, Jenna Caplette; and my great-grandmother, Daisy Clark Wear.

3. Scholars of Britain and its empire (especially India) have been exceptionally attentive to the social, economic, and cultural history of hunger (Sen 1981; Davis 2002; Russell 2005; Trentmann 2006; Vernon 2007; Amrith 2008; Otter 2020).

4. Emily Yates-Doerr (2015a, 232) suggests that hunger functions as a "multi-object" enfolding multiple versions that stick to particular contexts and experiences.

5. Prior to the 1980s, "food security" referred to national food stocks, which experts measured to judge a country's ability to provide for its citizens (in the same way that experts measured energy security by the amount of national oil reserves) (Jarosz 2011; Stedman 2014; Fullbrook 2010).

6. A word of clarification: of course hunger is a biological function, which under ideal conditions serves to maintain bodily homeostasis (stability). As the chapters suggest, homeostasis alone cannot explain what is happening with hunger, eating, and metabolism in the twentieth and twenty-first centuries. Some scientists have proposed that food cravings and metabolic disease are caused by evolutionary maladaptation to the modern world (the "feast and fast hypothesis"). However, such genetic and evolutionary theories lack empirical evidence and structural awareness (Simmons 2024).

## 1. THE STARVING PROCESS

1. Hunt was Indian agent at the Kiowa, Comache, and Wichita Agency. He made a point to disagree with "those who advocate the starving process," thereby describing it clearly as the prevailing assumption.

2. On refusal, see Simpson 2014 and 2016.

3. Ideologies of hunger as stimulus to work were pervasive in the nineteenth-century United States (Stanley 1998, 99–109).

4. Hartman (1997) points out that this form of debt/obligation also entails a sense of blameworthiness, as in "it's your own fault if you are hungry, for not working hard enough." A similar sense of blameworthiness echoes in General Smith's words to Maȟpíya Lúta quoted earlier in the chapter ("it is your own fault.").

5. Stanley (1998, 107) shows that Northern states instituted punitive antivagrancy laws at the same time as Union troops were emancipating enslaved people. Charity reformers praised the "discipline" imparted to unemployed vagrants by hunger and cold.

6. Native leaders emphasized their hospitality in their speeches, sharing food with visitors when they were hungry (Blaisdell 2000, 22, 77, 184, 191).

## 2. PUNISHMENT AND REWARD

1. I am following Nikolas Rose and Joelle M. Abi-Rached's (2013, 86, 104) call for "thinking with the animal" in scientific models of behavior.

2. Herbert Spencer defined hunger in his *Principles of Psychology* (1855, 163) as one of the simplest "units of feeling." Most states of mind, he claimed, were "compounds" of a few basic mental units. A few "really simple" feelings were unique in that they were "not decomposable by introspection" into smaller units.

3. For example: "The reward for successful choice was food; as punishment for failure the electric shock was used" (Casteel 1911, 1). "I used the well-known discrimination method, combining the motives of punishment and reward" (Johnson 1914, 342).

4. Of course the feminine-marked lab worker would be in charge of the well-nourished rat!

5. The apparatus became popularly known as a "Skinner box," although Skinner contributed only the lever-press and a great deal of publicity. See Moss 1924 and Woodworth 1918.

## 3. FIGHT—DON'T STARVE

1. Author John Dos Passos coined the term "starvationist" in reference to the Harlan County mines ("Red Cross Named 'Starvationist'" 1931).

2. Gates belonged to the woman's branch of the National Miners Union of Straight Creek and gave this testimony at a public hearing by the Dreiser Commission (Dreiser et al. 2008 [1932]).

3. Another such hearing in Harlem examined cases of child malnutrition and marched to the local Charity Association to demand aid ("Open Hearing" 1931).

4. The *Boston Globe* claimed to identify a characteristic "Slavic" typology among the marchers, a not-so-subtle reference to Communist infiltration ("Police Meeting" 1932).

5. Leab (1967, 314) notes that the Unemployed Councils peaked in 1930 and began to decline thereafter, as they became more visibly associated with the Communist Party and radical tactics, and as alternative organizations arose.

6. On the medical politics of malnutrition in the 1930s, see Brosco 2001, Meckel 2008, and Ruis 2013.

7. In 1932, Taliaferro Clark initiated the Study of Untreated Syphilis in Tuskegee, Alabama, as chief officer of the US Public Health Service. Traces of racial eugenics can be found already in his work on nutrition: he surveyed a population of white, "native-born" children to find a baseline measure of nutritional health (Clark 1921).

8. Annelise Orleck (1993) and Lashawn Harris (2009) are important exceptions, and have opened these histories to much broader issues around gender, race, labor, and consumer politics.

## 5. CRAVING AND CONTROL

1. I salute Christine Kearns, DDS, MBA, for her work on building this archive (Kearns, Glantz, and Apollonio 2019).

2. At the first meeting of the Sugar Research Foundation scientific advisory committee in 1960, Dr. Charles King (executive director of the Nutrition Foundation) suggested that "the foundation's publications could be more cautious" regarding their claims about sugar and the appestat (Hickson and Sugar Association 1960, 20). The appestat ad ran for the following ten years.

3. Many thanks to Nancy Campbell (2007) for directing my attention to Vincent Dole (1959, 1965, and 1989).

## 6. WEAPON OF WHITE SUPREMACY

1. In April 1967 the federal Civil Rights Commission calculated that "in the eight Mississippi counties that changed from commodity distribution to food stamps, there was a total decrease in participation one year after the change of almost 36,000 residents" (Citizens' Board 1968, 12; Smith 2023, 29–43).

2. Taking a different angle on the Citizens' Board's *Hunger USA* and Carr and Davies's "Hunger in America," Frohlich (2024, 79–84) tracks the federal Food and Drug Administration's role in mediating claims about deficiencies in the American diet: either Americans ate too much or too little (also see LeBlanc 2019, 160–179).

3. Rachel Moran (2018, 123–131) offers a fantastic archival analysis of letters sent by the public to the USDA in response to "Hunger in America."

4. Frohlich (2024, 88) suggests that some of Pollack's critiques of *Hunger USA* echoed the FDA's argument that American diets were not as deficient as sellers of dietary supplements wanted people to believe. So Pollack may not have been motivated only by personal or political pique.

## 7. CARCERAL HUNGER

1. The Vermont Supreme Court ruled in 2009 that the Nutraloaf violated the State Constitution.

2. In 2012 an Appeals Court did enter a judgment against Nutraloaf but only because one particular recipe used in a Milwaukee jail was shown to cause vomiting and an anal fistula. Tellingly, in that particular case the complainant had lost weight while in jail (*Prude v. Clarke* 2012).

3. It is important to note that starvation has not disappeared from US prisons. A 2015 investigation found that people incarcerated in a privately-run prison in Georgia were so hungry they were eating toothpaste and toilet paper (Santo and Iaboni 2015).

## 8. OZEMPIC

1. Charlotte Biltekoff (2013, 121) has noted that the use of the term "epidemic" reflected both a population-level approach to nutrition and a sense of collective danger or peril.

2. Megan McCullogh and Jessica Hardin (2013, 4) have asked, Why do public health calculations never take into account the psychological, social, and economic costs of trying to be thinner?

3. Nicolas Rasmussen (2012, 882) has pointed out that early twentieth-century medicine already associated fatness with hormonal deficiencies.

4. Amanda Lynch has noted that there was wide variation in responses to hunger (Lynch, Kozak, and Zalesin 2022). About a third of the patients she and her colleagues interviewed had intense, painful, and uncontrollable feelings of hunger before surgery; others had no such feelings. Similarly many patients lost all sense of hunger after surgery, whereas others did not feel a change.

5. These questions resonate strongly with what Laura Stark and Nancy Campbell (2018) have named the "methods of ingression" in contrast to methods that extract knowledge from others.

## CONCLUSION: THEY WERE HUNGRY

1. I recognize that hunger has a biological function. My aim here is to expand the realm of explanation to include political, economic, cultural, and critical theory. Hunger and scarcity are not predestined by genetics (or anything else for that matter). Hunger is the result of regimes of knowledge and power.

BIBLIOGRAPHY

ARCHIVAL COLLECTIONS

Archives of the History of American Psychology (Cummings Center for the History of Psychology)
Civil Rights Movement Archive
Eliot Stellar Papers, University of Pennsylvania Archives and Records Center
Food and Agriculture Organization (FAO) Archives
Industry Documents Library
National Museum of African American History and Culture
Prints and Photographs Division, Library of Congress
Robert Mearns Yerkes Papers, 1822–1985 (inclusive), Manuscripts & Archives, Yale University Library
Southern Rural Poverty Collection
US National Archives and Records Administration
United Nations Relief and Rehabilitation Administration (UNRRA) Photographs, United Nations Archives

LEGAL CASES

*Becerra v. Kramer*. 2017. United States District Court for the Northern District of Illinois Eastern Division. "Becerra v. Kramer Case No. 16 C 1408 (N.D. Ill. Jan. 10, 2017)." Casetext. Accessed September 20, 2023. https://casetext.com/case/becerra-v-kramer.
*Finney v. Arkansas Board of Correction*. 1974. United States Court of Appeals, Eighth Circuit. "Finney v. Arkansas Board of Correction 505 F.2d 194 (8th Cir. 1974)." Casetext. Accessed September 15, 2023. https://casetext.com/case/finney-v-arkansas-board-of -correction/.

*Holt v. Sarver.* 1969. United States District Court, E.D. Arkansas, Pine Bluff Division. "Holt v. Sarver 300 F. Supp. 825 (E.D. Ark. 1969)." Casetext. Accessed September 16, 2023. https://casetext.com/case/holt-v-sarver-2.

*Holt v. Sarver.* 1970. United States District Court, E.D. Arkansas, Pine Bluff Division. "Holt v. Sarver 309 F. Supp. 362 (E.D. Ark. 1970)." Casetext. Accessed September 21, 2023. https://casetext.com/case/holt-v-sarver-3.

*Hutto et al. v. Finney et al.* 1978. John Paul Stevens, United States Supreme Court "Hutto et al. v. Finney et. al" 437 U.S. 678 (1978) 98 S. Ct. 2565. Casetext. Accessed September 15, 2023. https://casetext.com/case/hutto-v-finney?.

*Jackson v. Bishop.* 1967. United States District Court, E.D. Arkansas, Pine Bluff Division. "Jackson v. Bishop 268 F. Supp. 804 (E.D. Ark. 1967)." Casetext. Accessed September 18, 2203. https://casetext.com/case/jackson-v-bishop.

*Johnson v. Williams.* 1991. United States District Court, E.D. Virginia, Alexandria Division. "Johnson v. Williams, 768 F. Supp. 1161, 1163–64 (E.D. Va. 1991)." Casetext. Accessed September 25, 2023. https://casetext.com/case/johnson-v-williams-22?.

*Landman v. Royster.* 1971. United States District Court, E.D. Virginia, Richmond Division. "Landman v. Royster 333 F. Supp. 621 (E.D. Va. 1971)." Casetext. Accessed September 20, 2023. https://casetext.com/case/landman-v-royster.

*LeMaire v. Maass.* 1993. United States Court of Appeals, Ninth Circuit. "LeMaire v. Maass 12 F.3d 1444 (9th Cir. 1993)." Casetext. Accessed September 24, 2023. https://casetext.com /case/lemaire-v-maass.

*Prude v. Clarke.* 2011. United States District Court, E.D. Wisconsin. "Prude v. Clarke, Case No. 10-CV-167 (E.D. Wis. Jul. 19, 2011)." Casetext Research. Accessed September 25, 2023. https://casetext.com/case/prude-v-clarke/.

*Prude v. Clarke.* 2012. United States Court of Appeals, Seventh Circuit. "Prude v. Clarke, 675 F.3d 732 (7th Cir. 2012)." Casetext. Accessed September 25, 2023. https://casetext.com /case/prude-v-clarke-3?.

*Skelton v. New Jersey Department of Corrections (NJDOC).* 2020. United States District Court District of New Jersey Camden Vicinage. "Skelton v New Jersey Department of Corrections CIV. NO. 19–18597 (RMB) (D.N.J. Oct. 30, 2020)." Casetext. Accessed September 25, 2023. https://casetext.com/case/skelton-v-nj-dept-of-corr.

*Smego v. Aramark Food Servs. Corp.* 2013. United States District Court Central District of Illinois Springfield Division. "Smego v. Aramark Food Servs. Corp. No. 10–3334 (C.D. Ill. May. 13, 2013)." Casetext. Accessed September 26, 2023. https://casetext.com /case/smego-v-aramark-food-servs-corp-1/.

*Talley v. Stephens.* 1965. United States District Court, E.D. Arkansas, Pine Bluff Division. "Talley v. Stephens 247 F. Supp. 683 (E.D. Ark. 1965)." Casetext. Accessed September 15, 2023. https://casetext.com/case/talley-v-stephens.

## OTHER SOURCES

Abbott, Grace. 1932. "Improvement in Rural Public Relief: The Lesson of the Coal-Mining Communities." *Social Service Review* 6 (2): 183–222.

AbolishUCR Collective. 2022. "Swipe Free, Tuition Free, Cop Free University." Accessed December 20, 2022. https://drive.google.com/file/d/1XEZ3IU_r5dWCHkBtuTDwhSWJ k86DC22e/view.

Adams, David Wallace. 1988. "Fundamental Considerations: The Deep Meaning of Native American Schooling, 1880–1900." *Harvard Educational Review* 58 (1): 1–29. https://doi .org/10.17763/haer.58.1.h5715211105l7nm65.

Adams, Jane, and D. Gorton. 2009. "This Land Ain't My Land: The Eviction of Sharecroppers by the Farm Security Administration." *Agricultural History* 83 (3): 323–351. https:// doi.org/10.2307/40607494.

Agamben, Giorgio. 1998. *Homo Sacer: Sovereign Power and Bare Life*. Translated by Daniel Heller-Roazen. Stanford, CA: Stanford University Press.

Agricultural Packing and Allied Workers of America United Cannery (UCAPAWA), Congress of Industrial Organizations (CIO), and C.L.R. James. 1942. "Down with Starvation Wages in South-East Missouri: 30 Cents an Hour, White and Colored Together." [Missouri]: Local 313, UCAPAWA–CIO.

Ahlberg, Kristin L. 2008. *Transplanting the Great Society: Lyndon Johnson and Food for Peace*. Columbia: University of Missouri Press.

Alkon, Alison Hope, and Julian Agyeman, eds. 2014. *Cultivating Food Justice : Race, Class, and Sustainability*. Cambridge, MA: MIT Press.

Allen, Patricia. 2007. "The Disappearance of Hunger in America." *Gastronomica* 7 (3): 19–23.

Amrith, Sunil S. 2008. *Food and Welfare in India, c. 1900–1950*. Cambridge, UK: Cambridge University Press.

Anand, Bal K., and John R. Brobeck. 1951. "Hypothalamic Control of Food Intake in Rats and Cats." *Yale Journal of Biology and Medicine* 24 (2): 123.

Apple, Rima. 1996. *Vitamania: Vitamins in American Culture*. New Brunswick, NJ: Rutgers University Press.

Ashman, Linda, Jaime de la Vega, Marc Dohan, Andy Fisher, Rosa Hippler, and Bill Romain. 1993. "Seeds of Change: Strategies for Food Security for the Inner City," University of California–Los Angeles.

Associated Press. 2013. "Guantanamo Detainees' Hunger Strikes Will No Longer Be Disclosed by U.S. Military." *Washington Post*, December 4.

Avila, Joseph. 2016. "UCR Student Goes on 115-Hour Hunger Strike for Food Security." *The Highlander*, May 30.

Baily, Brianna. 2020. "Oklahoma Spends Less Than a Dollar a Meal Feeding Prisoners." *The Frontier*, October 20.

Baker, Phillip, Priscilla Machado, Thiago Santos, Katherine Sievert, Kathryn Backholer, Michalis Hadjikakou, Cherie Russell, Oliver Huse, Colin Bell, Gyorgy Scrinis, Anthony Worsley, Sharon Friel, and Mark Lawrence. 2020. "Ultra-processed Foods and the Nutrition Transition: Global, Regional and National Trends, Food Systems Transformations and Political Economy Drivers." *Obesity Reviews* 21 (12): e13126. https://doi.org/10.1111 /obr.13126.

Banu, Bargu. 2014. *Starve and Immolate: The Politics of Human Weapons*. New York: Columbia University Press.

Barksdale, Kevin T. 2009. *The Lost State of Franklin: America's First Secession*. Lexington: University Press of Kentucky.

Barrett, Kim E. 2014. "Neurohumoral Regulation of Gastrointestinal Function." In *Gastrointestinal Physiology*. New York: McGraw Hill. https://accessmedicine.mhmedical.com /content.aspx?bookid=691§ionid=45431400.

Bass, Manda. 2022. "Cummins Farm Named Century Farm." Arkansas Department of Corrections, October 5. Accessed September 13, 2023. https://doc.arkansas.gov/stories/cummins-farm-named-century-farm/.

Bauer, Lauren. 2020. "About 14 Million Children in the US Are Not Getting Enough To Eat." Brookings Institution. July 9. www.brookings.edu/blog/up-front/2020/07/09/about-14-million-children-in-the-us-are-not-getting-enough-to-eat/.

Bauer, Shane. 2018a. *American Prison: A Reporter's Undercover Journey into the Business of Punishment*. New York: Penguin.

Bauer, Shane. 2018b. "Today It Locks Up Immigrants. But CoreCivic's Roots Lie in the Brutal Past of America's Prisons." *Mother Jones* (September–October).

Bearden, Bessye. 1932. "Louise Thompson, Back from Russia, in 'Hunger' March." *Chicago Defender*, December 10.

Belluz, Julia. 2023. "What New Weight Loss Drugs Teach Us about Fat and Free Will." *New York Times*, January 21.

Benjamin, Ruha. 2019. "Introduction: Discriminatory Design, Liberating Imagination." In *Captivating Technologies: Race, Carceral Technoscience and Liberatory Imagination in Everyday Life*, edited by Ruha Benjamin, 1–22. Durham, NC: Duke University Press.

Berlant, Lauren. 2011. *Cruel Optimism*. Durham, NC: Duke University Press.

Berntson, Gary G., and Sahib S. Khalsa. 2021. "Neural Circuits of Interoception." *Trends in Neurosciences* 44 (1): 17–28. https://doi.org/10.1016/j.tins.2020.09.011.

Berridge, Kent C. 1996. "Food Reward: Brain Substrates of Wanting and Liking." *Neuroscience & Biobehavioral Reviews* 20 (1): 1–25.

Berridge, Kent C. 2004. "Motivation Concepts in Behavioral Neuroscience." *Physiology & Behavior* 81 (2): 179–209.

Berridge, Kenneth C., and Terry E. Robinson. 2003. "Parsing Reward." *Trends in Neuroscience* 26 (9): 507–513. https://doi.org/10.1016/S0166-2236(03)00233-9.

Biltekoff, Charlotte. 2013. *Eating Right in America. The Cultural Politics of Food and Health*. Durham, NC: Duke University Press.

Biltekoff, Charlotte. 2024. *Real Food, Real Facts: Processed Food and the Politics of Knowledge*. Berkeley: University of California Press.

"The Black Hills." 1875. *Minneapolis Tribune*, June 5, p. 2.

Black Panther Community News Service. 1969. *The Black Panther* (April 27, 1968), 3 (1): 1–5.

Blackhawk, Ned. 1997. "Julian Steward and the Politics of Representation: A Critique of Anthropologist Julian Steward's Ethnographic Portrayals of the American Indians of the Great Basin." *American Indian Culture and Research Journal* 21 (2): 61–81.

Blaisdell, Bob, ed. 2000. *Great Speeches by Native Americans*. Mineola, NY: Dover Publications.

Bloom, Stephen R., and J. M. Polak. 1978. "Gut Hormones." *Proceedings of the Nutrition Society* 37 (3): 259–271.

Blundell, John E. 2018. "Behaviour, Energy Balance, Obesity and Capitalism." *European Journal of Clinical Nutrition* 72 (9): 1305–1309. https://doi.org/10.1038/s41430-018-0231-x.

Blundell, John, Graham Finlayson, Mads Axelsen, Axel Flint, Catherine Gibbons, Trine Kvist, and Julie B. Hjerpsted. 2017. "Effects of Once-weekly Semaglutide on Appetite, Energy Intake, Control of Eating, Food Preference and Body Weight in Subjects with Obesity." *Diabetes Obesity and Metabolism* 19 (9): 1242–1251. https://doi.org/10.1111/dom.12932.

Blundell, John E., and Graham Finlayson. 2004. "Is Susceptibility to Weight Gain Characterized by Homeostatic or Hedonic Risk Factors for Overconsumption?." *Physiology and Behavior* 82 (1): 21–25.

Blundell, John E., and Graham Finlayson. 2011. "Food Addiction Not Helpful: The Hedonic Component—Implicit Wanting—Is Important." *Addiction* 106 (7): 1216–8; discussion 1219. https://doi.org/10.1111/j.1360-0443.2011.03413.x.

Born, Molly. 2018. "In Some States, Drug Felons Still Face Lifetime Ban on SNAP Benefits." National Public Radio. June 20. www.npr.org/sections/thesalt/2018/06/20/621391895/in-some-states-drug-felons-still-face-lifetime-ban-on-snap-benefits.

Braun, Lundy. 2014. *Breathing Race into the Machine: The Surprising Career of the Spirometer from Plantation to Genetics*. Minneapolis: University of Minnesota Press.

Brenner, Joseph, Robert Coles, Alan Mermann, Milton J. E. Senn, Cyril Walwayn, Raymond Wheeler, and Southern Regional Council. 1967. *Hungry Children*. Atlanta, GA: Southern Regional Council.

Brobeck, John R. 1993. "Remembrance of Experiments Almost Forgotten." *Appetite* 21 (3): 225–231.

Brosco, Jeffrey P. 2001. "Weight Charts and Well-Child Care: How the Pediatrician Became the Expert in Child Health." *Archives of Pediatrics and Adolescent Medicine* 155 (12): 1385–1389. https://doi.org/10.1001/archpedi.155.12.1385.

Brown, Maud A. 1920. "A Study of Malnutrition of Schoolchildren." *Journal of the American Medical Association* 75 (1): 27–30. https://doi.org/10.1001/jama.1920.02620270031008.

Bueltzingsloewen, Isabelle von. 2005. "Le sort des vieillards des hospices: Aperçu d'une hécatombe." In *Morts sans ordonnance: les aliénés et la faim dans un hôpital psychiatrique départemental du Rhône*, edited by Isabelle von Bueltzingsloewen, 149–161. Rennes: Presses Universitaires de Rennes.

"A Buffalo Campaign." 1869. *United States Army and Navy Journal and Gazette of the Regular and Volunteer Forces* 6 (45): 1.

Burnham, Grace M., and Labor Research Association. 1930. "Starve or Fight! A Challenge to the Unemployed." *The Daily Worker*, February 10.

Camacho, Angélica. 2023. "Unbroken Spirit: California SHU Prisoner Hunger Strikes and the Promise of Rebirth." *Kalfou* 10 (2): 165–92. Accessed November 15, 2024. www.proquest.com/scholarly-journals/unbroken-spirit/docview/3075726938/se-2.

Campbell, Nancy D. 2007. *Discovering Addiction: The Science and Politics of Substance Abuse Research*. Ann Arbor: University of Michigan Press.

Camplin, Erika. 2016. *Prison Food in America*. Lanham, MD: Rowman and Littlefield.

Canfield, Marsha. 1970. "Protesters Ask Action, Less Talk." *St. Louis Globe-Democrat*, October 9.

Cannon, Walter. 1916. *Bodily Changes in Pain, Hunger, Fear, and Rage: An Account of Recent Researches into the Function of Emotional Excitement*. New York: D. Appleton.

Cannon, Walter B. 1932. *Wisdom of the Body*. New York: W. W. Norton.

Cannon, Walter B. 1941. "The Body Physiologic and the Body Politic." *Science* 93 (2401): 1–10.

Carney, Megan. 2015. *The Unending Hunger: Tracing Women and Food Insecurity across Borders*. Berkeley: University of California Press.

Carolan, Michel. 2013. *Reclaiming Food Security*. Oxon: Routledge.

Carr, Martin, and Peter Davies. 1968. "Hunger in America." *CBS Reports*.

Carson, Jack. 1931. "Starvation Plus Slavery on Farms of the South." *Southern Worker*, October 3.

Carson, John. 2007. *The Measure of Merit: Talents, Intelligence, and Inequality in the French and American Republics, 1750–1940*. Princeton, NJ: Princeton University Press.

Cassady, Bridget A., Robert V. Considine, and Richard D. Mattes. 2012. "Beverage Consumption, Appetite, and Energy Intake: What Did You Expect." *American Journal of Clinical Nutrition* 95 (3): 587–593. https://doi.org/10.3945/ajcn.111.025437.

Casteel, D. B. 1911. "The Discriminative Ability of the Painted Turtle." *Journal of Animal Behavior* (1): 1–28.

Celio, Adam C., and Walter J. Pories. 2016. "A History of Bariatric Surgery." *Surgical Clinics of North America* 96 (4): 655–667. https://doi.org/10.1016/j.suc.2016.03.001.

"Charity Grafters Carry on Fake at Workers' Expense. By a Worker Correspondent." 1931. *Southern Worker*, December 5, p. 2.

Chen, Wen G., Dana Schloesser, Angela M. Arensdorf, Janine M. Simmons, Changhai Cui, Rita Valentino, James W. Gnadt, Lisbeth Nielsen, Coryse St. Hillaire-Clarke, Victoria Spruance, Todd S. Horowitz, Yolanda F. Vallejo, and Helene M. Langevin. 2021. "The Emerging Science of Interoception: Sensing, Integrating, Interpreting, and Regulating Signals within the Self." *Trends in Neurosciences* 44 (1): 3–16. https://doi.org/10.1016/j.tins.2020.10.007.

Cheon, Bobby K. 2021. "The Obesogenic Properties of Social Inequality: Perceived Socioeconomic Disadvantage Stimulates Appetite and Energy Intake." *Appetite* 157: 104969. https://doi.org/10.1016/j.appet.2020.104969.

Chilton, Mariana, and Jenny Rabinowich. 2012. "Toxic Stress and Child Hunger over the Life Course: Three Case Studies." *Journal of Applied Research on Children: Informing Policy for Children at Risk* 3 (1): 3.

Choudhury, Athia N. 2022. "The Making of the American Calorie and the Metabolic Metrics of Empire." *Journal of Transnational American Studies* 13 (1): 15–44. https://doi.org/10.5070/t813158578.

Citizens' Board of Inquiry into Hunger and Malnutrition in the United States. 1968. *Hunger USA: A Report by the Citizens' Board of Inquiry into Hunger and Malnutrition in the United States, with an Introductory Comment by Robert F. Kennedy*. Boston: Beacon Press.

Clark, Taliaferro. 1921. "Malnutrition." *Public Health Reports* 36 (17): 923–930.

Clarke, Adele E., and Joan H. Fujimura, eds. 1992. *The Right Tools for the Job: At Work in the Twentieth-century Life Sciences*. Princeton, NJ: Princeton University Press.

Cobb, Charlie. 1966. "Memo to: SNCC Communications. Re: Discussions at Mount Beulah Poor Peoples Meetings." Civil Rights Movement Archive. Accessed February 15, 2020. www.crmvet.org/docs/650209_sncc_cobb_pp.pdf.

Coleman, Beth. 2009. "Race as Technology." *Camera Obscura: Feminism, Culture, and Media Studies* 24 (1): 177–207. https://doi.org/10.1215/02705346-2008-018.

Collingham, Lizzie. 2011. *The Taste of War: World War II and the Battle for Food*. New York: Penguin.

"Color Line Missing As Hunger Marchers Besiege Capitol." 1932. *Pittsburgh Courier*, December 10, p. 1.

"Communists Behind the 'Hunger March' Moving on Capital." 1931. *New York Times*, November 29, pp. 1, 20.

Cook, C. W. 1971. "Statement by CW Cook Chairman of General Foods Corporation in Behalf of the Joint ANA-AAAA Committee before the Federal Trade Commission." Center for Science in the Public Interest, CSPI Collection, Industry Documents Library. Accessed Jun 15, 2022. www.industrydocuments.ucsf.edu/docs/fgvw0229.

Cook-Lynn, Elizabeth, and Mario Gonzales. 1999. *The Politics of Hallowed Ground: Wounded Knee and the Struggle for Indian Sovereignty*. Urbana: University of Illinois Press.

Cottom, Tressie McMillan. 2023. "Ozempic Can't Fix What Our Culture Has Broken." *New York Times*, October 9.

Crawford, James, and Mutop (aka Bow Low) DuGuya. 2011. "Why Prisoners Are Protesting: Pelican Bay State Prison Security Housing Units Peaceful Protest Hunger Strike Starting July 1, 2011." Accessed June 1, 2023. https://prisonerhungerstrikesolidarity.wordpress.com/voices-from-inside/why-prisoners-are-protesting/.

Cuellar, Jackie. 2022. "Gruel and Unusual: Prison Punishment Diets and the Eighth Amendment." *Minnesota Law Review* 107: 475–527.

Cullather, Nick. 2010. *The Hungry World: America's Cold War Battle against Poverty in Asia*. Cambridge, MA: Harvard University Press.

Cummings, David E. 2015. "Taste and the Regulation of Food Intake: It's Not Just about Flavor." *American Journal of Clinical Nutrition* 102 (4): 717–718. https://doi.org/10.3945/ajcn.115.120667.

"Curtis Silences Hunger Parade Leaders' Slur: 3,000 Demanding 'Make the Rich Pay' March to Capitol as Red Protest Hunger Marchers' on Peaceful Invasion of Capital." 1932. *New York Herald Tribune*, December 7.

Dagher, A. 2009. "The Neurobiology of Appetite: Hunger as Addiction." *International Journal of Obesity* 33: 30–33.

Damon, Anna. 1931. "Women's Role in the National Hunger March." *The Daily Worker*, November 6, p. 4.

Daschuk, James. 2014. *Clearing the Plains: Disease, Politics of Starvation and the Loss of Indigenous Life*. Regina: University of Regina Press.

Davidson, Thomas. 1947. "Interview with Mr. Thomas Davidson. Team Director, D.P. Operations, Germany. 10 April 1947." United Nations Archives and Records Management Section. Accessed March 15, 2023. https://search.archives.un.org/inteviews-various-officials-10.

Davis, Dána Ain. 2007. "Narrating the Mute: Racializing and Racism in a Neoliberal Moment." *Souls* 9 (4): 346–360. https://doi.org/10.1080/10999940701703810.

Davis, Mike. 2002. *Late Victorian Holocausts: El Niño Famines and the Making of the Third World*. London: Verso.

The Debt Collective. 2020. *Can't Pay Won't Pay: The Case for Economic Disobedience and Debt Abolition*. Chicago: Haymarket Books.

De Jong, Greta. 2000. "'With the Aid of God and the F.S.A.': The Louisiana Farmers' Union and the African American Freedom Struggle in the New Deal Era." *Journal of Social History* 34 (1): 105–139.

De Jong, Greta. 2016. *You Can't Eat Freedom: Southerners and Social Justice after the Civil Rights Movement*. Chapel Hill: University of North Carolina Press.

De Silva, Akila, and Stephen R. Bloom. 2012. "Gut Hormones and Appetite Control: A Focus on PYY and GLP-1 as Therapeutic Targets in Obesity." *Gut Liver* 6 (1): 10–20. https://doi.org/10.5009/gnl.2012.6.1.10.

De Waal, Alex. 2005. *Famine That Kills: Darfur, Sudan*. Oxford, UK: Oxford University Press.

DeParle, Jason. 2020. "As Hunger Swells, Food Stamps Become a Partisan Flash Point." *New York Times*, May 6.

DeVault, Marjorie L., and James P. Pitts. 1984. "Surplus and Scarcity: Hunger and the Origins of the Food Stamp Program." *Social Problems* 31 (5): 545–557. https://doi.org/10.2307/800240.

Dewsbury, Donald A. 2003. "Conflicting Approaches: Operant Psychology Arrives at a Primate Laboratory." *The Behavior Analyst* 26 (2): 253–265.

Di Marzo, V., A. Ligresti, and L. Cristino. 2009. "The Endocannabinoid System As a Link between Homoeostatic and Hedonic Pathways Involved in Energy Balance Regulation." *International Journal of Obesity* 33 (Suppl 2): S18–S24. https://doi.org/10.1038/ijo.2009.67.

Dickinson, Maggie. 2019. *Feeding the Crisis: Care and Abandonment in America's Food Safety Net*. Berkeley: University of California Press.

Dittmer, John. 2009. *The Good Doctors: The Medical Committee for Human Rights and the Struggle for Social Justice in Health Care*. New York: Bloomsbury Press.

Dodson, John D. 1917. "Relative Values of Reward And Punishment in Habit Formation." *Psychobiology* 1 (3): 231–276. https://doi.org/10.1037/h0072287.

Dole, Vincent P. 1959. "Body Fat." *Scientific American* 201 (6): 70–77.

Dole, Vincent P. 1965. "Thoughts on Narcotics Addiction." *Bulletin of the New York Academy of Medicine* 41 (2): 211–213.

Dole, Vincent P. 1989. "Vincent Dole." In *Addicts Who Survived: An Oral History of Narcotic Use in America Before 1965*, edited by David T. Courtwright, Herman Joseph, Don Des Jarlais, and Claude Brown, 331–343. Knoxville: University of Tennessee Press.

Dole, Vincent P., Irving L. Schwartz, Jorn Hess Thaysen, Niels A Thorn, and Lawrence Silver. 1954. "Treatment of Obesity with a Low Protein Calorically Unrestricted Diet." *American Journal of Clinical Nutrition* 2 (6): 381–391. https://doi.org/10.1093/ajcn/2.6.381.

Dorsey, L. C. 1992. "L. C. Dorsey." Duke University Sanford School of Public Policy. Accessed February 29, 2020. http://livinghistory.sanford.duke.edu/interviews/l-c-dorsey/.

Douglass, Frederick. 1882. "Speech at Elmira. West India Emancipation." In *Life and Times of Frederick Douglass Written by Himself*, 601–618. Hartford: Park Publishing.

Dove, W. Franklin. 1946. "Developing Food Acceptance Research." *Science* 103 (2668): 187–190. https://doi.org/10.1126/science.103.2668.187.

Downs, Jim. 2012. *Sick from Freedom, African-American Illness and Suffering during the Civil War and Reconstruction*. Oxford: Oxford University Press.

Drake, Samuel Gardner. 1851. *Biography and History of the Indians of North America, from Its First Discovery*. Boston: B.B. Mussey.

Dreiser, Theodore, Lester Cohen, Melvin P. Levy, Charles Walker, Adelaide Walker, Jessie Wakefield, Anna Rochester, Arnold Johnson, Bruce Crawford, Boris Israel, and Sherwood Anderson. 2008 [1932]. *Harlan Miners Speak: Report on Terrorism in the Kentucky Coal Fields Prepared by Members of the National Committee for the Defense of Political Prisoners*. Lexington: University Press of Kentucky.

Drewnowski, Adam, and M.R.C. Greenwood. 1983. "Cream and Sugar: Human Preferences for High-Fat Foods." *Physiology and Behavior* 30 (4): 629–633. https://doi.org/10.1016/0031-9384(83)90232-9.

Drèze, Jean. 1991. "Famine Prevention in India." In *The Political Economy of Hunger: Volume 2: Famine Prevention*, edited by Amartya Sen and Jean Drèze, 13–122. Oxford: Oxford University Press.

Drier, Peter, Megan Bomba, and Rosa Romero. 2016. *Food Insecurity among University of California Employees*. Los Angeles: Urban and Environmental Policy Institute, Occidental College.

Dror, Otniel E. 2016. "Cold War 'Super-Pleasure': Insatiability, Self-Stimulation, and the Postwar Brain." *Osiris* 31 (1): 227–249.

Drummond, Jack. 1950. Foreword in *The Biology of Human Starvation*, edited by Ancel Keys, Brožek Josef, Austin Henschel, Olaf Mickelsen, and Henry Longstreet Taylor, xiii–xvi. Minneapolis: University of Minnesota Press.

Du Bois, Cora. 1944. *The People of Alor: A Social-Psychological Study of an East Indian Island*. Minneapolis: University of Minnesota Press.

E.R.O. 1946. "International Mutual Aid: The Task of UNRRA." *The World Today* 2 (1): 35–44.

East, Elyssa. 2016. "Ballad of Harlan County." *Oxford American* 93.

"Economic Trends and the Weight of Children." 1933. *Journal of the American Medical Association* 101 (23): 1804. https://doi.org/10.1001/jama.1933.02740480036012.

Egan, Paul. 2016. "Prisoners Protest Food under New Contractor Trinity." *Detroit Free Press*, March 22.

Ellis, Fred. 1930. "Work or Wages." *Daily Worker*, February 18, p. 4.

Emberton, Carole. 2013. *Beyond Redemption: Race, Violence and the American South after the Civil War*. Chicago: University of Chicago Press.

Escobar, Arturo. 2011. *Encountering Development: The Making and Unmaking of the Third World*. Princeton, NJ: Princeton University Press.

Esquibel, Catriona Rueda, and Luz Calvo. 2013. "Decolonize Your Diet: A Manifesto." *nineteen sixty nine* 2 (1): 5.

Estes, Nick. 2019. *Our History Is the Future: Standing Rock versus the Dakota Access Pipeline, and the Long Tradition of Indigenous Resistance*. London: Verso.

Eyer, Joseph, and Peter Sterling. 1977. "Stress-related Mortality and Social Organization." *Review of Radical Political Economics* 9 (1): 1–44.

Farmer-Kaiser, Mary. 2010. *Freedwomen and the Freedmen's Bureau: Race, Gender, and Public Policy in the Age of Emancipation*. New York: Fordham University Press.

Fausto-Sterling, Anne. 2008. "The Bare Bones of Race." *Social Studies of Science* 38 (5): 657–694.

"FBI Probes Clash of Marchers, Police: Relief Official Says Hunger Marchers Will Not Have To Sleep in Fields." 1934. *Atlanta Constitution*, November 1, p. 20.

Feldman, Allen. 1991. *Formations of Violence: The Narrative of the Body and Political Terror in Northern Ireland*. Chicago: University of Chicago Press.

Ferguson, James. 1994. *The Anti-politics Machine: "Development," Depoliticization, and Bureaucratic Power in Lesotho*. Minneapolis: University of Minnesota Press.

Ferster, Charles. n.d. [ca. 1958]. "Procedure Wt. Con. Gp., Nov. 21" Charles Ferster archive, Archives of the History of American Psychology, M239.

Ferster, Charles B. 1958. "Control of Behavior in Chimpanzees and Pigeons by Time Out from Positive Reinforcement." *Psychological Monographs: General and Applied* 72 (8): 1–38. https://doi.org/10.1037/h0093787.

Ferster, Charles B., and Marian K. DeMyer. 1962. "A Method for the Experimental Analysis of the Behavior of Autistic Children." *American Journal of Orthopsychiatry* 32 (1): 89–98. https://doi.org/10.1111/j.1939-0025.1962.tb00267.x.

Ferster, Charles B., John I. Nurnberger, and Eugene B. Levitt. 1996 [1962]. "The Control of Eating." *Obesity Research* 4: 401–410.

"55 Stop Here for Hunger Demonstration." 1931. *Hartford Courant*, December 3, p. 22.

Finlayson, Graham, Neil King, and John E. Blundell. 2007. "Liking vs. Wanting Food: Importance for Human Appetite Control and Weight Regulation." *Neuroscience and Biobehavioral Reviews* 31 (7): 987–1002. https://doi.org/10.1016/j.neubiorev.2007.03.004.

Finlayson, Graham, Neil King, and John E. Blundell. 2008. "The Role of Implicit Wanting in Relation to Explicit Liking and Wanting for Food: Implications for Appetite Control." *Appetite* 50 (1): 120–127.

Firth, Caisin L., Elizabeth Sazie, Katrina Hedberg, Linda Drach, and Julie Maher. 2015. "Female Inmates with Diabetes: Results from Changes in a Prison Food Environment." *Women's Health Issues* 25 (6): 732–738. https://doi.org/10.1016/j.whi.2015.07.009.

Fisher, Andrew. 2017. *Big Hunger: The Unholy Alliance between Corporate America and Anti-Hunger Groups*. Cambridge, MA: MIT Press.

Food and Agriculture Organization (FAO), International Fund for Agricultural Development, UNICEF, World Food Programme, and World Health Organization. 2020. *State of Food Security and Nutrition in the World 2020: Transforming Food Systems for Affordable Healthy Diets*. Rome: FAO.

Food and Drug Administration (FDA). 2023. "Medications Containing Semaglutide Marketed for Type 2 Diabetes or Weight Loss." Accessed September 10, 2023. www.fda.gov/drugs/postmarket-drug-safety-information-patients-and-providers/medications-containing-semaglutide-marketed-type-2-diabetes-or-weight-loss.

"Forced Labor in Arkansas Cotton Fields. By Worker Correspondent." 1931. *Southern Worker*, October 31, p. 3.

"Forced Negroes to Work at Starvation Wages for 'Free' U.S. Red Cross Flour, Claim Floridians Forced To Do Laborious Work To Get Flour Provided by Congress." 1932. *Pittsburgh Courier*, August 27, p. 2.

Forney, Jacob. 1858. "Office of Superintendent of Indian Affairs, W.T., Great Salt Lake City, Utah Territory, September 6, 1858." In *Annual Report of the Commissioner for Indian Affairs Accompanying the Annual Report of the Secretary of the Interior for the Year 1858*, 317. Washington, DC: Wm. A. Harris.

Fortin, Kelsey, Susan Harvey, and Stacey Swearingen White. 2021. "Hidden Hunger: Understanding the Complexity of Food Insecurity Among College Students." *Journal of the American College of Nutrition* 40 (3): 242–252. https://doi.org/10.1080/07315724.2020.1754304.

Foucault, Michel. *Security, Territory, Population: Lectures At the Collège De France 1977–1978*. Translated by Graham Burchell. New York: St. Martin's Press, 2009.

Fraser, Nancy, and Linda Gordon. 1994. "A Genealogy of Dependency: Tracing a Keyword of the US Welfare State." *Signs: Journal of Women in Culture and Society* 19 (2): 309–336.

Friedman, Jeffrey. 2012. "Leading the Charge in Leptin Research: An Interview with Jeffrey Friedman." *Disease Models and Mechanisms* 5: 576–579. https://doi.org/10.1242/dmm.010629.

Frohlich, Xaq. 2024. *From Label to Table: Regulating Food in America in the Information Age*. Berkeley: University of California Press.

"From the Archives: Virginia State Prison Farm." 2023. *Richmond Times-Dispatch*, May 21.

Fullbrook, David. 2010. "Food as Security." *Food Security* 2 (1): 5–20. https://doi.org/10.1007/s12571-009-0050-y.

Gálvez, Alyshia. 2019. "Transnational Mother Blame: Protecting and Caring in a Globalized Context." *Medical Anthropology Quarterly* 38 (7): 574–587. https://doi.org/10.1080/01459740.2019.1653866.

Gannes, Harry. 1931. "Diet and 'Health' in the Harlan Coal Fields." *The Daily Worker*, November 21, p. 4.

Garcia, Heriberto Sharky. 2018. "If the Future Is Now: Revolutionary Abolitionist Art and Praxis from the Underside of White-American Civil Society." Accessed September 10, 2023. https://trueleappress.files.wordpress.com/2020/02/16.-sharky-if-the-future-is-now.pdf.

Garth, Hanna. 2013. "Obesity in Cuba: Memories of the Special Period and Approaches to Weight Loss Today." In *Reconstructing Obesity*, edited by Megan B. McCullogh and Jessica A. Hardin, 89–106. London: Berghahn Books.

Garth, Hanna. 2020. "Blackness and 'Justice' in the Los Angeles Food Justice Movement." In *Black Food Matters: Racial Justice in the Wake of Food Justice*, edited by Hanna Garth and Ashanté M. Reese, 107–130. Minneapolis: University of Minnesota Press.

Geiger, H. Jack. 1969. "The Endlessly Revolving Door." *American Journal of Nursing* 69 (11): 2436–2445.

Geiger, H. Jack, and Louise Cohen. 2017. "In Conversation with a Pioneer: Dr. Jack Geiger." Primary Care Development Corporation. Accessed September 10, 2023. www.pcdc.org/public-health-pioneer-conversation-dr-jack-geiger/.

Gere, Cathy. 2017. *Pain, Pleasure, and the Greater Good: From the Panopticon to the Skinner Box and Beyond*. Chicago: University of Chicago Press.

Gerlach, Hans Christian. 1998. *Krieg, Ernährung, Völkermord: Forschungen zur deutschen Vernichtungspolitik im Zweiten Weltkrieg*. Hamburg: Hamburger Edition.

Gibbs, James, and Gerard P. Smith. 1982. "Gut Peptides and Food in the Gut Produce Similar Satiety Effects." *Peptides* 3 (3): 553–557. https://doi.org/10.1016/0196-9781(82)90125-5.

Gibbs, James, Robert C. Young, and Gerard P. Smith. 1973. "Cholecystokinin Decreases Food Intake in Rats." *Journal of Comparative and Physiological Psychology* 84 (3): 488.

Gilbreth, Frank B. 1911. *Motion Study: A Method for Increasing the Efficiency of the Workman*. New York: D. Van Nostrand.

Gil-Campos, Mercedes, Concepción María Aguilera, Ramón Cañete, and Angel Gil. 2006. "Ghrelin: A Hormone Regulating Food Intake and Energy Homeostasis." *British Journal of Nutrition* 96 (2): 201–226. https://doi.org/10.1079/bjn20061787.

Glickman, Larry. 1997. *The Living Wage: American Workers and the Making of Consumer Society*. Ithaca, NY: Cornell University Press.

"Going Hungry for Freedom." 1968. *The Progressive* 32 (6): 8–9.

Goldrick-Rab, Sara, Jeb Richardson, and Anthony Hernandez. 2017. *Hungry and Homeless in College*. Madison, WI: Association of Community College Trustees.

Goldstein, Alyosha. 2018. "The Ground Not Given: Colonial Dispositions of Land, Race, and Hunger." *Social Text* 36 (2): 83–106. https://doi.org/10.1215/01642472-4362373.

Goldstein, Joseph. 2023. "The N.Y.C. Neighborhood That's Getting Even Thinner on Ozempic." *New York Times*, August 26.

Green, John J., Eleanor M. Green, and Anna M. Kleiner. 2014. "From the Past to the Present: Agricultural Development and Black Farmers in the American South." In *Cultivating Food Justice: Race, Class, and Sustainability*, edited by Alison Hope Alkon and Julian Agyeman, 47–64. Cambridge, MA: MIT Press.

Green, Laurie B. 2017. "The Media Matters: 50 Years after the "Discovery" of Hunger in the U.S." University of Texas at Austin. Accessed September 15, 2019. http://notevenpast .org/the-media-matters-reflections-on-the-fiftieth-anniversary-of-the-discovery-of -hunger-in-the-u-s/.

Greenough, Paul. 1982. *Prosperity and Misery in Modern Bengal. The Famine of 1943–1944.* Oxford, UK: Oxford University Press.

Grigson, Patricia Sue. 2002. "Like Drugs for Chocolate." *Physiology and Behavior* 76 (3): 389–395. https://doi.org/10.1016/S0031-9384(02)00758-8.

Guebenlian, Shane. 1947. "Hunger Strike Over." *Palestine Post*, April 23.

Guetzkow, Harold Steere, and Paul Hoover Bowman. 1946. *Men and Hunger: A Psychological Manual for Relief Workers*. Elgin, IL: Brethren Publishing House.

Guthman, Julie. 2011. *Weighing In: Obesity, Food Justice and the Limits of Capitalism*. Berkeley: University of California Press.

Guthman, Julie. 2015. "Binging and Purging: Agrofood Capitalism and the Body as Socioecological Fix." *Environment and Planning A: Economy and Space* 47 (12): 2522–2536. https://doi.org/10.1068/a140005p.

Haasberg, Analena Hope. 2020. "Nurturing the Revolution: The Black Panther Party and the Early Seeds of the Food Justice Movement." In *Black Food Matters: Racial Justice in the Wake of Food Justice*, edited by Hanna Garth and Ashanté M. Reese, 82–106. Minneapolis: University of Minnesota Press.

Halford, Jason C., Emma J. Boyland, John E. Blundell, Tim C. Kirkham, and Joanne A. Harrold. 2010. "Pharmacological Management of Appetite Expression in Obesity." *Nature Reviews Endocrinology* 6 (5): 255–269. https://doi.org/10.1038/nrendo.2010.19.

Halford, Jason C., Emma J. Boyland, Gillian D. Cooper, T. M. Dovey, C. J. Smith, N. Williams, C. L. Lawton, and J. E. Blundell. 2008. "Children's Food Preferences: Effects of Weight Status, Food Type, Branding and Television Food Advertisements (Commercials)." *International Journal of Pediatric Obesity* 3 (1): 31–38. https://doi.org /10.1080/17477160701645152.

Hall, Kevin D., A. Ayuketah, R. Brychta, H. Cai, T. Cassimatis, K. Y. Chen, S. T. Chung, E. Costa, A. Courville, V. Darcey, L. A. Fletcher, C. G. Forde, A. M. Gharib, J. Guo, R. Howard, P. V. Joseph, S. McGehee, R. Ouwerkerk, K. Raisinger, I. Rozga, M. Stagliano, M. Walter, P. J. Walter, S. Yang, and M. Zhou. 2019. "Ultra-Processed Diets Cause Excess Calorie Intake and Weight Gain: An Inpatient Randomized Controlled Trial of Ad Libitum Food Intake." *Cell Metabolism* 30 (1): 67–77.e3. https://doi .org/10.1016/j.cmet.2019.05.008.

Hamilton, Laura T., and Kelly Nielsen. 2021. *Broke: The Racial Consequences of Underfunding Public Universities*. Chicago: University of Chicago Press.

Hampl, Sarah E., Sandra G. Hassink, Ashley C. Skinner, S. C. Armstrong, S. E. Barlow, C. F. Bolling, K. C. Avila Edwards, I. Eneli, R. Hamre, M. M. Joseph, D. Lunsford, E. Mendonca, M. P. Michalsky, N. Mirza, E. R. Ochoa, M. Sharifi, A. E. Staiano,

A. E. Weedn, S. K. Flinn, J. Lindros, and K. Okechukwu. 2023. "Clinical Practice Guideline for the Evaluation and Treatment of Children and Adolescents With Obesity." *Pediatrics* 151 (2): e2022060640. https://doi.org/10.1542/peds.2022-060640.

Haraway, Donna. 2015. "Anthropocene, Capitalocene, Plantationocene, Chthulucene: Making Kin." *Environmental Humanities* 6 (1): 159–165. https://doi.org/10.1215/22011919 -3615934.

Hardy, Kathy. 2016. "Nutrition Services in Correctional Facilities." *Today's Dietician* 18 (6): 32.

Harlow, Harry F. 1953. "Mice, Monkeys, Men, and Motives." *Psychological Review* 60 (1): 23–32. https://doi.org/10.1037/h0056040.

Harris, Lashawn. 2009. "Running with the Reds: African American Women and the Communist Party during the Great Depression." *Journal of African American History* 94 (1): 21–43.

Harrison, Da'Shaun L. 2021. *Belly of the Beast: The Politics of Anti-Fatness as Anti-Blackness.* Berkeley: North Atlantic Books.

Harshaw, Christopher. 2008. "Alimentary Epigenetics: A Developmental Psychobiological Systems View of the Perception of Hunger, Thirst and Satiety." *Developmental Review* 28 (4): 541–569. https://doi.org/10.1016/j.dr.2008.08.001.

Hartford, Bruce. 1965. "Letter from Bruce Hartford (SCLC field staff, Selma) to Lynn Bush (UCLA CORE)." Civil Rights Movement Archive. Accessed February 15, 2020. www .crmvet.org/lets/650412_hartford-let.pdf.

Hartman, Saidiya V. 1997. *Scenes of Subjection: Terror, Slavery, and Self-Making in Nineteenth-century America.* Oxford, UK: Oxford University Press.

Hatch, Anthony Ryan. 2019. "Billions Served: Prison Food Regimes, Nutritional Punishment, and Gastronomical Resistance." In *Captivating Technologies: Race, Carceral Technoscience and Liberatory Imagination in Everyday Life,* edited by Ruha Benjamin, 67–84. Durham, NC: Duke University Press.

Hatch, Anthony Ryan, Sonya Sternlieb, and Julia Gordon. 2019. "Sugar Ecologies: Their Metabolic and Racial Effects." *Food, Culture and Society* 22 (5): 595–607. https://doi.org /10.1080/15528014.2019.1638123.

Hatch, John. 1992. "Interview with John Hatch." Rutherford Living History Collection. Accessed February 28, 2020. http://livinghistory.sanford.duke.edu/interviews/john-hatch/.

*Hearing before the Committee on Agriculture.* 1931. *Seventy-first Congress, third session. January 26, 27, 29, and February 2, 1931. Reforestation Act Amendment, Peanut Statistics, Farm and Unemployment Relief, Agricultural Credit Corporations, Experimental Farm in Mobile County, Alabama, National Arboretum Appropriations.* Washington, DC: Government Printing Office.

*Hearings before the Special Subcommittee on the Employment, Manpower and Poverty of the Committee on Labor and Public Welfare.* 1967. *United States Senate, Ninetieth Congress. First session on Examining the War on Poverty. Part 2. Jackson, Mississippi, April 10, 1967.* Washington, DC: Government Printing Office.

Heaton, John W. 2005. *The Shoshone-Bannocks: Culture and Commerce at Fort Hall, 1870–1940.* Lawrence: University Press of Kansas.

Hebb, Donald O. 1949. *The Organization of Behavior: A Neuropsychological Theory.* New York: John Wiley and Sons.

Hecht, Gabrielle, ed. 2011. *Entangled Geographies: Empire and Technopolitics in the Global Cold War.* Cambridge, MA: MIT Press.

Hennen, John C. 2008. Introduction to the New Edition. In *Harlan Miners Speak: Report on Terrorism in the Kentucky Coal Fields Prepared by Members of the National Committee for the Defense of Political Prisoners*, 7–32. Lexington: University Press of Kentucky.

Henry, Lisa. 2017. "Understanding Food Insecurity among College Students: Experience, Motivation, and Local Solutions." *Annals of Anthropological Practice* 41 (1): 6–19. https://doi.org/10.1111/napa.12108.

Hernandez, Kelly Lytle. 2017. *City of Inmates: Conquest, Rebellion, and the Rise of Human Caging in Los Angeles, 1771–1965*. Chapel Hill: University of North Carolina Press.

Hervey, G. R. 1959. "The Effects of Lesions in the Hypothalamus in Parabiotic Rats." *Journal of Physiology* 145 (2): 336–352. https://doi.org/10.1113/jphysiol.1959.sp006145.

Hetherington, A. W., and S. W. Ranson. 1940. "Hypothalamic Lesions and Adiposity in the Rat." *The Anatomical Record* 78 (2): 149–172. https://doi.org/10.1002/ar.1090780203.

Hicks, Vinnie C. 1911. "The Relative Values of the Different Curves of Learning." *Journal of Animal Behavior* 1 (2): 138–156.

Hickson, John L., and Sugar Association, Inc. 1960. "[Letter from John L Hickson on March 17, 1960 enclosing report of the first meeting of the Scientific Advisory Committee]." Roger Adams Papers, University of Illinois Archives, Industry Documents Library. www.industrydocuments.ucsf.edu/docs/yzvk0226.

Hillyer, Reiko. 2019. "'Going Up on the Way Down': The Virginia State Penitentiary, *Landman v. Royster*, and the Rise and Fall of Prison Litigation." *Journal of Civil and Human Rights* 5 (1): 1–42.

Hinton, Elizabeth. 2016. *From the War on Poverty to the War on Crime: The Making of Mass Incarceration in America*. Cambridge, MA: Harvard University Press.

Hobart, Hiʻilei Julia, ed. 2019. *The Foodways of Hawaiʻi*. Routledge.

Hoffman, David. 1983. "Discussing Hunger in U.S., Meese Sparks a Firestorm: Meese Sparks a Political Firestorm with Remarks about Hunger in U.S." *Washington Post*, December 10.

Hoge, Mildred A., and Ruth J. Stocking. 1912. "A Note on the Relative Value of Punishment and Reward As Motives." *Journal of Animal Behavior* 2 (1): 43–50.

Holian, Anna. 2011. *Between National Socialism and Soviet Communism: Displaced Persons in Postwar Germany*. Ann Arbor: University of Michigan Press.

Hoover, Herbert. 1931a. "Annual Message to the Congress on the State of the Union. December 8, 1931." In *Public Papers of the Presidents of the United States. Herbert Hoover. Containing the Public Messages, Speeches and Statements of the President. January 1 to December 31, 1931*, pp. 580–597. Washington, DC: Government Printing Office.

Hoover, Herbert. 1931b. "The President's News Conference of September 11, 1931: Unemployment and Relief." In *Public Papers of the Presidents of the United States. Herbert Hoover. Containing the Public Messages, Speeches and Statements of the President. January 1 to December 31, 1931*, 417–419. Washington, DC: Government Printing Office.

Hopkins, Mark, and John E. Blundell. 2017. "Energy Metabolism and Appetite Control: Separate Roles for Fat-Free Mass and Fat Mass in the Control of Food Intake in Humans." In *Appetite and Food Intake: Central Control*, edited by Ruth B. S. Harris, 67–90. Boca Raton, FL: CRC Press.

Hubbard, Tasha. 2014. "Buffalo Genocide in Nineteenth-Century North America: 'Kill, Skin, and Sell.'" In *Colonial Genocide in Indigenous North America*, edited by Alexander

Laban Hinton, Andrew Woolford, and Jeff Benvenuto, 292–305. Raleigh, NC: Duke University Press.

"'Hunger Hikers' Halt at Brickpile, but Throw None." 1931. *New York Herald Tribune*, December 4, p. 2.

*Hunger and Malnutrition in US*. 1968. *Hearings Before the United States Senate Committee on Labor and Public Welfare, Subcommittee on Employment, Manpower, and Poverty, Ninetieth Congress, Second Session, on May 23, 29, June 12, 14, 1968*. Washington, DC: Government Printing Office.

"Hunger March in St. Louis Is Ended by Riot." 1931. *Washington Post*, January 17, p. 1.

"Hunger March Spurs Relief." 1931. *Los Angeles Times*, July 20, p. 3.

"Hunger March Squelched: Radicals Get Free Rides to Jail While Unemployed Show No Inclination to Parade." 1932. *Los Angeles Times*, October 4, p. A18.

"Hunger Marcher?" 1932. *Austin Statesman*, December 5, p. 4.

"Hunger Marchers Speak for 12,000,000 Jobless! Fight for Unemployment Insurance!" 1931. *The Daily Worker*, November 23, p. 1.

"Hunger Parade Today Allowed by Washington: Marchers to Present Plea to Congress, Then Depart, by Agreement with Police." 1932. *New York Herald Tribune*, December 6, p. 3.

"Hunger Strike." 1947. *Atlanta Constitution*, June 20, p. 7.

"Hunger Strike Over." 1946. *Palestine Post*, July 18, p. 1.

Hunt, P. B. 1881. "Kiowa, Comanche and Wichita Agency; September 1, 1881." In *Annual Report of the Commissioner of Indian Affairs to the Secretary of the Interior for the Year 1881*, 77–82. Washington, DC: Government Printing Office, https://digitalcommons.csumb.edu/hornbeck_usa_2_e/19.

Ibrahim, Baher. 2021. "Uprooting, Trauma, and Confinement: Psychiatry in Refugee Camps, 1945–1993." Glasgow University.

Imamura, M., I. Sasaki, J. Kameyama, and T. Sato. 1984. "Response of Gastric Acid and Gut Hormones in Biliary Tract Reconstruction Using an Interposed Jejunum or Ileum in Dogs." *Surgical Gastroenterology* 3 (1): 51–58.

Incarcerated Workers Organizing Committee Research (IWOC)/Action Cooperative. 2018. "Cruel and Usual: A National Prisoner Survey of Prison Food and Health Care Quality." Incarcerated Workers Organizing Committee. Accessed September 15, 2023. https://incarceratedworkers.org/sites/default/files/resource_file/iwoc_report_04-18_final.pdf.

Ismail, Evan. 2017a. "How the R'Pantry Is Working to Combat Food Insecurity." *The Highlander*, February 6.

Ismail, Evan. 2017b. "'Hunger Does Not Equal Profit': Feed the People Protest Food Insecurity at the Bell Tower." *The Highlander*, March 6.

Ismail, Evan. 2017c. "The Seeds of Change: How the R'Garden Is Doing Its Part for Food Insecure Students." *The Highlander*, February 27.

Jackson, Aunt Molly, and John Greenway. 1961. *Songs and Stories of Aunt Molly Jackson*. Smithsonian Folkways Recordings FW05457, FH 5457. https://folkways.si.edu/aunt-molly-jackson-and-john-greenway/the-songs-and-stories-of/american-folk-struggle-protest/music/album/smithsonian.

Jacob, Margaret D. 2006. "Indian Boarding Schools in Comparative Perspective: The Removal of Indigenous Children in the United States and Australia, 1880–1940." In *Boarding School Blues: Revisiting American Indian Educational Experiences*, edited by

Clifford E. Trafzer, Jean A. Keller, and Lorene Sisquoc, 202–231. Lincoln: University of Nebraska Press.

"Japan Bans Hunger Strike: Declares Weapons Illegal and Evicts Electrical Workers." 1946. *New York Times*, November 14, p. 6.

Jarosz, Lucy. 2011. "Defining World Hunger: Scale and Neoliberal Ideology in International Food Security Policy Discourse." *Food, Culture and Society* 14 (1): 117–139.

Jarosz, Lucy. 2014. "Comparing Food Security and Food Sovereignty Discourses." *Dialogues in Human Geography* 4 (2): 168–181. https://doi.org/10.1177/2043820614537161.

Johnson, Albert Prodigy, and Kathy Iandoli. 2016. *Commissary Kitchen: My Infamous Prison Cookbook*. New York: Infamous Books.

Johnson, H. M. 1914. "Visual Pattern-Discrimination in the Vertebrates-II. Comparative Visual Acuity in the Dog, the Monkey and the Chick." *Journal of Animal Behavior* 4 (5): 340–361.

Jonçich, Geraldine M. 1968. *The Sane Positivist: A Biography of Edward L. Thorndike*. Middletown, CT: Wesleyan University Press.

Jones, Brennon. 1979. "Feeding the Workers." *New York Times*, p. A21.

Joseph A. Myers Center for Research on Native American Issues and Native American Student Development. 2021. "The University of California Land Grab: A Legacy of Profit from Indigenous Land." University of California–Berkeley. Accessed January 6, 2022. https://indd.adobe.com/view/7cdb5d0a-47e1-4811-8538-39bb255f0928.

Kalina, Kasia. 2019. "Rehabilitation as the Wage of Starvation: The 1941 Local 313 Sharecropper Strike's Critical Theory of Normativity." *International Labor and Working-Class History* 96: 60–78. https://doi.org/10.1017/s014754791900022x.

Kare, Morley R. 1969. "Sensory Perception Research" in *Research Symposium: Seeking New Approaches to Old Problems*. Bethesda, MD: International Sugar Research Foundation. Roger Adams Papers, University of Illinois Archives, Industry Documents Library. www.industrydocuments.ucsf.edu/docs/mkbk0226.

Kay, Helen. 1932. "The Fight of the Hunger Children." *The Daily Worker*, December 3, p. 3.

Kearns, Cristin E., Stanton A. Glantz, and Dorie E. Apollonio. 2019. "In Defense of Sugar: A Critical Analysis of Rhetorical Strategies Used in the Sugar Association's Award-Winning 1976 Public Relations Campaign." *BMC Public Health* 19 (1): 1150. https://doi.org/10.1186/s12889-019-7401-1.

Kelley, Robin D. G. 1991. *Hammer and Hoe: Alabama Communists during the Great Depression*. Chapel Hill: University of North Carolina Press.

Kennedy, G. C. 1953. "The Role of Depot Fat in the Hypothalamic Control of Food Intake in the Rat." *Proceedings of the Royal Society of London. Series B—Biological Sciences* 140 (901): 578–592. https://doi.org/10.1098/rspb.1953.0009.

Keys, Ancel. 1946. "Battle of Hunger: What happens to the Minds and Bodies of the Millions Starving Today?." *New York Times*, June 23.

Keys, Ancel, Josef Brožek, Austin Henschel, Olaf Mickelsen, and Henry Longstreet Taylor. 1950. *The Biology of Human Starvation*. 2 vol. Minneapolis: University of Minnesota Press.

"The Klan Rides against the Hunger Marchers." 1932. *Pittsburgh Courier*, December 10, p. 4.

Klinger, Alfred D., Robert Mendelsohn, and Jaqui Alberts. 1970. "A Reply to Dr. Herbert Pollack Re: Hunger USA." *American Journal of Clinical Nutrition* 23 (6): 677–683.

Kohler-Hausmann, Julilly. 2017. *Getting Tough: Welfare and Imprisonment in 1970s America.* Princeton, NJ: Princeton University Press.

Kohler-Hausmann, Julilly. 2015. "Guns and Butter: The Welfare State, the Carceral State, and the Politics of Exclusion in the Postwar United States." *Journal of American History* 102 (1): 87–99. https://doi.org/10.1093/jahist/jav239.

Kojima, M., H. Hosoda, Y. Date, M. Nakazato, H. Matsuo, and K. Kangawa. 1999. "Ghrelin Is a Growth-Hormone-Releasing Acylated Peptide from Stomach." *Nature* 402 (6762): 656–660. https://doi.org/10.1038/45230.

Kornbluh, Felicia. 2015. "Food as a Civil Right: Hunger, Work, and Welfare in the South after the Civil Rights Act." *Labor* 12 (1–2): 135–158. https://doi.org/10.1215/15476715-2837640.

Krieger, Nancy. 2011. *Epidemiology and the People's Health: Theory and Context.* Oxford, UK: Oxford University Press.

Labor Research Association. 1931. "Capitalism Kills Children." *The Daily Worker.*

Lagemann, Ellen Condliffe. 1989. "The Plural Worlds of Educational Research." *History of Education Quarterly* 29 (2): 185–214.

Latham, Michael C. 1968. "The Hunger USA Debate." William F. Darby Papers, Eskind Biomedical Library Manuscripts Collection Repository, Vanderbilt, Industry Documents Library. Accessed February 30, 2020. www.industrydocuments.ucsf.edu/docs/stkd0228.

Laurent, Sylvie. 2018. *King and the Other America: The Poor People's Campaign and the Quest for Economic Equality.* Berkeley: University of California Press.

Leab, Daniel J. 1967. "'United We Eat': The Creation and Organization of the Unemployed Councils in 1930." *Labor History* 8 (3): 300–315. https://doi.org/10.1080/00236566708584023.

LeBlanc, Hannah Findlen. 2019. "Nutrition for National Defense: American Food Science in World War II and the Cold War." Stanford University.

Leigh Smith, Jenny. 2015. "The Awkward Years: Defining and Managing Famines, 1944–1947." *History and Technology* 31 (3): 206–219. https://doi.org/10.1080/07341512.2015.1129810.

Lemov, Rebecca. 2005. *World as Laboratory: Experiments with Mice, Mazes, and Men.* New York: Hill and Wang.

"Letter from Field Secretary, American Eugenics Association to Fair Associations asking education exhibit space." 1930. Image Archive on the American Eugenics Movement, Dolan DNA Learning Center, Cold Spring Harbor Laboratory. Accessed June 30, 2018. www.eugenicsarchive.org/html/eugenics/index2.html?tag=704.

Levitt, Eugene. 1958. "Notes on the Meeting of the Weight Control Group, December 12, 1958." Charles Ferster collection, Archives of the History of American Psychology, M239.

Lewis, David Rich. 1994. *Neither Wolf nor Dog: American Indians, Environment, and Agrarian Change.* Oxford, UK: Oxford University Press.

London, Jenny, and Alexi Jones. 2021. "Food Insecurity Is Rising, and Incarceration Puts Families at Risk." Prison Policy Initiative. Accessed September 15, 2023. www.prisonpolicy.org/blog/2021/02/10/food-insecurity/.

Luissier, Kira. 2018. "The Entrepreneurial Work Ethic: the Racial Politics of Motivation," in "Personality, Incorporated: Psychological Capital in American Management, 1960–1995," 80–92. PhD diss., University of Toronto 2018. Proquest (10936855).

Lynch, Amanda, Andrea T. Kozak, and Kerstyn C. Zalesin. 2022. "'The Stomach I Have Now Has a Brain Connection': Changes in Experiences of Hunger and Fullness Following Bariatric Surgery." *Appetite* 179: 106271. https://doi.org/10.1016/j.appet.2022.106271.

MacLean, Paul S., John E. Blundell, J. A. Mennella, and R. L. Batterham. 2017. "Biological Control of Appetite: A Daunting Complexity." *Obesity* 25 (Suppl 1): S8–S16. https://doi.org/10.1002/oby.21771.

Magat, Mela. 2015. "UCR Takes Steps To End Food Insecurity among Students." *The Highlander*, June 1.

"Malnutrition and Hunger in the United States." 1970. *Journal of the American Medical Association* 213 (2): 272–275. https://doi.org/10.1001/jama.1970.03170280032006.

*Malnutrition and Starvation in Western Netherlands: September 1944—July 1945.* 1948. The Hague: General State Publishing Office.

Manley, Rebecca. 2015. "Nutritional Dystrophy: The Science and Semantics of Starvation in WWII." In *Hunger and War: Food Provisioning in the Soviet Union during World War II*, edited by Wendy Z. Goldman and Donald A. Filtzer, 206–264. Indianapolis: Indiana University Press.

Mannie, Kathryn. 2023. "'It Changed My Life': Ozempic Patient Shares Her Good, Bad and Scary Side Effects." *Global News*, July 5.

Marcus, Ruth. 2023. "I Lost 40 Pounds on Ozempic. But I'm Left with Even More Questions." *Washington Post*, June 6.

Marcuse, Herbert. 1991 [1964]. *One-Dimensional Man: Studies in the Ideology of Advanced Industrial Society*. Boston: Beacon Press.

Martin, Ernest F. 1972. "The 'Hunger in America' Controversy." *Journal of Broadcasting* 16 (2): 185–194. https://doi.org/10.1080/08838157209386342.

Martinez, Suzanna M., Karen Webb, Edward A. Frongillo, and Lorrene D. Ritchie. 2018. "Food Insecurity in California's Public University System: What Are the Risk Factors." *Journal of Hunger and Environmental Nutrition* 13 (1): 1–18. https://doi.org/10.1080/19320248.2017.1374901.

Marya, Rupa, and Raj Patel. 2021. *Inflamed: Deep Medicine and the Anatomy of Injustice*. London: Penguin.

Maryland Food and Prison Abolition Project (MFPAP). 2021. "'I Refuse to Let Them Kill Me': Food, Violence, and the Maryland Correctional Food System." Accessed September 10, 2023. https://static1.squarespace.com/static/5cfbd4669f33530001eeeb1e/t/614a994382003d4b88ba44d9/1632278867753/Food%2C+Violence%2C+and+the+Maryland+Correctional+Food+System+%E2%80%94+Full+Report.pdf.

Maslow, Abraham H. 1943. "Preface to Motivation Theory." *Psychosomatic Medicine* 5: 85–92.

Maslow, Abraham H. 1970. *Motivation and Personality*. New York: Harper & Row.

Mayer, Jean. 1953. "Glucostatic Mechanism of Regulation of Food Intake." *New England Journal of Medicine* 249: 13–16.

Mayer, Jean. 1955. "Regulation of Energy Intake and Body Weight: The Glucostatic Theory and the Lipogenic Hypothesis." *Annals of the New York Academy of Sciences* 63 (1): 15–43. https://doi.org/10.1111/j.1749-6632.1955.tb36543.x.

Mayer, Jean. 1966a. "Some Aspects of the Problem of Regulation of Food Intake and Obesity." *New England Journal of Medicine* 274 (13): 722–731.

Mayer, Jean. 1966b. "Why People Get Hungry." *Nutrition Today* 2–8.

Mayer, Jean. 1971. "Jean Mayer on the Hunger Documentary." *Washington Post*.

Mayer, Jean. 1972. "Nutrition: Substitute a Bit of Roquefort for a Dousing of Salt." *Washington Post*.

Mayer, Jean. 1977. "My Life as a Physiologist and Nutritionist." In *Discovery Processes in Modern Biology: People and Processes in Biological Discovery*, edited by William Robert Klemm, 175–192. New York: RE Krieger Publishing Company.

Mayer, Jean, Leonore F. Monello, and Carl C. Seltzer. 1965. "Hunger and Satiety Sensations in Man." *Postgraduate Medicine* 37: 97–102. https://doi.org/10.1080/00325481.1965.11695562.

"Mayor Evades Hunger Meet. By a Worker Correspondent." 1931. *Southern Worker*, December 12, p. 4.

McCarty, Maclyn. 1984. "Presentation of the Academy Medal to Vincent P. Dole, MD." *Bulletin of the New York Academy of Medicine* 60 (8): 790.

McClelland, David C., and John W. Atkinson. 1948. "The Projective Expression of Needs: I. The Effect of Different Intensities of the Hunger Drive on Perception." *Journal of Psychology* 25 (2): 205–222.

McCullogh, Megan B., and Jessica A. Hardin. 2013. Introduction in *Reconstructing Obesity: The Meaning of Measures and the Measure of Meanings*, edited by Jessica A. Hardin and Megan B. McCullogh, 1–26. New York: Berghahn Books.

McDowell, Robin, and Margie Mason. 2024. "Prisoners in the US Are Part of a Hidden Workforce Linked To Hundreds of Popular Food Brands." *AP News*, January 29.

McKeithen, Will. 2022. "Carceral Nutrition: Prison Food and the Biopolitics of Dietary Knowledge in the Neoliberal Prison." *Food and Foodways* 30 (1–2): 58–81. https://doi.org/10.1080/07409710.2022.2030938.

McKinley, Jesse. 2018. "Goodbye, Prison Loaf: Reporter's Notebook." *New York Times*, December 28.

McKittrick, Katherine. 2013. "Plantation Futures." *Small Axe: A Caribbean Journal of Criticism* 17 (3) (42): 1–15. https://doi.org/10.1215/07990537-2378892.

Mead, Margaret. 1943. "The Problem of Changing Food Habits: With Suggestions for Psychoanalytic Contributions." *ETC: A Review of General Semantics* 1 (1): 47–50.

Meckel, Richard A. 2008. "Politics, Policy, and the Measuring of Child Health: Child Malnutrition in the Great Depression." In *Healing the World's Children: Interdisciplinary Perspectives on Child Health in the Twentieth Century*, edited by Cynthia Comacchio, Janet Golden, and George Weisz, 235–252. Montreal: McGill-Queen's University Press.

Meehl, Paul E. 1992. "Needs (Murray, 1938) and State-variables (Skinner, 1938)." *Psychological Reports* 70 (2): 407–450. https://doi.org/10.2466/pro.1992.70.2.407.

Meerloo, Joost A. M. 1945. *Total War and the Human Mind: A Psychologist's Experiences in Occupied Holland*. New York: International Universities Press.

Meerloo, Joost A. M. 1952. "Contribution of the Psychiatrist to the Management of Crisis Situations." *American Journal of Psychiatry* 109 (5): 352–355. https://doi.org/10.1176/ajp.109.5.352.

Meiselman, Herbert L., and Howard G. Schutz. 2003. "History of Food Acceptance Research in the US Army." *Appetite* 40 (3): 199–216. https://doi.org/10.1016/s0195-6663(03)00007-2.

Meza, Anthony, Emily Altman, Suzanna Martinez, and Cindy W. Leung. 2019. "'It's a Feeling That One Is Not Worth Food': A Qualitative Study Exploring the Psychosocial Experience and Academic Consequences of Food Insecurity Among College Students." *Journal of the Academy of Nutrition and Dietetics* 119 (10): 1713–1721. https://doi.org/10.1016/j.jand.2018.09.006.

"Mill Slavery for Women in Mills of Danville, Va. By a Worker Correspondent." 1931. *Southern Worker*, December 5, p. 3.

Miller, Neal E., Clark J. Bailey, and James A. F. Stevenson. 1950. "Decreased 'Hunger' but Increased Food Intake Resulting from Hypothalamic Lesions." *Science* 112 (2905): 256–259.

Miller, Neal E., Gardner L. Hart, and Yale University Institute of Human Relations. 1948. *Motivation and Reward in Learning*. Yale University.

Mills, Wesley. 1899. "The Nature of Animal Intelligence and the Methods of Investigating It." *Psychological Review* 6 (3): 262–274.

Mink, Gwendolyn. 1996. *The Wages of Motherhood: Inequality in the Welfare State, 1917–1942*. Ithaca, NY: Cornell University Press.

Mintz, Sidney W. 1986. *Sweetness and Power: The Place of Sugar in Modern History*. New York: Penguin.

Mississippi Freedom Democratic Party (MFDP). 1966. "Why We Are Here at the Greenville Air Force Base." Wisconsin Historical Society. Accessed February 15, 2020. http://content.wisconsinhistory.org/cdm/ref/collection/p15932coll2/id/40550.

Mita, Tore J. 1969. "Letters to the Editor: Role of the Public Health Nutritionist." *American Journal of Clinical Nutrition* 22 (9): 1157–1159. https://doi.org/10.1093/ajcn/22.9.1157.

Montange, Leah. 2017. "Hunger Strikes, Detainee Protest, and the Relationality of Political Subjectivization." *Citizenship Studies* 21 (5): 509–526. https://doi.org/10.1080/13621025.2017.1316702.

Moodie, Rob, David Stuckler, Carlos Monteiro, Nick Sheron, Bruce Neal, Thaksaphon Thamarangsi, Paul Lincoln, Sally Casswell, and NCD Action Group Lancet. 2013. "Profits and Pandemics: Prevention of Harmful Effects of Tobacco, Alcohol, and Ultra-Processed Food and Drink Industries." *Lancet* 381 (9867): 670–679. https://doi.org/10.1016/S0140-6736(12)62089-3.

Moraes, Amanda Guarino. 2019. "Treating Hunger: Medical Expertise, Nutritional Science and the Development of Technical Food Solutions," PhD diss., Queens University. Proquest (13910042).

Moran, Rachel Louise. 2011. "Consuming Relief: Food Stamps and the New Welfare of the New Deal." *Journal of American History* 97 (4): 1001–1022. https://doi.org/10.1093/jahist/jaq067.

Moran, Rachel Louise. 2018. *Governing Bodies: American Politics and the Shaping of the Modern Physique*. Philadelphia: University of Pennsylvania Press.

Morris-Suzuki, Tessa. 2005. *The Past within Us: Media, Memory, History*. London: Verso.

Morrison, Margaret, and Mary S. Morgan. 1999. "Models as Mediating Instruments." In *Models as Mediators: Perspectives on Natural and Social Science*, edited by Mary S. Morgan and Margaret Morrison, 10–38. Cambridge, UK: Cambridge University Press.

Moses, Robert P. 1962. "Letter from Bob Moses to Martha Prescod re Hunger & Food Need in Mississippi, December 1962." Civil Rights Movement Archives. Accessed February 1, 2020. www.crmvet.org/lets/6212_moses-prescod-letter.pdf.

Moses, Robert P. 2001. *Radical Equations: Civil Rights from Mississippi to the Algebra Project*. Boston: Beacon Press.

Moskowitz, Howard R. 1971. "The Sweetness and Pleasantness of Sugars." *American Journal of Psychology* 84 (3): 387–405.

Moskowitz, Howard R., and Joel L. Sidel. 1971. "Magnitude and Hedonic Scales of Food Acceptability." *Journal of Food Science* 36 (4): 677–680.

Moss, Fred A. 1924. "Study of Animal Drives." *Journal of Experimental Psychology* 7 (3): 165–185. https://doi.org/10.1037/h0070966.

Moss, Michael. 2013. *Salt Sugar Fat: How the Food Giants Hooked Us.* Toronto: McClelland & Stewart.

Mozaffarian, Dariush. 2022. "Perspective: Obesity—An Unexplained Epidemic." *American Journal of Clinical Nutrition* 115 (6): 1445–1450. https://doi.org/10.1093/ajcn/nqac075.

Mudry, Jessica J. 2009. *Measured Meals: Nutrition in America.* Albany: State University of New York Press.

Mueller, John F. 1969. "The Conscience of a Scientific Society." *American Journal of Clinical Nutrition* 22 (11): 1411–1414. https://doi.org/10.1093/ajcn/22.11.1411.

Mukherjee, Trisha. 2017. "Panther, Poet, Professor: Jamal Joseph on Columbia and Harlem." Columbia University. Accessed February 25, 2020. www.columbiaspectator.com/the -eye/2017/11/09/panther-prisoner-poet-professor-jamal-joseph-on-columbia-and-harlem/.

Murphy, M. 2011. "Distributed Reproduction." In *Corpus: An Interdisciplinary Reader on Bodies and Knowledge,* edited by Monica J. Casper and Paisley Currah, 21–38. New York: Palgrave Macmillan.

Murphy, M. 2017. *The Economization of Life.* Durham, NC: Duke University Press.

Nadasen, Premilla. 2004. *Welfare Warriors: The Welfare Rights Movement in the United States.* New York: Routledge.

"National Hunger March Parades Thru Washington. Fight for Unemployment Insurance! Support the Demands of the Hunger March! (Statement of the Central Committee, CPUSA)." 1931. *The Daily Worker,* December 7, pp. 1–2.

"National Hunger March to Washington. Four Main Columns Will Reach Capitol Dec 7th. Unemployed Councils Issue Nation-Wide Call to Intensify Fight Against Starvation." 1931. *Southern Worker,* October 24, p. 2.

National Museum of African American History and Culture (NMAAHC). 2021. "Grounds for Solidarity: Resurrection City." Smithsonian Museum. Accessed February 1, 2021. https://nmaahc.si.edu/explore/manylenses/grounds-solidarity.

Native American Food Sovereignty Alliance (NAFSA). 2020. Accessed June 15, 2023. https:// nativefoodalliance.org/.

Nazmi, Aydin, Suzanna Martinez, Ajani Byrd, Derrick Robinson, Stephanie Bianco, Jennifer Maguire, Rashida M. Crutchfield, Kelly Condron, and Lorrene Ritchie. 2019. "A Systematic Review of Food Insecurity among US Students in Higher Education." *Journal of Hunger and Environmental Nutrition* 14 (5): 725–740. https://doi.org/10.1080 /19320248.2018.1484316.

Nelson, Alondra. 2011. *Body and Soul: The Black Panther Party and the Fight Against Medical Discrimination.* Minneapolis: University of Minnesota Press.

Nelson, Eshe. 2023. "How Ozempic and Weight Loss Drugs Are Reshaping Denmark's Economy." *New York Times,* August 28.

Nelson, Melissa. 2002. "Arkansas Prison Still Shackled to Dark Past." *Los Angeles Times,* January 6.

Nelson, Stanley, dir. 2016. *The Black Panthers: Vanguard of the Revolution.* New York: Firelight Films.

Nestle, Marion, and Sally Guttmacher. 1992. "Hunger in the United States: Rationale, Methods, and Policy Implications of State Hunger Surveys." *Journal of Nutrition Education* 24 (1): 18S–22S.

"Newark Hunger Hearing Today. Jobless Council Finds Babies Starving." 1931. *The Daily Worker*, November 20, p. 2.

Nichols, Robert. 2020. *Theft Is Property!: Dispossession and Critical Theory*. Durham, NC: Duke University Press.

Nikolaus, Cassandra J., Ruopeng An, Brenna Ellison, and Sharon M. Nickols-Richardson. 2020. "Food Insecurity among College Students in the United States: A Scoping Review." *Advances in Nutrition* 11 (2): 327–348. https://doi.org/10.1093/advances/nmz111.

Nordsiek, Frederic W. 1964. "An Epidemiological Approach to Obesity." *American Journal of Public Health and the Nation's Health* 54 (10): 1689–1698.

Norgaard, Kari Marie. 2019. *Salmon and Acorns Feed Our People: Colonialism, Nature, and Social Action*. Newark, NJ: Rutgers University Press.

Norgaard, Kari Marie, Ron Reed, and Carolina Van Horn. 2011. "A Continuing Legacy: Institutional Racism, Hunger, and Nutritional Justice on the Klamath." In *Cultivating Food Justice*, edited by Alison Hope Alkon and Julian Agyeman, 23–45. Cambridge, MA: MIT Press.

Ó Grada, Cormac. 2009. *Famine: A Short History*. Princeton, NJ: Princeton University Press.

Office of the United Nations High Commissioner for Human Rights and Food and Agriculture Organization (FAO). 2010. *The Right to Adequate Food*. Geneva: United Nations.

Olson, Christine M. 2010. "Hunger and Food Insecurity in the US: History, Correlates and Dynamics." Cornell University. Accessed June 15, 2023. www.cornell.edu/video/christine-olson-hunger-and-food-insecurity-in-the-us.

Olsson, Tore C. 2017. *Agrarian Crossings: Reformers and the Remaking of the US and Mexican Countryside*. Princeton, NJ: Princeton University Press.

"Open Hearing in Harlem on Hunger. March to Charity Outfit; Demand Relief." 1931. *The Daily Worker*, November 13, p. 2.

Oreskes, Naomi, and Eric Conway. 2010. *Merchants of Doubt: How a Handful of Scientists Obscured the Truth on Issues from Tobacco Smoke to Global Warming*. New York: Bloomsbury.

"Organize for National Hunger March on Washington. Winter Relief Demand before U.S. Government." 1931. *Southern Worker*, November 7, p. 1.

Orleck, Annelise. 1993. "'We Are That Mythical Thing Called the Public': Militant Housewives during the Great Depression." *Feminist Studies* 19 (1): 147. https://doi.org/10.2307/3178357.

Orleck, Annelise. 2011. Introduction in *War on Poverty: A New Grassroots History, 1964–1980*, edited by Annelise Orleck and Lisa Gayle Hazirjian, 1–30. Athens: University of Georgia Press.

Ošancova, Kateřina, and Stanislav Hejda. 1975. "Epidemiology of Obesity." In *Obesity: Its Pathogenesis and Management*, 57–91. Dordrecht: Springer Netherlands.

Oshinsky, David. 1997. *Worse Than Slavery: Parchman Farm and the Ordeal of Jim Crow Justice*. New York: Free Press.

Ostler, Jeffrey. 2001. "'The Last Buffalo Hunt' and Beyond: Plains Sioux Economic Strategies in the Early Reservation Period." *Great Plains Quarterly* 21 (2): 115–130.

Otter, Chris. 2020. *Diet for a Large Planet: Industrial Britain, Food Systems and World Ecology*. Chicago: University of Chicago Press.

Ownby, Ted. 1999. *American Dreams in Mississippi: Consumers, Poverty, and Culture, 1830–1998*. Durham, NC: University of North Carolina Press.

"Ozempic User Reviews and Ratings." 2023. *Drugs.com*. Accessed September 10, 2023. www.drugs.com/comments/semaglutide/ozempic.html.

Palmer, William P., ed. 1884. *Calendar of Virginia State Papers and Other Manuscripts from January 1, 1785 to July 2, 1789, Preserved in the Capitol at Richmond*. Richmond, VA: R.U. Derr.

Pangborn, Rose Marie. 1957. "How Sugar Enhances Flavors." *Sugar Molecule* 10 (4): 1–7.

"Paul Thomas Young: Distinguished Scientific Contribution Award." 1965. *American Psychologist* 20 (12): 1084–1088.

Pelchat, Marcia Levin. 2002. "Of Human Bondage: Food Craving, Obsession, Compulsion, and Addiction." *Physiology and Behavior* 76 (3): 347–352.

Perkins, Tom. 2018. "Michigan's Failed Effort to Privatize Prison Kitchens and the Future of Institutional Food." *Civil Eats*, August 20.

Perry, Imani. 2018. "Sticks Broken at the River: The Security State and the Violence of Manhood." In *Vexy Thing: On Gender and Liberation*, 150–176. Durham, NC: Duke University Press.

Philip Morris. 2000. "Hunger Communications Group Recommendations." Philip Morris Records, Industry Documents Library. Accessed September 15, 2019. www.industrydocuments.ucsf.edu/docs/fqvd0069.

Phillips, Erica, Anne McDaniel, and Alicia Croft. 2018. "Food Insecurity and Academic Disruption among College Students." *Journal of Student Affairs Research and Practice* 55 (4): 353–372. https://doi.org/10.1080/19496591.2018.1470003.

Phillips, Lynne, and Suzan Ilcan. 2003. "'A World Free from Hunger': Global Imagination and Governance in the Age of Scientific Management." *Sociologia Ruralis* 43 (4): 434–453. https://doi.org/10.1046/j.1467-9523.2003.00254.x.

Pieratos, Nikki A., Sarah S. Manning, and Nick Tilsen. 2021. "Land Back: A Meta Narrative To Help Indigenous People Show Up As Movement Leaders." *Leadership* 17 (1): 47–61. https://doi.org/10.1177/1742715020976204.

Pilkington, Ed. 2018. "Major Prison Strike Spreads across US and Canada As Inmates Refuse Food." *The Guardian*, August 23.

Piven, Frances Fox, and Richard Cloward. 1977. *Poor People's Movements: Why They Succeed, How They Fail*. New York: Pantheon Books.

"Police Meeting 'Hunger Marchers' Vanguard at the District of Columbia Line." 1932. *Daily Boston Globe*, December 6, p. 15.

Pollack, Herbert. 1968. "Hunger USA 1968—A Critical Review." William F. Darby Papers, Eskind Biomedical Library Manuscripts Collection Repository, Vanderbilt University, Industry Documents Library. 1968. Accessed February 15, 2020. www.industrydocuments.ucsf.edu/docs/nhkm0227.

Pollack, Herbert. 1969. "Hunger USA 1968: A Critical Review." *American Journal of Clinical Nutrition* 22 (4): 480–489.

Poppendieck, Janet. 1999. *Sweet Charity? Emergency Food and the End of Entitlement*. New York: Penguin.

Poppendieck, Janet. 2014. *Breadlines Deep in Wheat: Food Assistance in the Great Depression*. Berkeley: University of California Press.

Potorti, Mary. 2017. "'Feeding the Revolution': The Black Panther Party, Hunger, and Community Survival." *Journal of African American Studies* 21 (1): 85–110. https://doi .org/10.1007/s12111-017-9345-9.

Proctor, Robert. 1988. *Racial Hygiene: Medicine under the Nazis.* Cambridge, MA: Harvard University Press.

Quadagno, Jill. 1990. "Race, Class, and Gender in the US Welfare State: Nixon's Failed Family Assistance Plan." *American Sociological Review* 55 (1): 11–28.

Radimer, Kathy L. 1990. "Understanding Hunger and Developing Indicators to Assess It." PhD diss., Cornell University. Proquest (9106199).

Radimer, Kathy L. 2002. "Measurement of Household Food Security in the USA and Other Industrialised Countries." *Public Health Nutrition* 5 (6A): 859–864. https://doi .org/10.1079/PHN2002385.

Radimer, Kathy L., Christine M. Olson, and Cathy C. Campbell. 1990. "Development of Indicators To Assess Hunger." *Journal of Nutrition* 120 (suppl 11): 1544–1548.

Rasmussen, Nicolas. 2009. *On Speed: From Benzedrine to Adderall.* New York: New York University Press.

Rasmussen, Nicolas. 2012. "Weight Stigma, Addiction, Science, and the Medication of Fatness in Mid-Twentieth Century America." *Sociology of Health and Illness* 34 (6): 880–895. https://doi.org/10.1111/j.1467-9566.2011.01444.x.

Raz, Mical. 2013. *What's Wrong with the Poor?: Psychiatry, Race, and the War on Poverty.* Durham, NC: University of North Carolina Press.

Red Cloud. 2000 [1866]. "Shall We Permit Ourselves To Be Driven To and Fro?" In *Great Speeches by Native Americans*, edited by Bob Blaisdell, 130–131. Mineola, NY: Dover Publications.

"Red Cross Held 'Starvationist,' 'Strike Breaker.'" 1931. *New York Herald Tribune*, December 4, p. 3.

"Red Cross in Vile Plot To Enslave Labor (By Worker Correspondent)." 1931. *Southern Worker*, October 31, p. 2.

"Red Cross, Police, Charities Drive Unemployed to Slavery." 1931. *Southern Worker*, October 31, p. 4.

Redfield, Peter. 2013. *Life in Crisis: The Ethical Journey of Doctors without Borders.* Berkeley: University of California Press.

"Reds Lead Jobless in Lodging Demand." 1931. *New York Times*, January 4, p. 2.

Reese, Ashanté M. 2021. "Tarry with Me: Reclaiming Sweetness in an Anti-Black World." *Oxford American* 112. https://oxfordamerican.org/magazine/issue-112-spring-2021/tarry -with-me.

Reese, Ashanté M. 2022. "Incarceration, Abolition, and Liberating the Food System." *Civil Eats*, January 7. https://civileats.com/2022/01/17/incarceration-abolition-prison-liberating -food-system/.

Reese, Ashanté M., and Randolph Carr. 2020. "Op-ed: Overthrowing the Food System's Plantation Paradigm." *Civil Eats*, June 9. https://civileats.com/2020/06/19/op-ed-over throwing-the-food-systems-plantation-paradigm/.

Reese, Ashanté M., and Dara Cooper. 2021. "Making Spaces Something Like Freedom: Black Feminist Praxis in the Re/Imagining of a Just Food System." *ACME: An International Journal for Critical Geographies* 20 (4): 450–459.

Reese, Ashanté M., and Hanna Garth. 2020. "Black Food Matters: An Introduction." In *Black Food Matters: Racial Justice in the Wake of Food Justice*, edited by Hanna Garth and Ashanté M. Reese. Minneapolis: University of Minnesota Press.

Reese, Ashanté M., and Joshua Sbicca. 2022. "Food and Carcerality: From Confinement to Abolition." *Food and Foodways* 30 (1–2): 1–15. https://doi.org/10.1080/07409710.2022.2030931.

Reinisch, Jessica. 2011. "Internationalism in Relief: The Birth (and Death) of UNRRA." *Past and Present* 210 (Suppl 6): 258–289. https://doi.org/10.1093/pastj/gtq050.

Reinisch, Jessica. 2013. "'Auntie UNRRA' at the Crossroads." *Past and Present* 218 (8): 70–97. https://doi.org/10.1093/pastj/gts035.

Reiter, Keramet. 2014. "The Pelican Bay Hunger Strike: Resistance within the Structural Constraints of a US Supermax Prison." *South Atlantic Quarterly* 113 (3): 579–611. https://doi.org/10.1215/00382876-2692191.

*Report of the Commissioner of Indian Affairs to the Secretary of the Interior for the Year 1872*. 1872. Washington, DC: Government Printing Office.

*Report of the Commissioner of Indian Affairs to the Secretary of the Interior for the Year 1878*. 1878. Washington, DC: Government Printing Office.

Reuter, David L. 2010. "Food Problems Contribute to Riot at Kentucky Prison." *Prison Legal News*, April 15. www.prisonlegalnews.org/news/2010/apr/15/food-problems-contribute-to-riot-at-kentucky-prison/.

Riley, Barry. 2017. *The Political History of American Food Aid: An Uneasy Benevolence*. Oxford, UK: Oxford University Press.

Ring, Wilson. 2008. "Prison Calls It Food, Inmates Disagree." *Huffington Post*, March 23. Accessed September 20, 2023. www.huffingtonpost.com/2008/03/23/prison-calls-it-food inma_n_92953.html.

Roberts, Lydia J. 1927. *What Is Malnutrition?* Washington, DC: Government Printing Office.

Roberts-Pedersen, Elizabeth. 2021. "POWs into Citizens: Repatriation, Gender and Civil Resettlement Units in Great Britain." In *Gender and Trauma Since 1900*, edited by Christina Twomey and Paula A. Michaels, 101–122. London: Bloomsbury.

Robertson, Ruth H. 2022. "The New Black Hills Gold Rush." Accessed June 15, 2023. https://atmos.earth/the-new-black-hills-gold-rush-lakota-people/.

Roediger, David R. 2006. *Working toward Whiteness: How America's Immigrants Became White: The Strange Journey from Ellis Island to the Suburbs*. New York: Basic Books.

Rose, Nikolas, and Joelle M. Abi-Rached. 2013. *Neuro: The New Brain Sciences and the Management of the Mind*. Princeton, NJ: Princeton University Press.

Rosenthal, Caitlyn. 2018. *Accounting for Slavery: Masters and Management*. Cambridge, MA: Harvard University Press.

Rothberg, Michael. 2019. *The Implicated Subject: Beyond Victims and Perpetrators*. Palo Alto, CA: Stanford University Press.

Ruby, Jeff. 2010. "Dining Critic Tries Nutraloaf, the Prison Food for Misbehaving Inmates." *Chicago Magazine*, August 26. www.chicagomag.com/chicago-magazine/september-2010/dining-critic-tries-nutraloaf-the-prison-food-for-misbehaving-inmates/.

Ruis, Andrew R. 2013. "'Children with Half-Starved Bodies' and the Assessment of Malnutrition in the United States, 1890–1950." *Bulletin of the History of Medicine* 87 (3): 378–406.

"Ruleville Miss.: Surplus Food Denied to Registrants." 1962. *The Student Voice*, December 19, p. 2.

Russell, Sharman Apt. 2005. *Hunger: An Unnatural History*. New York: Basic Books.

Ruth, Michael. "Memory of a Miner: A True-Life Story From Harlan County's Heyday." Accessed July 27, 2024. www.memoryofaminer.com/harlanhistory.

Rutherford, Alexandra. 2009. *Beyond the Box: B. F. Skinner's Technology of Behavior from Laboratory to Life, 1950s–1970s*. Toronto: University of Toronto Press.

Salvatici, Sylvia. 2012. "'Help the People To Help Themselves': UNRRA Relief Workers and European Displaced Persons." *Journal of Refugee Studies* 25 (3): 428–451. https://doi .org/10.1093/jrs/fes019.

Sanabria, Emilia. 2015a. "Circulating Ignorance: Complexity and Agnogenesis in the Obesity 'Epidemic.'" *Cultural Anthropology* 31 (1): 131–158. https://doi.org/10.14506/ca31.1.07.

Sanabria, Emilia. 2015b. "Sensorial Pedagogies, Hungry Fat Cells and the Limits of Nutritional Health Education." *Biosocieties* 10 (2): 125–142. https://doi.org/10.1057 /biosoc.2015.5.

*Santa Cruz Sentinel*. 1889. May 30, p. 3.

Santo, Alysia, and Lisa Iaboni. 2015. "What's in a Prison Meal?." *The Marshall Project*, July 7. Accessed September 25, 2023. www.themarshallproject.org/2015/07/07/what-s-in -a-prison-meal.

Saville, Julie. 1994. *The Work of Reconstruction: From Slave to Wage Laborer in South Carolina, 1860–1870*. Cambridge, UK: Cambridge University Press.

Sawyer, Wendy, and Peter Wagner. 2023. "Mass Incarceration: The Whole Pie 2023." Prison Policy Initiative. Accessed January 15, 2024. www.prisonpolicy.org/reports /pie2023.html#:~:text=The%20United%20States%20has%20the,that%20something %20needs%20to%20change.

Schwartz, Michael W., Stephen C. Woods, Daniel Porte, Randy J. Seeley, and Denis G. Baskin. 2000. "Central Nervous System Control of Food Intake." *Nature* 404 (6778): 661–671. https://doi.org/10.1038/35007534.

Scott-Smith, Tom. 2017. "Sticky Technologies: Plumpy'nut®, Emergency Feeding and the Viscosity of Humanitarian Design." *Social Studies Science* 306312717747418. https://doi .org/10.1177/0306312717747418.

Seager, Henry Rogers. 1913. "Theory of the Minimum Wage." *American Labor Legislation Review* 3 (1): 81–91.

Sen, Amartya. 1981. *Poverty and Famines : An Essay on Entitlement and Deprivation*. Oxford, UK: Clarendon Press.

"Session 2B. Metabolism and Effects of Sweetness. W. Darby, Chairperson." n.d. William F. Darby Papers, Eskind Biomedical Library Manuscripts Collection Repository, Vanderbilt University, Industry Documents Library. Accessed September 15, 2022. www.industry documents.ucsf.edu/docs/tzfw0228.

Sharp, J. A. 2014a. "Old Fort Wear." Accessed October 27, 2024. https://sevier.tngenealogy .net/about-sevier/48-local-info/227-old-fort-wear.

Sharp, J. A. 2014b. "Sevier County Settlers vs. Cherokee Indians." Accessed October 27, 2024. https://sevier.tngenealogy.net/about-sevier/44-history/155-sevier-county-settlers -vs-the-cherokee-indians.

Shaviro, Steven. 2016. *Discognition*. London: Repeater Books.

Sheets, Connor. 2017. "'I'm not a dog': Hunger Strikes Inside Alabama Prisons, from Protests to Force-Feeding." *AL.com*, April 30.

"Sheriff Drives Food Truck out of Cal. Strike." 1930. *Daily Worker*, January 18, p. 1.

Sherman, William Tecumseh. 1875. *Memoirs of General William T. Sherman by Himself. March to the Sea*. New York: D. Appleton.

Shils, Edward A. 1946. "Social and Psychological Aspects of Displacement and Repatriation." *Journal of Social Issues* 2 (3): 3–18. https://doi.org/10.1111/j.1540-4560.1946.tb02709.x.

Simmons, Dana. 2008. "Starvation Science from Colonies to Metropole." In *Food and Globalization*, edited by Frank Trentmann and Alexander Nützenadel, 173–192. London: Berg.

Simmons, Dana. 2015. *Vital Minimum: Needs, Science and Politics in Modern France*. Chicago: University of Chicago Press.

Simmons, Dana. 2016. "Impostor Syndrome, a Reparative History." *Engaging Science, Technology, and Society* 2: 106–127.

Simmons, Dana. 2017. "The Living Wage, 'That Reproductive Ferment.'" *History of the Present* 7 (1): 96–96.

Simmons, Dana. 2024. "Paleofantasies and Original Affluence." Unpublished ms.

Simpson, Audra. 2014. *Mohawk Interruptus: Political Life across the Borders of Settler States*. Durham, NC: Duke University Press.

Simpson, Audra. 2016. "Consent's Revenge." *Cultural Anthropology* 31 (3): 326–333. https://doi.org/10.14506/ca31.3.02.

Simpson, Leanne Betasamosake. 2017. *As We Have Always Been: Indigenous Freedom through Radical Resistance*. Minneapolis: University of Minnesota Press.

Sivaraman, Subash, and Mohandas Kozhippally. 2020. "Letter. Are we moving towards direct-to-consumer medication?." *Practical Diabetes* 37 (5): 166–166. https://doi.org/10.1002/pdi.2302.

Skinner, B. F. 1953. *Science and Human Behavior*. New York: Simon and Schuster.

Skinner, B. F. 1981. "Charles B. Ferster—A Personal Memoir." *Journal of the Experimental Analysis of Behavior* 35 (3): 259–261.

Small, Dana M., and Alexandra G. DiFeliceantonio. 2019. "Processed Foods and Food Reward." *Science* 363 (6425): 346–347. https://doi.org/10.1126/science.aav0556.

Small, Willard S. 1900. "An Experimental Study of the Mental Processes of the Rat." *American Journal of Psychology* 11 (2): 133–165.

Smith, Andrew F. 2011. *Starving the South: How the North Won the Civil War*. New York: St. Martin's Press.

Smith, Bobby J., II. 2019. "Mississippi's War against the War on Poverty: Food Power, Hunger and White Supremacy." Center for the Study of Southern Culture at the University of Mississippi. Accessed February 15, 2020. https://southernstudies.olemiss.edu/study-the-south/ms-war-against-war-on-poverty/.

Smith, Bobby J., II. 2023. *Food Power Politics: The Food Story of the Mississippi Civil Rights Movement*. Chapel Hill: University of North Carolina Press.

Smith, Gerard P. 1982. "Satiety and the Problem of Motivation." In *The Physiological Mechanisms of Motivation*, 133–143. New York: Springer New York.

Smith, J. Y. 1990. "Herbert Pollack Dies." *Washington Post*, January 5.

Smith, [Mrs.] Jim. 1931. "Three Men in Family Work, yet All Face Starvation (from the Wife of a Striker at Straight Creek, Ky.)." *Southern Worker*, October 17, p. 3.

Smith, Mrs. S. J. 1961. "Letter to Charles B. Ferster, January 16, 1961." Charles Ferster collection, Archives of the History of American Psychology, M239.

Smithsonian's National Zoo and Conservation Institute. n.d. "Gila Monster." Smithsonian's National Zoo and Conservation Institute. Accessed November 15, 2023. https://national zoo.si.edu/animals/gila-monster.

Smits, David D. 1994. "The Frontier Army and the Destruction of the Buffalo: 1865–1883." *Western Historical Quarterly* 25 (3): 312–338.

Smoyer, Amy B., and Giza Lopes. 2017. "Hungry on the Inside: Prison Food As Concrete and Symbolic Punishment in a Women's Prison." *Punishment and Society* 19 (2): 240–255. https://doi.org/10.1177/1462474516665605.

Snyder, Timothy. 2012. *Bloodlands: Europe between Hitler and Stalin*. New York: Basic Books.

Soble, Leslie, Kathryn Stroud, and Marika Weinstein. 2020. *Eating Behind Bars: Ending the Hidden Punishment of Food in Prison*. Oakland, CA: Impact Justice. https://impact justice.org/wp-content/uploads/IJ-Eating-Behind-Bars.pdf.

Spackman, Christy, and Jacob Lahne. 2019. "Sensory Labor: Considering the Work of Taste in the Food System." *Food, Culture and Society* 22 (2): 142–151. https://doi.org/10.1080/15528014.2019.1573039.

Spencer, Herbert. 1855. *The Principles of Psychology*. New York: D. Appleton.

Spragg, S.D.S. 1940. "Morphine Addiction in Chimpanzees." *Comparative Psychology Monographs* 79: 132.

Stanley, Amy Dru. 1998. *From Bondage to Contract: Wage Labor, Marriage, and the Market in the Age of Slave Emancipation*. Cambridge, UK: Cambridge University Press.

Stark, Laura, and Nancy D. Campbell. 2018. "The Ineffable: A Framework for the Study of Methods through the Case of Mid-Century Mind-Brain Sciences." *Social Studies of Science* 48 (6): 789–820. https://doi.org/10.1177/0306312718816807.

Stark, Louis. 1931a. "Deprival of Rights Charged in Harlan." *New York Times*, September 30, p. 3.

Stark, Louis. 1931b. "Harlan Coal Fields Face Civil War." *New York Times*, September 28, p. 1.

"Starvation and Death to Labor." 1876. *Chicago Daily Tribune*, November 1, p. 4.

Stedman, Stephen John. 2014. "Food and Security." In *The Evolving Sphere of Food Security*, edited by Rosamond L. Naylor, 349–367. Oxford, UK: Oxford University Press.

Stein, Karen. 2000. "Foodservice in Correctional Facilities." *Journal of the American Dietetic Association* 100 (5): 508–509. https://doi.org/10.1016/S0002-8223(00)00153-X.

Stilt, Larry. 1963. "Step Up Drive to Aid Hungry Miss. Negroes: Economic Pressure against 5000 Families Affects 22,000 People." *JET* 23 (18): 1–2.

Strings, Sabrina. 2019. *Fearing the Black Body: The Racial Origins of Fat Phobia*. New York: NYU Press.

Student Nonviolent Coordinating Committee (SNCC). 1963. "Violence Stalks Voter Registration Workers in Mississippi." Civil Rights Movement Archive, Tougaloo College. Accessed February 1, 2020. www.crmvet.org/docs/6303_sncc_ms-violence.pdf.

"Sub-Committee on Psychometry." 1928. *Eugenics Research Association 16th Annual Meeting*, p. 4.

Sugar Information Inc. 1953. "What Makes People Fat?" Braga Brothers Collection; Industry Documents Library. Accessed September 15, 2019. www.industrydocuments.ucsf.edu/docs/yznl0226.

Sugar Information Inc. 1954. "Why Don't People Stick To Their Diets?." *Life Magazine*, July 12, p. 87.

Sugar Information Inc. 1968. "Your Appestat, Sugar and You." *Better Homes and Gardens*, January, p. 73.

Sugar Information Inc. 1973. "The Plain Truth about Your Sweet Tooth." *Time Magazine*, February 19, p. 42.

Sugar Association Inc. and Neil Kelly. 1967. "Letter from Neil Kelly Regarding Next Sugar Information Advertisement." Great Western Sugar Company Collection, Colorado State University Libraries Archives and Special Collections, Industry Documents Library. Accessed September 15, 2019. www.industrydocuments.ucsf.edu/docs/sqyv0228.

Sugar Association Inc. and John W. Tatum Jr. 1968. "Letter from John W Tatem Jr to Sugar Association, Inc, The Concerning Sugar Information Advertisement." Great Western Sugar Company Collection, Colorado State University Libraries Archives and Special Collections, Industry Documents Library. Accessed September 15, 2019. www.industry documents.ucsf.edu/docs/qqyv0228.

Sugar Research Foundation. 1969. "Research Symposium; Seeking New Approaches to Old Problems." Sugar Research Foundation, Roger Adams Papers, University of Illinois Archives, Industry Documents Library. Accessed September 20, 2019. www.industry documents.ucsf.edu/docs/mkbk022.

Sydenstricker, Edgar. 1933. "Health and the Depression." *The Milbank Memorial Fund Quarterly Bulletin* 11 (4): 273. https://doi.org/10.2307/3347444.

Synott, Amy. 2023. "Those Weight Loss Drugs May Do a Number on Your Face." *New York Times*, January 24.

Szalavitz, Maia. 2023. "What Ozempic Reveals about Desire." *New York Times*, June 4.

Tani, Karen. 2016. *States of Dependency: Welfare, Rights, and American Governance, 1935–1972*. Cambridge, UK: Cambridge University Press.

Tappan, Jennifer. 2017. *The Riddle of Malnutrition: The Long Arc of Biomedical and Public Health Interventions in Uganda*. Toledo: Ohio University Press.

"Tenant Organization to Stop Evictions. By a Farmer Correspondent." 1931. *Southern Worker*, December 5, p. 3.

Testa, Alexander, and Dylan B. Jackson. 2019. "Food Insecurity among Formerly Incarcerated Adults." *Criminal Justice and Behavior* 46 (10): 1493–1511. https://doi.org/10.1177/0093854819856920.

Thain, Gerald J. 1971. "Advertising: The FTC Response." William F. Darby Papers, Eskind Biomedical Library Manuscripts Collection Repository, Vanderbilt University, Industry Documents Library. Accessed November 15, 2019. www.industrydocuments.ucsf.edu/docs/lrcb0228.

Theoharis, Liz. 2020. "A Jubilee Moment in Pandemic America? The Poetry of a Movement to Change This Country." Kairos: The Center for Religions, Rights and Social Justice. Accessed June 15, 2022. https://kairoscenter.org/a-jubilee-moment-in-pandemic-america/.

Thorndike, Edward L. 1907. *The Elements of Psychology*. New York: A.G. Selier.

Thorndike, Edward L. 1911. *Animal Intelligence: Experimental Studies*. New York: Macmillan.

Thorndike, Edward L. 1919. *Educational Psychology: A Briefer Course*. New York: Columbia University Teachers College.

Tolentino, Jia. 2023. "Will the Ozempic Era Change How We Think about Being Fat and Being Thin?." *New Yorker*, March 20.

Tomlinson, Stephen. 1997. "Edward Lee Thorndike and John Dewey on the Science of Education." *Oxford Review of Education* 23 (3): 365–383.

"Too Many Thugs in Harlan, Says Fighting Miner (By a Worker Correspondent)." 1931. *Southern Worker*, October 24, p. 3.

Trafzer, Clifford E., Jean A. Keller, and Lorene Sisquoc. 2006. *Boarding School Blues: Revisiting American Indian Educational Experiences.* Lincoln: University of Nebraska Press.

Trentmann, Frank. 2006. "Coping with Shortage: The Problem of Food Security and Global Visions of Coordination, c. 1890s–1950." In *Food and Conflict in Europe in the Age of the Two World Wars*, edited by Frank Trentmann and Flemming Just, 13–48. London: Palgrave Macmillan UK.

Tribole, Evelyn, and Elyse Resch. 2012. *Intuitive Eating: A Revolutionary Program That Works.* New York: St. Martin's Griffin.

Ugelvik, Thomas. 2011. "The Hidden Food: Mealtime Resistance and Identity Work in a Norwegian Prison." *Punishment and Society* 13 (1): 47–63. https://doi.org/10.1177/1462 474510385630.

"Unemployed March on Chicago's South Side." 1931. *The Chicago Defender*, February 14, p. 3.

United Nations Relief and Rehabilitation Administration (UNRRA). 1945. "Psychological Problems of Displaced Persons: A Report Prepared for the Welfare Division of the European Regional Office of the United Nations Relief and Rehabilitation Administration by the Inter-Allied Psychological Study Group." United Nations Archives and Records Management Section. Accessed June 15, 2023. https://search.archives.un.org/psycholo gical-problems-of-displaced-persons-5.

United Nations Relief and Rehabilitation Administration, Welfare Division. 1945. "Welfare Guide: Services to United Nations Nationals Displaced in Germany." United Nations Archives and Records Management Section. Accessed June 15, 2023. https://search .archives.un.org/uploads/r/united-nations-archives/c/d/6/cd68acf0b503c54300735de41 28d27225586ebe47fdc4e41a1bdf8980b8ac058/S-1129-0000-0956-00001.PDF.

"United States of America; Before Federal Trade Commission; In the Matter of Sugar Information, Inc., Sugar Association, Inc., and Leo Burnett Company, Inc., corporations. Docket C-2309." 1972. CSPI Collection. Center for Science in the Public Interest, Industry Documents Library. Accessed June 15, 2019. www.industrydocuments.ucsf.edu /docs/qlvl0229.

University of California. 2024. "Student Basic Needs." University of California. Accessed July 3, 2024. www.universityofcalifornia.edu/about-us/information-center/student-basic -needs.

University of North Carolina at Chapel Hill. 2007. "Drug Derived from Gila Monster Saliva Helps Diabetics Control Glucose, Lose Weight." *ScienceDaily*, July 12.

"User Reviews for Ozempic subcutaneous." 2023. WebMD. Accessed September 10, 2023. https://reviews.webmd.com/drugs/drugreview-174491-ozempic-subcutaneous.

Valaoras, V. G. 1946. "Some Effects of Famine on the Population of Greece." *Milbank Memorial Fund Quarterly* 24 (3): 215–234.

Valdez, Natali. 2021. *Weighing the Future: Race, Science, and Pregnancy Trials in the Postgenomic Era.* Berkeley: University of California Press.

Vaughn, Rachel A. 2017. "'Choosing' Wisely: Paralleling Food Sovereignty and Reproductive Justice." *Frontiers: A Journal of Women Studies* 38 (3): 22. https://doi.org/10.5250 /fronjwomestud.38.3.0022.

Veracini, Lorenzo. 2021. *The World Turned Inside Out: Settler Colonialism as a Political Idea.* London: Verso.

Vernon, James. 2007. *Hunger: A Modern History.* Cambridge, MA: Harvard University Press.

Virchow, Rudolf Carl. "Report on the Typhus Epidemic in Upper Silesia." *American Journal of Public Health* 96, no. 12 (2006 [1848]): 2102–5.

Vogt, William. 1948. *Road to Survival.* New York: William Sloane.

Vrecko, Scott. 2010a. "'Civilizing Technologies' and the Control of Deviance." *BioSocieties* 5 (1): 36–51. https://doi.org/10.1057/biosoc.2009.8.

Vrecko, Scott. 2010b. "Global and Everyday Matters of Consumption: On the Productive Assemblage of Pharmaceuticals and Obesity." *Theory and Society* 39 (5): 555–573. https://doi.org/10.1007/s11186-010-9122-4.

Wainaina, Binyavanga. 2005. "How to Write about Africa." *Granta* 92. Accessed September 15, 2018. https://granta.com/how-to-write-about-africa/.

Wallach, Jennifer Jensen. 2019. *Getting What We Need Ourselves: How Food Has Shaped African American Life.* Lanham, MD: Rowman and Littlefield.

Warnes, Andrew. 2004. *Hunger Overcome?: Food and Resistance in Twentieth-century African American Literature.* Athens: University of Georgia Press.

Washburn, Margaret Floy. 1908. *The Animal Mind: A Text-book of Comparative Psychology.* New York: MacMillan.

Wassum, K. M., S. B. Ostlund, N. T. Maidment, and B. W. Balleine. 2009. "Distinct Opioid Circuits Determine the Palatability and the Desirability of Rewarding Events." *Proceedings of the National Academy of Sciences of the United States of America* 106 (30): 12512–12517. https://doi.org/10.1073/pnas.0905874106.

Watson, John B. 1903. *Animal Education: An Experimental Study on the Psychical Development of the White Rat, Correlated with the Growth of Its Nervous System.* Chicago: University of Chicago Press.

Watson, John B. 1914. *Behavior: An Introduction to Comparative Psychology.* New York: Henry Holt.

Weidman, Nadine. 2016. "Between the Counterculture and the Corporation: Abraham Maslow and Humanistic Psychology in the 1960s." In *Groovy Science: Knowledge, Innovation and American Counterculture,* edited by David Kaiser and W. Patrick McCray, 109–141. Chicago: University of Chicago Press.

Weinreb, Alice. 2012. "'For the Hungry Have No Past nor Do They Belong to a Political Party': Debates over German Hunger after World War II." *Central European History* 45 (1): 50–78. https://doi.org/10.1017/s0008938911000987.

Weyl, Nathaniel. 1932. "Organizing Hunger." *New Republic* 73 (941): 117–120.

White House. 1970. *White House Conference on Food, Nutrition and Health: Final Report.* Washington, DC: Government Printing Office.

White, Monica M. 2017. "'A Pig and a Garden': Fannie Lou Hamer and the Freedom Farms Cooperative." *Food and Foodways* 25 (1): 20–39. https://doi.org/10.1080/07409710.2017.1270647.

White, Monica M. 2018. *Freedom Farmers: Agricultural Resistance and the Black Freedom Movement.* Chapel Hill: University of North Carolina Press Books.

Whyte, Kyle Powys. 2016. "Indigenous Food Sovereignty, Renewal and U.S. Settler Colonialism." In *The Routledge Handbook of Food Ethics,* edited by Mary C. Rawlinson and Caleb Ward, 354–365. London: Routledge.

Williams-Forson, Psyche A. 2022. *Eating While Black: Food Shaming and Race in America.* Chapel Hill: University of North Carolina Press.

Williams, Brian, and Carrie Freshour. 2022. "Carceral Geographies of Pesticides and Poultry." *Food and Foodways* 30 (1–2): 38–57. https://doi.org/10.1080/07409710.2022.2030936.

Williams, Elizabeth A. 2020. *Appetite and its Discontents: Science, Medicine and the Urge to Eat, 1750–1950.* Chicago: University of Chicago Press.

Williams, Patricia. 1988. "On Being the Object of Property." *Signs* 14 (1): 5–24.

Wilson, Elizabeth A. 2015. *Gut Feminism.* Durham, NC: Duke University Press.

Winslow, Gordon. 1882. "Hoopa Valley Agency, July 31, 1882." In *Annual Report of the Commissioner of Indian Affairs to the Secretary of the Interior for the Year 1882*, p. 525. Washington, DC: Government Printing Office.

Wise, M. Norton. 1993. "Mediations: Enlightenment Balancing Acts, or the Technologies of Rationalism." In *World Changes: Thomas Kuhn and the Nature of Science*, edited by Paul Horwich, 207–258. Cambridge, MA: MIT Press.

Wolf-Meyer, Matthew. 2011. "Natural Hegemonies: Sleep and the Rhythms of American Capitalism." *Current Anthropology* 52 (6): 876–895.

Wolf-Meyer, Matthew J. 2012. *The Slumbering Masses: Sleep, Medicine, and Modern American Life.* Minneapolis: University of Minnesota Press.

Woodbridge, George. 1950. *UNRRA: The History of the United Nations Relief and Rehabilitation Administration.* 2 vols. New York: Columbia University Press.

Woods-Brown, Clair, Kate Hunt, and Helen Sweeting. 2023. "Food and the Prison Environment: A Meta-Ethnography of Global First-Hand Experiences of Food, Meals and Eating in Custody." *Health and Justice* 11 (1): 23. https://doi.org/10.1186/s40352-023-00222-z.

Woodward, Ellen S. 1945. "UNRRA and War's Aftermath." *Social Security Bulletin* 8: 10.

Woodworth, Robert S. 1918. *Dynamic Psychology.* New York: Columbia University Press.

Woody, William Douglas. 2022. "Tracing the Career Arc of Joost A. M. Meerloo: Prominence, Fading, and Premonitions of Menticide." *History of the Human Sciences* OnlineFirst 1–28. https://doi.org/10.1177/09526951221121227.

Wren, A. M., and Stephen R. Bloom. 2007. "Gut Hormones and Appetite Control." *Gastroenterology* 132 (6): 2116–2130. https://doi.org/10.1053/j.gastro.2007.03.048.

Wright, Richard. 2005 [1944]. *Black Boy (American Hunger).* New York: Harper Perennial.

Wynter, Sylvia. 2003. "Unsettling the Coloniality of Being/Power/Truth/Freedom: Towards the Human, after Man, Its Overrepresentation—An Argument." *CR: The New Centennial Review* 3 (3): 257–337.

XLIV Congress. 1876. "The Situation in the South. Speech of Senator Morton. Debate on the Centennial Bill. Cochran, of Pennsylvania, and Tucker, of Virginia, Oppose the Appropriation." *The Pittsburgh Commercial*, January 29, p. 1.

Yates-Doerr, Emily. 2015a. "Intervals of Confidence: Uncertain Accounts of Global Hunger." *BioSocieties* 10 (2): 229–246. https://doi.org/10.1057/biosoc.2015.9.

Yates-Doerr, Emily. 2015b. *The Weight of Obesity: Hunger and Global Health in Postwar Guatemala.* Berkeley: University of California Press.

Yates-Doerr, Emily. 2024. *Mal-Nutrition: Maternal Health Science and the Reproduction of Harm.* Berkeley: University of California Press.

Yerkes, Robert M. 1907. *The Dancing Mouse: A Study in Animal Behavior.* New York: Macmillan.

Yerkes, Robert M., and John D. Dodson. 1908. "The Relation of Strength of Stimulus To Rapidity of Habit-Formation." *Journal of Comparative Neurology* 18 (5): 459–482. https://doi.org/10.1002/cne.920180503.

Youmans, John B. 1970. "Hunger and Malnutrition." *JAMA: The Journal of the American Medical Association* 214 (6): 1123. https://doi.org/10.1001/jama.1970.03180060097035.

Young, Paul Thomas. 1941. "The Experimental Analysis of Appetite." *Psychological Bulletin* 38 (3): 129–164. https://doi.org/10.1037/h0053492.

Young, Paul Thomas. 1947. "Studies of Food Preference, Appetite and Dietary Habit; Palatability in Relation To Learning and Performance." *Journal of Comparative and Physiological Psychology* 40 (2): 37–72. https://doi.org/10.1037/h0061360.

Young, Paul Thomas. 1948a. "Appetite, Palatability and Feeding Habit: A Critical Review." *Psychological Bulletin* 45 (4): 289–320. https://doi.org/10.1037/h0063233.

Young, Paul Thomas. 1948b. "Studies of Food Preference, Appetite and Dietary Habit. VIII. Food-seeking Drives, Palatability and the Law of Effect." *Journal of Comparative and Physiological Psychology* 41 (4): 269–300. https://doi.org/10.1037/h0056529.

Young, Paul Thomas. 1949. "Food-seeking Drive, Affective Process, and Learning." *Psychological Review* 56 (2): 98–121. https://doi.org/10.1037/h0060312.

Young, Paul Thomas. 1952. "The Role of Hedonic Processes in the Organization of Behavior." *Psychological Review* 59 (4): 249–262. https://doi.org/10.1037/h0057176.

Young, Robert C., James Gibbs, Joseph Antin, Jonathan Holt, and Gerard P. Smith. 1974. "Absence of Satiety during Sham Feeding in the Rat." *Journal of Comparative and Physiological Psychology* 87 (5): 795–800. https://doi.org/10.1037/h0037210.

"Youth Starving in No. Carolina Must Organize." 1931. *Southern Worker*, October 10, p. 3.

Zahra, Tara. 2011. "'The Psychological Marshall Plan': Displacement, Gender, and Human Rights after World War II." *Central European History* 44 (1): 37–62. https://doi.org/10.1017/s0008938910001172.

Zeller, Mrs. G. R. 1961. "Letter to Dr. C.B. Ferster, January 11, 1961." Charles Ferster collection, Archives of the History of American Psychology, M239.

Founded in 1893,
UNIVERSITY OF CALIFORNIA PRESS
publishes bold, progressive books and journals
on topics in the arts, humanities, social sciences,
and natural sciences—with a focus on social
justice issues—that inspire thought and action
among readers worldwide.

The UC PRESS FOUNDATION
raises funds to uphold the press's vital role
as an independent, nonprofit publisher, and
receives philanthropic support from a wide
range of individuals and institutions—and from
committed readers like you. To learn more, visit
ucpress.edu/supportus.

www.ingramcontent.com/pod-product-compliance
Ingram Content Group UK Ltd.
Pitfield, Milton Keynes, MK11 3LW, UK
UKHW041934310325
456955UK00001B/6